## Investment Treaty Arbitration as Public International Law

Investment treaty arbitration is fast becoming one of the most common methods of dispute settlement in international law. Despite having ancient roots, tensions remain between the private interests in international investment relations and the public international law features of the arbitral procedure. This book, which presents an account of investment treaty arbitration as a part of public international law – as opposed to commercial law – provides an important contribution to the literature on this subject. Eric De Brabandere examines the procedural implications of conceiving of investment treaty arbitration in such a way, with regard to issues such as the principles of confidentiality and privacy, and remedies. The author demonstrates how the public international law character of investment treaty arbitration derives from, and has impacted upon, the dispute settlement procedure.

**Eric De Brabandere** is Associate Professor of International Law at the Grotius Centre for International Legal Studies at Leiden University, and is a Member of the Brussels Bar.

CAMBRIDGE STUDIES IN INTERNATIONAL AND COMPARATIVE LAW

Established in 1946, this series produces high quality scholarship in the fields of public and private international law and comparative law. Although these are distinct legal sub-disciplines, developments since 1946 confirm their interrelations.

Comparative law is increasingly used as a tool in the making of law at national, regional and international levels. Private international law is now often affected by international conventions, and the issues faced by classical conflicts rules are frequently dealt with by substantive harmonization of law under international auspices. Mixed international arbitrations, especially those involving state economic activity, raise mixed questions of public and private international law, while in many fields (such as the protection of human rights and democratic standards, investment guarantees and international criminal law) international and national systems interact. National constitutional arrangements relating to 'foreign affairs', and to the implementation of international norms, are a focus of attention.

The series welcomes works of a theoretical or interdisciplinary character, and those focusing on the new approaches to international or comparative law or conflicts of law. Studies of particular institutions or problems are equally welcome, as are translations of the best work published in other languages.



*A list of books in the series can be found at the end of this volume.*

# Investment Treaty Arbitration as Public International Law

## Procedural Aspects and Implications

Eric De Brabandere

CAMBRIDGE
UNIVERSITY PRESS

CAMBRIDGE
UNIVERSITY PRESS

University Printing House, Cambridge CB2 8BS, United Kingdom

Cambridge University Press is part of the University of Cambridge.

It furthers the University's mission by disseminating knowledge in the pursuit of education, learning and research at the highest international levels of excellence.

www.cambridge.org
Information on this title: www.cambridge.org/9781107066878



First published 2014

Printed in the United Kingdom by Clays, St Ives plc

*A catalogue record for this publication is available from the British Library*

*Library of Congress Cataloging in Publication data*
Brabandere, Eric de, author.
Investment treaty arbitration as public international law : procedural aspects and implications / Eric De Brabandere.
pages cm – (Cambridge studies in international and comparative law)
ISBN 978-1-107-06687-8 (hardback)
1. Arbitration and award, International. 2. Investments, Foreign (International law) 3. Investments, Foreign – Law and legislation. 4. Commercial treaties. I. Title.
K3830.B73 2014
346′.092–dc23

2014012734

ISBN 978-1-107-06687-8 Hardback

# Contents

# Acknowledgements

This book has been written as part of a three-year VENI research grant from the Netherlands Organization for Scientific Research (NWO), entitled 'Resolution of Contemporary Investment Disputes: Conciliating Private Rights and Public Interests in Internationalized Commercial Relation'. This grant has enabled me to focus on and further explore this fascinating topic, and I am greatly indebted to the NWO for this.

I would like to thank my colleagues from the Grotius Centre for International Legal Studies at Leiden University, in particular Larissa van den Herik, Nico Schrijver, Yannick Radi (whom I also thank for commenting on certain parts of the book) and Vid Prislan for their support and for the numerous discussions and debates we have had on international investment law and arbitration, and international law generally, which have shaped some of the thoughts and arguments developed in this book.

Several arguments presented in this book have been shared and tested at international guest lectures, conferences and seminars, *inter alia*, at the universities of Edinburgh, Frankfurt, Geneva, Ghent, Leiden, Luxembourg, Ottawa and Trento, the British Institute for International and Comparative Law, CEPINA-CEPANI (Belgian International Arbitration Institute) and the 2012 VIAC/YAAP/ArbAut Joint Conference. My thanks extend to the organizers and participants of these gatherings for engaging with my thoughts and for their constructive criticism on my ideas. They are too many to name, those concerned will recognize themselves.

I would also like to thank Hilde Roskam for her editorial assistance.

Finally, and most importantly, I thank Katia Gevaert for her encouragement, trust and understanding throughout the writing of this book.

# Table of cases

INVESTMENT ARBITRATION

## ICSID

## Non-ICSID

## PERMANENT COURT OF INTERNATIONAL JUSTICE



## INTERNATIONAL COURT OF JUSTICE

OTHER DECISIONS OF INTERNATIONAL COURTS AND ARBITRAL TRIBUNALS

# List of abbreviations

| | |
|---|---|
| BIT | bilateral investment treaty |
| ECHR | European Convention on Human Rights |
| ECT | Energy Charter Treaty |
| ECtHR | European Court of Human Rights |
| FET | fair and equitable treatment |
| FPS | (full) protection and security |
| ICC | International Chamber of Commerce |
| ICJ | International Court of Justice |
| ICSID Convention | Convention on the Settlement of Investment Disputes between States and Nationals of Other States (Washington Convention) |
| ICSID | International Centre for Settlement of Investment Disputes |
| ILC | International Law Commission |
| ITLOS | International Tribunal for the Law of the Sea |
| MFN | most-favoured-nation |
| NAFTA | North American Free Trade Agreement |
| NGO | non-governmental organization |
| NT | national treatment |
| PCA | Permanent Court of Arbitration |
| PCIJ | Permanent Court of International Justice |
| SCC | Stockholm Chamber of Commerce |
| UNCITRAL | United Nations Commission on International Trade Law |
| UNCTAD | United Nations Conference on Trade and Development |

| | |
|---|---|
| UNTS | United Nations Treaty Series |
| VCLT | Vienna Convention on the Law of Treaties |
| WTO | World Trade Organization |
| WTO DSU | World Trade Organization Dispute Settlement Understanding |

# Introduction

Investment treaty arbitration is nowadays one of the most important dispute settlement mechanisms in international law. Despite having fairly ancient roots, the protection of foreign investors has over the past two decades evolved from a rather peripheral branch of the law, which had attracted little attention in scholarship and practice, to one of the most vibrant areas of research, interest and concern in public international law.

Since the decision of the Arbitral Tribunal in *AAPL* v. *Sri Lanka*,[1] the first tribunal established on the basis of a dispute settlement provision contained in an investment treaty that provided foreign investors direct access to arbitration under the ICSID Convention,[2] investment arbitration has shifted from a relatively private or commercial dispute settlement method to an essentially public international law one. Factually, investment treaty arbitration has become one of the most important dispute settlement mechanisms in international law.

Attempts to characterize investment treaty arbitration as private or public, that is, as a private dispute settlement mechanism essentially regulated by private and commercial law principles, or as a dispute settlement mechanism regulated by public (international) law principles, have thrived since the rise of the use of investment treaty arbitration in the 1990s.[3] In this book, I argue that investment treaty arbitration is a public international law dispute settlement

[1] *Asian Agricultural Products Ltd (AAPL)* v. *Republic of Sri Lanka*, ICSID Case No. ARB/87/3, Award, 27 June 1990. All cited cases are available at www.italaw.com unless otherwise indicated.

[2] Convention on the Settlement of Investment Disputes between States and Nationals of Other States, 18 March 1965, 575 UNTS 159.

[3] See Jan Paulsson, 'Arbitration without Privity', *ICSID Review – Foreign Investment Law Journal*, 10(2) (1995): 232. See, more recently, Anthea Roberts, 'Clash of Paradigms: Actors

mechanism that is fundamentally concerned with the international legal obligations of states under public international law, and is founded on an international treaty containing the consent of states. The main feature of investment treaty arbitration today is the public international law character of the instrument containing the consent of states to arbitration and state obligations granting substantive protection to foreign investors. The dispute is thus one that is directed at the international legal obligations of states and, hence, is a public international law dispute, the settlement of which occurs within the framework of public international law. Secondly, this intrinsic feature, it is argued, is visible from and impacts the procedure applicable to investment treaty arbitration, despite the latter being derived from arbitral rules applicable to the settlement of commercial disputes. While certain of these aspects are already clearly present in contemporary investment treaty arbitral procedure – which both reveals the public international law character of investment treaty arbitration, and at the same time shows the influence that the public international law character of investment treaty arbitration has had on the procedure – others, it will be argued, have yet to be fully incorporated.

My argument that investment treaty arbitration as a public international law dispute settlement mechanism implies that I move away, in this book, from other theories about the nature of contemporary investment treaty arbitration, notably those theories that either characterize investment treaty arbitration as a 'hybrid' legal system or equate it with public/administrative law dispute settlement. While these theories may certainly be of assistance in, for example, questions of interpretation, they do not fully reflect the contemporary nature of investment treaty arbitration.

## Disentangling the 'hybridity' of investment disputes

The claim that investment treaty arbitration is a 'hybrid' dispute settlement mechanism results from the use in investment treaty arbitration of elements derived from both public international law and international commercial law and arbitration.[4] The 'hybrid' foundation of investment

and Analogies Shaping the Investment Treaty System', *American Journal of International Law*, 107(1) (2013): 45.

4 See, generally, Zachary Douglas, 'The Hybrid Foundations of Investment Treaty Arbitration', *British Yearbook of International Law*, 74 (2004): 151, and Daniel Kalderminis, 'Investment Treaty Arbitration as Global Administrative Law: What this Might Mean in

treaty arbitration is then coupled to the claim that neither international commercial arbitration, private law, public international law nor public law are adequate legal paradigms that cover the settlement of international investment disputes.[5] The 'hybridity' is essentially based on two interconnected features of investment treaty arbitration.

First, international investment law and investment treaty arbitration are characterized by a dual layer of obligations that exist in the investment relations between a foreign investor and a host state. When investors decide to develop their activities in a foreign state, they typically sign an investment contract with the host state. At the same time, and although the contract in itself may contain protection mechanisms for the investors, such as stabilization clauses and access to arbitration, the foreign investor may benefit concomitantly from protection offered under an investment treaty, to which the host state and the home state of the investor are parties.[6] The contract is a private law instrument, which is regulated by private and commercial law – despite some lingering controversy in respect of state contracts that I will further address in Chapter 1[7] – while the treaty obligations are without doubt state obligations regulated by public international law. There are, consequently, two layers of obligations resting on the host state: the contractual obligations towards the foreign investor based on the investment contract; and the public international law obligations based on the investment treaty.

Secondly, the 'hybrid' system of investment treaty arbitration would result from the procedural way in which investment disputes are settled.[8] The majority of investment protection treaties offer foreign investors the possibility of bringing claims for violations of that treaty directly against host states before an international arbitral tribunal. Then, investment tribunals are mandated to establish whether the

Practice', in Chester Brown and Kate Miles (eds.), *Evolution in Investment Treaty Law and Arbitration* (Cambridge University Press, 2011), p. 149.

5 Roberts, 'Clash of Paradigms', p. 49; and Kalderminis, 'Investment Treaty Arbitration as Global Administrative Law', pp. 145–59.

6 See, generally, Patrick Dumberry, 'International Investment Contracts', in Tarcisio Gazzini and Eric De Brabandere (eds.), *International Investment Law. Sources of Rights and Obligations* (Leiden: Martinus Nijhoff, 2012), pp. 215–44.

7 See for the claim that state contracts are a particular kind of international legal act, Prosper Weil, '*Droit international et contrat d'Etat*', in *Mélanges offerts à Paul Reuter. Le droit international: unité et diversité* (Paris: Pedone, 1981), p. 562, and Francis A. Mann, 'The Theoretical Approach Towards the Law Governing Contracts Between States and Private Persons', *Revue Belge de Droit International*, 11(2) (1975): 563, 564–5.

8 Douglas, 'The Hybrid Foundations of Investment Treaty Arbitration', pp. 151–290.

host state has violated its treaty obligations and thus engaged its international responsibility under public international law. Such disputes are settled through a form of arbitration that is largely based on the rules and principles of international commercial arbitration.[9] The mandate of the arbitral tribunals and the rules and procedure applicable to the arbitral proceedings are thus a combination of both public international law and international commercial or private law.

These features of investment treaty arbitration, however, do not suffice to qualify investment treaty arbitration as a dispute settlement mechanism that lies in between public international law and commercial or private law, or to disqualify it as an essentially public international law dispute settlement mechanism. The 'hybridity' of investment treaty arbitration may be factually valid as explained above, but the normative claims associated with this 'hybridity' are largely unwarranted. As will be argued, categorizing investment law and arbitration as 'hybrid' fails to take account of the fact that contemporary investment arbitration forms an integral part of public international law, and that (the recognition of) this feature is of paramount importance to the dispute settlement procedure. This book, accordingly, is based on the idea that it is both useful and legally necessary to distinguish between the public international law and private law dimensions of investment disputes and investment arbitration, and considers investment treaty arbitration to be a public international law dispute settlement mechanism. Although there is, indeed, as a matter of principle, nothing 'revolutionary in abandoning the simple dichotomy between public and private international law conceptions of dispute resolution',[10] the characterization of a certain situation as 'hybrid' is generally an easy way out of disentangling a complex web of legal relations and, in the case of investment treaty arbitration, tends to blur the underlying legal relations between foreign investors and host states.

## Investment treaty arbitration and public law analogies

International investment law and investment treaty arbitration have much in common with domestic administrative and public law, and, as

[9] See Gus van Harten and Martin Loughlin, 'Investment Treaty Arbitration as a Species of Global Administrative Law', *European Journal of International Law*, 17(1) (2006): 121, 139–45.

[10] Zachary Douglas, *The International Law of Investment Treaty Claims* (Cambridge University Press, 2009), p. 7.

a consequence, proponents of the public law paradigm of investment treaty arbitration, based on the *analogy* between both investment treaty arbitration and public law dispute settlement, have sought to import principles from the latter to the former.[11] However, the analogies made do not imply that investment arbitration should *ipso facto* be equated with administrative of public law litigation[12] or that, because it is generally not accepted in administrative or public law litigation in domestic courts, the principle of party autonomy, for instance, would be incompatible with the settlement of investment disputes.[13]

The public/administrative law analogy without doubt has much merit and may indeed be of assistance to the interpretation of certain substantive obligations of state parties,[14] but too easily discards differences between public/administrative law disputes and investment disputes, and the fundamental consent by states to have investment disputes settled through international arbitration. I do not therefore endorse the qualification of the regime of international investment law as a public law system as defended, *inter alia*, by Gus van Harten.[15]

From a substantive perspective, there is certainly a similarity between investment disputes and public/administrative law disputes. Both are concerned with regulatory acts or measures taken by states, but the *types* of state conduct that may amount to a breach of the state's international investment obligations are different from those that may form the basis for domestic administrative/public law litigation.[16] Secondly, in domestic public/administrative law, such state conduct is tested against different domestic standards that may, depending on the constitutional system, also include international law principles. Investment treaty arbitration, on the other hand, is essentially concerned with assessing the conformity of state conduct with specific public international law standards governing the protection of foreign investors, which are not necessarily the same as those governing domestic public/administrative law disputes.

[11] See for a discussion: Roberts, 'Clash of Paradigms', p. 63.

[12] See, however, Gus van Harten, *Investment Treaty Arbitration and Public Law* (Oxford University Press, 2007), pp. 44 ff.

[13] *Ibid.*, pp. 130 ff.

[14] See the various contributions in Stephan W. Schill (ed.), *International Investment Law and Comparative Public Law* (Oxford University Press, 2010).

[15] Van Harten, *Investment Treaty Arbitration and Public Law*, pp. 44 ff. See also Kalderminis, 'Investment Treaty Arbitration as Global Administrative Law', pp. 145–59.

[16] See Andreas Kulick, *Global Public Interest in International Investment Law* (Cambridge University Press, 2012), pp. 84–5.

Procedurally, investment treaty arbitration resembles more interstate arbitration than administrative or public litigation,[17] not the least because it has developed as an alternative to international dispute settlement as part of a state's exercise of diplomatic protection, which is an intrinsically interstate mechanism. Investment treaty arbitration, in essence, has resulted in the elimination of the procedural limitations of diplomatic protection by removing the requirement to exhaust domestic remedies, and by the prospective consent of states to arbitrate such disputes by giving a direct claims right to foreign investors. But this does not imply that the (formerly interstate) dispute is actually transformed into a public/administrative law dispute on the international level.

It does not seem very helpful simply to transpose the rules and regulations applicable to public/administrative law dispute settlement to investment treaty arbitration. Doing so might indeed jeopardize the very basic foundations and characteristics of arbitral proceedings. One should, on the contrary, respect the general intent of states to settle investment disputes through international arbitration rather than through a standing international court or tribunal, and, consequently, respect the inevitable implications that the use of arbitration has on the settlement of investment disputes. There is thus nothing wrong as a matter of principle with the idea that party autonomy generally applies to investor–state disputes, and, as an application thereof, the freedom of the parties to define the law to be applied by the tribunal.[18] Such principles are inherent in the choice of arbitration as the dispute settlement mechanism. It is, therefore, of little usefulness to criticize generally the use of arbitration as a method to settle investor–state disputes and to propose systemic reforms of this procedure. The choice of international arbitration as the method of settling investment disputes should be respected. The question rather is how the public international law character of investment disputes has been incorporated in investment treaty arbitration, which is modelled on international commercial arbitration, and how, in certain areas of the procedure, this incorporation should be effectuated more efficiently. International

[17] As noted by one author, ICSID proceedings are 'conceptually no different to proceedings taking place between two sovereign states, where the law of the arbitration is international law' (Georgios Petrochilos, *Procedural Law in International Arbitration* (Oxford University Press, 2004), p. 218).

[18] See, however, for a criticism Van Harten, *Investment Treaty Arbitration and Public Law*, pp. 130 ff.

arbitration is not premised on a fixed set of rules and regulations as are national courts and tribunals. There are thus several ways in which the public international law character of international investment disputes has influenced, or has been visible through, the arbitral procedure.

The 'public interest' theory,[19] which broadly forms part of the public law analogy paradigm,[20] is nevertheless of high relevance, since the principles derived therefrom are equally applicable when investment treaty arbitration is viewed from its public international law foundation. Such a theory holds that because of the type of acts of the state that are subjected to scrutiny in investment treaty arbitration, the areas in which the activities of the foreign investor take place, and the importance of the pecuniary compensation usually awarded to foreign investors, investment treaty arbitration has a broader public interest that transcends that of the parties to the dispute only.[21] For example, a foreign investor may feel that a democratically and validly adopted law in the host state unduly affects its private rights under the investment contract, and even breach the state's obligations under the applicable investment treaty. In such situations, the general public interests of the state may, for example, warrant granting non-disputing parties access to the proceedings, militate in favour of conducting open and transparent proceedings, or impose certain conditions on the selection and qualification of arbitrators. Since these considerations are applicable to public international law dispute settlement as well, one may readily consider that, viewed from its public international law foundation, investment treaty arbitration has an important 'public interest', to which I will refer in particular in the second part of this book.

## Investment treaty arbitration as public international law

Treaty-based investment arbitrations currently outnumber contract-based arbitrations under the ICSID Convention.[22] The consent to

[19] See, generally, Kulick, *Global Public Interest in International Investment Law*.
[20] Roberts, 'Clash of Paradigms', p. 65. [21] *Ibid*.
[22] The 2013–2 issue of the ICSID statistics reports that an investment treaty formed the basis of consent to establish ICSID jurisdiction in 74 per cent of cases. Investment contracts accounted for 19 per cent of cases, while the national laws of the host state accounted for 7 per cent of cases. See *ICSID Caseload – Statistics*, Issue 2013–2, p. 10, available at: http://icsid.worldbank.org/ICSID/FrontServlet?requestType=ICSIDDocRH&actionVal=CaseLoad Statistics, accessed 30 August 2013. Similarly, the 2012 Permanent Court of Arbitration (PCA) Annual report states of the eighty-eight arbitrations on its docket in 2012, fifty-four were investor–state arbitrations under bilateral or multilateral investment treaties, or

arbitration which forms the basis of the vast majority of investment tribunals today is provided for in an investment treaty rather than in a contract. While a contract concluded under the municipal laws of a state may provide the basis for an international commercial arbitration claim, investment treaty arbitration is founded on an international treaty, and the consent to arbitration expressed by the state is a sovereign act of the state rooted in a public international law legal instrument. Consent to arbitration expressed in relation to commercial acts is fundamentally different in that both parties to the contract have expressed a clear wish to settle disputes by arbitration instead of by resort to the regular courts and tribunals of the host state, which is not the result of a state acting in the exercise of its functions under general public international law.[23] When involved in international commercial arbitration, the state is in essence acting in a private capacity, whereas a state involved in investment treaty arbitration will do so in a public or sovereign capacity.[24]

Contemporary treaty-based investment disputes relate to the international responsibility of states for alleged violations of international legal obligations contained in international legal instruments. The existence of two distinct layers of obligations – a contractual and a treaty level – does not imply that assessing the responsibility of a state for alleged violations of the state's international investment obligations ceases to be an exercise in applying public international law rules and principles. The use of the international commercial arbitration model to settle investment disputes has not altered the fact that in contemporary investment disputes investment tribunals are mandated to assess breaches by states of their obligations under public international law, which are laid down in international treaties granting protection to foreign investors.

national investment laws, with twenty-seven arbitrations and one expert determination being under contracts or other agreements to which at least one party is a state, a state-controlled entity, or an intergovernmental organization (PCA, 112th Annual Report, 2012, p. 12, available at: www.wx4all.net/pca/PCA-annualreport_2012.pdf). PCA Annual Report 2011 states that of the sixty-three investment arbitrations, forty were based on bilateral or multilateral investment treaties, twenty-four on 'contracts or other agreements to which at least one party is a state, state-controlled entity, or intergovernmental organization', and one case under a national investment law (PCA, 111th Annual Report, 2011, para. 3, available at: www.pca-cpa.org/showpage.asp?pag_id=1069).

23 See also Van Harten, *Investment Treaty Arbitration and Public Law*, pp. 48–9.

24 See the discussion on state contracts, below, Ch. 1, section 1.3.

Although it is beyond doubt that a state can engage its international responsibility when acting both in its sovereign and commercial capacity, as was recognized by the International Law Commission (ILC) in its Articles on the Responsibility of States for Internationally Wrongful Acts, the responsibility of a state remains a responsibility under public international law.[25] The tribunal's mandate in investment treaty arbitration thus consists in establishing whether the state has breached its international legal obligations, either through sovereign or commercial acts. While this mandate may thus include an analysis into the contractual relations between foreign investors and host states, this question is, in contemporary investment treaty arbitration, subsidiary or preliminary to the overall enquiry into the international legal responsibility of the host state. In other words, the examination of the international legal responsibility of a state for breaches of its international investment obligations, a matter regulated by public international law and not domestic law, is the principal object of investment treaty arbitration.[26]

My general claim that investment treaty arbitration is essentially a public international law dispute settlement mechanism does not imply that investment treaty arbitration has no private law dimension. Indeed, they are not incompatible and are present in investment treaty arbitration. However, the private law dimension is subsidiary to the public international law dimension, and one cannot equate investment treaty arbitration with a private or commercial dispute settlement method. Clearly, the principal beneficiary of the international instrument granting protection to the foreign investor is the investor itself, and that is why foreign investors are given a direct right of action against a state. This does not suffice to characterize the relation between the foreign investor and the host state as essentially private. As noted by Ian Brownlie in his separate opinion in *CME* v. *Czech Republic*:

> In this context, it is simply unacceptable to insist that the subject-matter is exclusively 'commercial' in character or that the interests in issue are, more or less, only those of the investor. Such an approach involves setting aside a number of essential elements in the Treaty relation. This first element is the

25 International Law Commission, 'Articles on the Responsibility of States for Internationally Wrongful Acts', Report of the International Law Commission on the Work of its 53rd Session, Official Records of the General Assembly, 56th Session, Supplement No. 10, UN Doc. A/56/10, November 2001.

26 Andrew Newcombe and Lluis Paradell, *Law and Practice of Investment Treaties: Standards of Treatment* (Alphen aan den Rijn: Kluwer Law International, 2009), para. 2.19.

significance of the fact that the Respondent is a sovereign State, which is responsible for the well-being of its people. This is not to confer a privilege on the Czech Republic but only to recognize its special character and responsibilities. The Czech Republic is not a commercial entity.[27]

The use of the method of international commercial arbitration to settle investment disputes that have a public international law character naturally results in a certain tension between the public international law nature of the dispute – because such disputes are concerned with the assessment of the exercise by a state of its sovereign powers under international law – and the private character of the dispute settlement method.

Equally, there is an opposition between the public and private functions of international dispute settlement. While the private function focuses on the settlement of the dispute between the parties, the public function of dispute settlement has a much broader ambit. Because of the general system of international investment protection, which goes beyond the mere bilateral relations between the host state and the home state of the foreign investor, investment treaty arbitration may influence generally the behaviour of states in the future, and may therefore, in terms of function, be equated with international interstate arbitration and litigation. The public function is inherent in public international law dispute settlement. However, it should be kept in mind that the choice of arbitration as a dispute settlement mechanism comes with certain intrinsic concepts and principles that may not be deviated from at the risk of denaturing the very essence of international arbitration. While it is undoubtedly true that because of the involvement of a state acting in its sovereign capacity international investment tribunals' decisions have a broader impact than awards in international commercial arbitration, this does not imply that international investment tribunals would have to respect the same principles as administrative courts. This book is not concerned, however, with the public function of investment treaty arbitration, but rather with the procedural implications of the public international law foundation of that system, since it is not necessarily the public function of investment treaty arbitration that affects the procedure, but rather its public international law character. The quality of the obligations at stake in investment treaty arbitration determines the public international law

[27] *CME Czech Republic BV* v. *Czech Republic*, UNCITRAL, Final Award, 14 March 2003, Separate Opinion of Ian Brownlie, para. 74.

character of investment treaty arbitration, and influences the rules and principles applicable to investment treaty arbitration.[28]

Also, that the foreign investor has certain specific private interests in international investment relations generally, namely to maximize the returns on its investment[29] and to have an efficient dispute settlement mechanism in case of disputes between itself and the host state to enable it to enforce the private rights is indisputable, but it is irrelevant for the conduct of the proceedings. The characteristics of the dispute, on the other hand, do influence the arbitral proceedings. Because of the involvement of a state acting in its sovereign capacity and the obligations it has contracted under treaties regulated by public international law, the review of the acts of the host state by arbitral tribunals is subjected to certain specific rules, such as the transparency of the proceedings, and the challenge criteria for appointed arbitrators. As a consequence also, and here the link between the 'public interest' approach discussed above is clearly visible, the dispute settlement mechanism established to judge and evaluate the exercise of this power by the state is of interest for a broader range of entities and individuals than the mere investor, and transcends the purely private or commercial interests of the parties to a dispute.

## Aim and scope of the book

This book aims at establishing that investment treaty arbitration is a public international law dispute settlement method, and demonstrating how the public international law character of investment treaty arbitration derives from, and has impacted on, the dispute settlement procedure. The fact that contemporary investment arbitration is a preponderantly public international law dispute settlement mechanism does, indeed, result from the procedural aspects of the dispute settlement method, and at the same time has influenced that procedure. Although Anthea Roberts argues that, of the three 'conceptions' of investment treaty arbitration - public international law, public law and international commercial arbitration - only the public law paradigm would offer an interpretative framework, while the others

[28] On this, see Stephan W. Schill, 'Crafting the International Economic Order: The Public Function of Investment Treaty Arbitration and its Significance for the Role of the Arbitrator', (2010) 23 *Leiden Journal of International Law*, 23(2) (2010): 401, 409 ff.

[29] See Jeswald W. Salacuse, *The Law of Investment Treaties* (Oxford University Press, 2009), p. 39.

would 'operate implicitly',[30] I will argue that, besides 'operating implicitly' – which it certainly does – the public international law foundation of investment treaty arbitration has in fact served explicitly as an interpretative and normative framework for procedural questions, as will be delineated in the second part of this book. The public international law character of investment treaty arbitration that I defend here is different from the public law paradigm, given that the latter is based essentially on the *analogy* between investment treaty arbitration and public law dispute settlement, and thus seeks to import principles from the latter to the former.[31] By contrast, the public international law paradigm adopted in this book is based on the claim that investment treaty arbitration essentially *is* public international law.

Underlying the book's main argument is the premise that the fundamental concepts on which international arbitration is based need to be respected. That international commercial arbitration as a dispute settlement method has been transposed to international investment disputes is not problematic as such, provided that one takes into consideration the public international law character of investment disputes. An overly broad focus on the private, commercial or 'hybrid' aspects of the dispute and the dispute settlement method, without sufficient consideration of the public international law dimension of the dispute and the procedural implications thereof results in a biased conception of the contemporary system of investment treaty arbitration, which this book seeks to review. Indeed, one cannot change the dispute settlement method chosen by the parties, and the inherent characteristics – both positive and negative – of arbitration. This book does not therefore aim to criticize the use of arbitration to settle investment disputes or to put an end to the current system of investment treaty arbitration.

The arguments developed in this book are valid for investment treaty arbitration generally, that is, investment arbitration based on an international investment *treaty*. Special consideration will be given to the ICSID Convention, which is justified as it constitutes an archetype that reveals clearly the public international law nature of investment treaty arbitration, in particular, because of the special features of the ICSID regime. Moreover, besides the possibility of having investment treaty arbitration conducted under the Permanent Court of Arbitration, or ad hoc by the application of existing sets of procedural rules such as the

[30] Roberts, 'Clash of Paradigms', p. 49. [31] *Ibid.*, p. 63.

UNCITRAL Arbitration Rules, the majority of investor–state disputes based on an investment treaty are settled through the facilities of the ICSID.[32] Because it creates a framework in which investors may directly access international arbitration, thereby avoiding the traditional recourse to diplomatic protection, and because it has completely 'internationalized' the arbitral proceedings, the ICSID Convention and Arbitration Rules contain several features that embody the public international law character of investment treaty arbitration. However, since my analysis is valid for investment treaty arbitration generally, I will point to the procedural rules of other institutions and to arbitration conducted outside the ICSID framework as well.

Because of its procedural perspective, this book is not concerned with substantive issues relating to the public international law character of, or the public interest in, international investment law generally.[33] Nor is this book envisaged as providing a general overview of the procedural rules applicable to international investment treaty arbitration. This book, instead, addresses investment treaty arbitration from a functional perspective. This implies that I will discuss only those issues and themes that are relevant to point to the influence of the public international law character of investment treaty arbitration on the applicable procedural rules, without engaging in a complete and general analysis of the various rules applicable to treaty arbitration.

## Structure of the book

The basic premise of this book, namely, that investment treaty arbitration is a public international law dispute settlement mechanism rather than a private or commercial dispute settlement mechanism, will be outlined and argued in Part I of this book, which is subdivided into two chapters. Chapter 1 addresses the public international law foundation of investment treaty arbitration by analysing the rationale of the direct access of foreign investors to investment treaty arbitration, the public international law regime governing investment treaty arbitration, the fundamental distinction between the contract and treaty levels of investment treaty arbitration, and, finally, the systemic distinction

32 For an overview of the various Model BITs and the dispute settlement forum made available to the parties, see Douglas, *The International Law of Investment Treaty Claims*, pp. 3–5.

33 On this, see Kulick, *Global Public Interest in International Investment Law*.

between investment treaty arbitration and international commercial arbitration. Chapter 2 zeroes in on the legal characterization of the right of access to investment treaty arbitration. Based on the distinction between substantive and procedural rights, Chapter 2, section 2.2, discusses the 'derivate rights' and 'direct rights' theories and the question of waiver of access to investment treaty arbitration.

Part II of this book addresses the procedural aspects and implications of the public international law dimension of investment treaty arbitration. Chapter 3 analyses the influence of the public international law dimension of investment treaty arbitration on the role, selection and qualification of arbitrations. Particular sections are devoted to the requirements of independence and impartiality, the legal reasoning of arbitral awards, and the autonomy of the parties and the powers of arbitral tribunals. Chapter 4 analyses the applicable law in investment treaty arbitration from a public international law perspective. In particular, this chapter discusses whether investment tribunals can, or should, take account of non-investment norms and principles. Chapter 5 concentrates on transparency and public access to investment treaty arbitration. Because of its public international law foundation, I argue in Chapter 5 that investment treaty arbitration has rightly moved away from the principles of confidentiality and privacy in international commercial arbitration by, first, allowing, at least as a matter of principle, public access to documents and to the hearing, and, secondly, by allowing non-disputing parties to participate as *amicus curiae* in investment treaty arbitration. Chapter 6 focuses on public international law remedies in investment treaty arbitration: section 6.1 sketches the main principles relating to remedies for internationally wrongful acts; section 6.2 discusses the award of non-pecuniary remedies as an alternative to pecuniary compensation; and section 6.3 addresses moral damages in investment treaty arbitration.

# PART I

# The public international law character of investment treaty arbitration

# 1 The public international law foundation of investment treaty arbitration

The characterization of investment treaty arbitration is closely interconnected with the foundation and function of international investment law. It is beyond doubt that today international investment law is not primarily or solely concerned with the private contractual relation between the foreign investor and the host state, but rather is principally founded on fundamental principles derived from international treaty law, and, to a lesser extent, on customary international law and general principles of law.[1]

This chapter will start with an analysis of the rationale of the direct access of foreign investors to investment treaty arbitration in order better to grasp the subsequent discussion of the specific characteristics of the claims rights of foreign investors (section 1.1). Section 1.2 will determine the public international law character and foundation of the disputes that arise in international investment law. Section 1.3 will make clear the distinction between the contract and treaty levels of the dispute. Section 1.4 will address the fundamental and systemic differences, which result from the previous sections, between investment treaty arbitration and international commercial arbitration.

## 1.1 The principle and rationale of the direct access of foreign investors to investment treaty arbitration

The access of foreign investors to international arbitration is perhaps one of the most important developments in contemporary international

[1] On the different sources of international investment law, see Tarcisio Gazzini and Eric De Brabandere (eds.), *International Investment Law: The Sources of Rights and Obligations* (Leiden: Martinus Nijhoff, 2012).

dispute settlement. However, before turning to the specific reasons behind this access, it is important to briefly delineate the general context in which this development has taken place.

### 1.1.1 *Non-state entities in international dispute settlement*

Dispute settlement procedures between non-state entities and states over the past two decades have increased substantially. From a historical perspective, the recent increase in the access of non-state entities to international judicial and arbitral procedures is, however, not unprecedented. Although since the end of the Second World War non-state entities have only very occasionally been involved in such proceedings, there are many pre-war precedents of international judicial and arbitral proceedings in which the participation of non-state entities was accepted or envisaged.[2] In the past decades, the number of procedures granting direct access to non-state entities has boomed, in particular through the so-called 'proliferation' of dispute settlement mechanisms. Although principally noticeable in the areas of human rights and investment law,[3] this development has been confirmed by various other international forums under which non-state entities can bring claims directly against states.[4] In those proceedings, non-state entities have been given the right to bring claims directly against a state for claims related to a specifically delineated dispute or factual situation. Next to the creation of new dispute settlement methods, the number of disputes involving non-state entities that are settled through existing international judicial and arbitral proceedings has also risen dramatically.[5]

[2] For a discussion, see Eric De Brabandere, 'Pragmatism in International Law: Non-State Actors and International Dispute Settlement', in Jean d'Aspremont (ed.), *Participants in the International Legal System. Multiple Perspectives on Non-State Actors in International Law* (London: Routledge, 2010), pp. 342–59, and Eric De Brabandere, 'Non-State Actors and the Proliferation and Individualization of International Dispute Settlement', in Bob Reinalda (ed.), *The Ashgate Research Companion to Non-State Actors* (Farnham: Ashgate, 2011), pp. 347–59.

[3] See John Merrills, 'The Means of Dispute Settlement', in M. N. Evans (ed.), *International Law* (Oxford University Press, 2011), p. 545.

[4] Several 'mass claims processes' have been established over the past decades, such as the UN Compensation Commission and the Iran–US Claims Tribunal. For an overview, see Howard M. Holtzmann and Edda Kristjánsdóttir (eds.), *International Mass Claims Processes. Legal and Practical Perspectives* (Oxford University Press, 2007). Another example of the standing of non-state actors outside the formal investment or human rights context is the access granted to companies and individuals of state parties to the Seabed Disputes Chamber of the ITLOS (Article 187(c)–(d) United Nations Convention on the Law of the Sea, 10 December 1982, 1833 UNTS 3).

[5] A brief look at the activities of the PCA easily illustrated this trend. The PCA's activities originally focused on interstate disputes only. However, as early as 1935 the PCA administered its first mixed dispute; for an overview of PCA activity in settling 'mixed'

Within this evolution, the access of foreign investors to international arbitration takes a prominent place. The direct access of foreign investors to an international remedy is inspired mainly by the ineffectiveness of the traditional system of diplomatic protection, and the fact that direct access of individuals and corporations to international arbitration has been granted as part of the protection offered by states to foreign investors. Direct access is not necessarily the direct consequence of the grant of direct rights to private parties, which I will further discuss in Chapter 2.

### *1.1.2 Diplomatic protection and the exhaustion of local remedies*

That investment treaty arbitration is fundamentally a public international law dispute settlement mechanism is confirmed by the rationale behind the advent of this system. Direct access to arbitration exists because the use of conventionally available dispute settlement mechanisms, in this case the domestic courts of the host state coupled with the possibility of the home state of the investor being able to resort to diplomatic protection, is of limited usefulness to settle investment disputes. From the perspective of the foreign investor, the obligation to submit disputes with the host state to the domestic courts of that state is, for reasons related to a perceived fear of lack of independence or bias of these tribunals, not attractive, and resort to diplomatic protection is a cumbersome, lengthy and uncertain procedure.

Customarily, conflicts between individuals and a state in the exercise of its sovereign authority can be brought only before the domestic courts of that state, since the application of state immunity would prevent the submission of such claims to the domestic courts of the individual's home state. Only in exceptional cases are private claims of

disputes, see James Crawford, 'The Permanent Court of Arbitration and Mixed Arbitration, Remarks on the Occasion of a Celebration of the Centenary of the PCA', 18 October 2007, available at: www.pca-cpa.org/upload/files/Crawford%20EN.pdf). In 1962, the PCA adopted a specific set of 'Optional Rules for Arbitrating Disputes between Two Parties of Which Only One is a State', which were superseded by a revised and modified version adopted in 1993 (Permanent Court of Arbitration Optional Rules for Arbitrating Disputes Between Two Parties of Which Only One is a State, available at: www.pca-cpa.org/upload/files/1STATENG.pdf). The total number of arbitrations in which the PCA acted as a registry remained relatively stable until 1999 (approximately thirty). Since then, the caseload has grown substantially, and in 2012 the PCA had a total of eighty-eight pending cases, only one of these being an interstate arbitration (PCA, 112th Annual Report, 2012, p. 12, available at: www.wx4all.net/pca/PCA-annualreport_2012.pdf).

individuals settled on the international level, namely, through the exercise of diplomatic protection. In those circumstances, the individual is nevertheless first required to exhaust all local remedies available in the host state.[6] Proceedings before the domestic courts and tribunals of the foreign state for conflicts between foreign investors and the host state, however, may not always prove to be an efficient dispute settlement method, essentially because it is time-consuming and unreliable, in particular, because of a fear of bias by the host state's judiciary towards the foreign investor.

Once the individual or corporation has exhausted all local remedies available in the host state, as required by the rules on diplomatic protection, private claims by individuals and corporations can be settled on the international level through the exercise by the home state of its right to diplomatic protection. The home state of the foreign investors can then 'espouse the claim' of its national, and bring a claim under international law against the host state. The state of the individual's nationality is not acting in the rights of the individual, but is acting in its own rights, namely, the right to see the law respected for its nationals. The traditional view thus holds that the state of the individual's or corporation's nationality is not acting in the rights of the individual or corporation, but is acting in its own right. As famously noted by the PCIJ in the *Mavrommatis Palestine Concessions* case:

> It is an elementary principle of international law that a State is entitled to protect its subjects, when injured by acts contrary to international law committed by another State, from whom they have been unable to obtain satisfaction through the ordinary channels. By taking up the case of one of its subjects and by resorting to diplomatic action or international judicial proceedings on his behalf, a State is in reality asserting its own rights – its right to ensure, in the person of its subjects, respect for the rules of international law.[7]

In other words, the 'mixed' conflict between the foreign investor and the host state is transformed into an interstate conflict between the host state and the state of nationality of the foreign investor. The individual therefore has no right to diplomatic protection and is thus dependent

[6] See, generally, International Law Commission, 'Draft Articles on Diplomatic Protection', Report on the Work of its 58th Session (1 May–9 June and 3 July–11 August 2006), General Assembly Official Records, 61st Session, Supplement No. 10, UN Doc A/61/10, 2006, p. 26.

[7] Permanent Court of International Justice, Judgment No. 2, 30 August 1924, *PCIJ Reports*, Series A (1924), p. 12.

on the political discretion of its government. As noted by the ICJ in the *Barcelona Traction* case:

> within the limits prescribed by international law, a State may exercise diplomatic protection by whatever means and to whatever extent it thinks fit, for it is its own right that the State is asserting ... The State must be viewed as the sole judge to decide whether its protection will be granted, to what extent it is granted, and when it will cease. It retains in this respect a discretionary power ...[8]

To avoid this rather cumbersome and uncertain procedure, modern investment treaties habitually grant investors the right to bring a claim against the host state directly before an international arbitral tribunal.[9] The direct standing of foreign investors in investment law is thus mainly motivated by the ineffectiveness of the traditional system of diplomatic protection, which not only requires the exhaustion of all domestic remedies, but, more importantly, is a discretionary right of the state only. The direct access to arbitration, on the contrary, provides a guarantee for the investor to have access to an effective international remedy while at the same time offering an interesting investor-friendly environment for the host state. This is precisely one of the rationales behind the ICSID Convention, namely, to remove investment disputes from the standard procedure of diplomatic protection by granting a direct access to an international remedy.[10] The specific characteristic of investment arbitration as a tailor-made mechanism part of the protection of foreign investment is further confirmed by the fact that ICSID has no facilities for arbitration of interstate disputes.

### *1.1.3 State consent and the direct access to investment treaty arbitration*

The direct claim rights of individual and corporate investors cannot be isolated from the general context of investment protection. The access of foreign investors to investment treaty arbitration is a pragmatic response to the need to have an adequate mechanism to settle investment disputes swiftly by an independent and impartial tribunal. As noted by the ICSID Arbitral Tribunal in *Maffezini* v. *Spain*:

[8] International Court of Justice, *Barcelona Traction* case, *Light and Power Co.* case *(Belgium* v. *Spain)*, Judgment, *ICJ Reports*, 1970, No. 3, paras 78–79.

[9] See, for example, the Model BITs of Canada, the United Kingdom, Chile, France, South Africa, Switzerland and the United States.

[10] Nigel Blackaby, 'Public Interest and Investment Treaty Arbitration', *Transnational Dispute Management*, 1(1) (2004): 2.

> there are good reasons to conclude that today dispute settlement arrangements are inextricably related to the protection of foreign investors, as they are also related to the protection of rights of traders under treaties of commerce ... International arbitration and other dispute settlement arrangements have replaced these older and frequently abusive practices of the past. These modern developments are essential, however, to the protection of the rights envisaged under the pertinent treaties; they are also closely linked to the material aspects of the treatment accorded.[11]

Other ICSID tribunals have adopted similar justifications for the direct access to arbitration.[12]

However, despite the link between investment protection and the access to arbitration, the direct access to investment treaty arbitration is by no means intended to be a generalized claims procedure to deal with any type of dispute between the host state and the foreign investor. Generally, in international law the grant of certain individual rights does not automatically entail the capacity to bring a claim for a violation of that right before an international tribunal or court, traditionally reserved to the state of the nationality of the individual through its right to exercise diplomatic protection and after the exhaustion by the foreign investor of the available local remedies. The direct access of foreign investors to arbitration in international investment disputes is,

[11] *Emilio Agustìn Maffezini* v. *Kingdom of Spain*, ICSID Case No. ARB/97/7, Decision of the Tribunal on Objections to Jurisdiction, 25 January 2000.

[12] The tribunal in *Siemens* v. *Argentina*, for example, mentioned that investment treaties have 'as a distinctive feature special dispute settlement mechanisms not normally open to investors. Access to these mechanisms is part of the protection offered under the Treaty. It is part of the treatment of foreign investors and investments' (*Siemens AG* v. *The Argentine Republic*, ICSID Case No. ARB/02/8, Decision on Jurisdiction, 3 August 2004, para. 102). The *Suez* Tribunal also noted that 'from the point of view of the promotion and protection of investments, the stated purposes of both the Argentina–Spain BIT and the Argentina–UK BIT, dispute settlement is as important as other matters governed by the BITs and is an integral part of the investment protection regime that the respective sovereign states have agreed upon' (*Suez, Sociedad General de Aguas de Barcelona SA and Vivendi Universal SA* v. *The Argentine Republic*, ICSID Case No. ARB/03/19, Decision on Jurisdiction, 3 August 2006, para. 59). Likewise, the tribunal in *Gas Natural* v. *Argentina* held that 'provision for international investor–state arbitration in bilateral investment treaties is a significant substantive incentive and protection for foreign investors' (*Gas Natural SDG SA* v. *The Argentine Republic*, ICSID Case No. ARB/03/10, Decision of the Tribunal on Preliminary Questions on Jurisdiction, 17 June 2005, para. 31). A different question, however, is whether the access to investment arbitration is to be considered as part of the *substantive* protection offered to foreign investors. This question, which has been at the core of the discussion on the extension of the most-favoured-nation (MFN) clause to dispute settlement provisions, however, falls outside the scope of this analysis.

simply put, the mere removal of these procedural requirements to enhance the effectiveness of remedies.

Because there is no automatic access to an international dispute settlement mechanism, even when foreign investors are given direct rights under a certain treaty, the express consent of the states is required, as is the case in general international law.[13] Therefore, the access of foreign investors to arbitration is granted only through the explicit consent by states which allow the individual of one or more states, depending on the bilateral or multilateral character of the treaty, to bring a claim directly related to the investment against another state without the former state's intervention. The consent to arbitration is given by states in advance of the dispute[14] to foreign investors of a particular state 'as a group'[15] by the signature of a treaty to this effect, or through the adoption of national legislation to that effect. Such consent is generally considered to constitute an 'offer to arbitrate' by the state,[16] which may then be accepted by the foreign investor[17] through the submission of a request for arbitration to the relevant institutional mechanism provided for in the instrument containing the consent of the host state.[18] Access to investment treaty arbitration may be restricted by the consent of the state,[19] most often expressed in the investment treaty. States, when expressing consent to direct

[13] See in this respect *Garanti Koza LLP* v. *Turkmenistan*, ICSID Case No. ARB/11/20, Decision on the Objection to Jurisdiction for Lack of Consent, Dissenting Opinion of Arbitrator Laurence Boisson de Chazournes, 2 July 2013, para. 5: 'Consent to jurisdiction in international adjudication must always be established. First, this is a necessary prerequisite to the exercise of the international judicial function. The principle of compétence de la compétence as defined under general international law, and under Article 41 of the ICSID Convention, empowers an arbitral tribunal or any other international court to determine *proprio motu* the extent and limits of its jurisdiction. At the same time, the principle of compétence de la compétence requires an arbitral tribunal or any other international court to establish the extent and limits of its jurisdiction objectively, i.e., on the basis of the title of jurisdiction that is conferred to the said tribunal, and not to go beyond it.'

[14] Francisco Orrego Vicuña, *International Dispute Settlement in an Evolving Global Society. Constitutionalization, Accessibility, Privatization* (Cambridge University Press, 2004), p. 66.

[15] Van Harten, *Investment Treaty Arbitration and Public Law*, p. 63.

[16] See, for example, *AAPL* v. *Sri Lanka*, ICSID Case No. ARB/87/3, paras 246 ff.

[17] See on the need for the consent of the foreign investor, *American Manufacturing and Trading, Inc.* v. *Zaire*, ICSID Case No. ARB/93/1, Award, 21 February 1997, paras 23 ff.

[18] See, generally, Christoph Schreuer, Loretta Malintoppi, August Reinisch and Anthony Sinclair, *The ICSID Convention. A Commentary* (Cambridge University Press, 2009), pp. 1279–82.

[19] As was also recalled by the International Court of Justice: 'the jurisdiction of the Court is based on the consent of States, under the conditions expressed therein' (International

investment arbitration, may condition their consent and, for example, require foreign investors to exhaust local remedies, either generally or for a limited time period, or insert a 'fork-in-the-road' clause which obliges investors to choose between international arbitration or domestic courts.[20]

## 1.2 The public international law regime of investment treaty arbitration

From the point of view of substantive legal obligations, the relation between the foreign investor and the host state is complex. There are several layers of obligations between these parties, which should clearly be distinguished one from the other, as will be explained in the next section. Because of the multilayered relation between the foreign investor and the host state, it is sometimes considered that this relation is a 'hybrid' or *sui generis* one.[21] It is indeed *sui generis* in the sense that the combination of the applicable legal frameworks may be unique and applied concomitantly in an international investment dispute, but the characterization of investment treaty arbitration as 'hybrid' fails to take account of the fact that the complex web of legal relations can, and should, be unravelled.

The different applicable legal frameworks, and accompanying rules and principles, should always be distinguished, and are always distinguishable even in the proceedings before an international investment tribunal. Despite the relative obviousness of the distinction between the contract and treaty levels of investment treaty claims, and the clear distinction made in international arbitral proceedings – either by counsel or by arbitrators – between treaty claims and claims based on the contractual relations between the disputing parties,[22] the interaction between these two levels of obligations has not always been unproblematic, in particular, in view of the concomitance of contract and treaty claims before international investment tribunals. However, this should not obfuscate the point that the treaty and contract levels may easily be differentiated and identified. I will here briefly expand upon

Court of Justice, *Certain Questions of Mutual Assistance in Criminal Matters (Djibouti* v. *France)*, Judgment, *ICJ Reports*, 2008, 177, p. 203, para. 60).

20 See Rudolf Dolzer and Christoph Schreuer, *Principles of International Investment Law* (Oxford University Press, 2008), pp. 214–26.

21 See, for instance, Douglas, *The International Law of Investment Treaty Claims*, p. 6.

22 *Ibid.*, p. 8.

the public international law regime governing foreign investment, before turning in the next section to the way in which the distinction between the contract and treaty levels has been dealt with by arbitral tribunals.

### *1.2.1 International investment treaties*

The first most obvious regime governing foreign investment is the international legal instrument granting protection to the foreign investor. This instrument usually takes the form of an international treaty;[23] most often a bilateral investment treaty (BIT), occasionally a multilateral treaty such as Chapter Eleven of the North American Free Trade Agreement (NAFTA) or the Energy Charter Treaty (ECT), and increasingly preferential trade and investment agreements (PTIAs).[24] These treaties' main objectives are to protect foreign investment in the post-entry phase, and, occasionally, also contain obligations aimed at liberalizing cross-border trade and investment. BITs, as most bilateral treaties, vary in content according to the specific needs of the negotiating states. However, since many states have developed 'model' investment treaties, and considering that the majority of the provisions on the protection of foreign investment are present in all modern BITs, there is certain uniformity both in the content and structure of BITs.[25] The majority of BITs thus contain provisions on the standards of treatment of foreign investors, such as fair and equitable treatment (FET), (full) protection and security (FPS), most-favoured-nation treatment

[23] Besides treaties, customary international law likewise provides for certain standards of protection of aliens, including foreign investors. On this, see Jean d'Aspremont, 'Customary International Investment Law: Story of a Paradox', in Tarcisio Gazzini and Eric De Brabandere (eds.), *International Investment Law. Sources of Rights and Obligations* (Leiden: Martinus Nijhoff, 2012), pp. 5–47. However, since direct access to investment treaty arbitration requires the explicit consent of states, breaches of international customary obligations of states towards foreign investors only will need to be claimed through the regular means of dispute settlement, namely, the domestic courts of the host state and, eventually, diplomatic protection. International investment tribunals may, of course, depending on the circumstances of the case, apply the relevant principles of international law, such as those provided for under customary international law and general principles of international law, as a matter of applicable law.

[24] See Eric De Brabandere, 'Co-existence and Conflict: Interaction between Preferential Trade and Investment Agreements and the BIT World', in Rainer Hofmann, Christian Tams and Stephan W. Schill (eds.), *Preferential Trade and Investment Agreements. A New Ordering Paradigm for International Investment Relations?* (Baden-Baden: Nomos, 2013), pp. 37–69.

[25] For the claim that international law is 'multilateralizing' despite the majority of treaties being bilateral, see Stephan W. Schill, *The Multilateralization of International Investment Law* (Cambridge University Press, 2010).

(MFN) and national treatment (NT). Provisions such as those related to expropriation and compensation, transfer of funds, protection from losses due to war, civil strife and other extraordinary circumstances, and, of course, access by the foreign investor to international arbitration are likewise very common in the majority of modern BITs.

The vast majority of contemporary BITs contain a dispute settlement clause granting foreign investors direct access to an international arbitral tribunal to settle disputes between that investor and the host state in relation to the obligations of the host state contained in the investment treaty.[26] Some tribunals have nevertheless considered, based on the broad language contained in BIT dispute settlement clauses, that the foreign investor can bring claims for contract breaches against a state before an international tribunal. As I will argue in Chapter 4, however, such decisions too easily overlook the distinction between contract and treaty levels, and the fact that the consent to arbitrate, being contained in an investment treaty, necessarily implies that such consent is in principle limited to the invocation by the foreign investor of the specific treaty rights contained in that treaty.[27] Foreign investors who claim that the state has breached the provisions of the contract indeed need to resort to the dispute settlement mechanisms provided for in that contract.[28] This may include international arbitration, but obviously, since the obligations invoked are contractual obligations regulated by municipal law and private law, and since the consent is founded on a contract rather than a treaty, the jurisdiction of the tribunal will be very different. Then, the tribunal is not concerned with an assessment of the international legal obligations of the state under the relevant international investment treaty, but solely with the liability of the state for breaches of the contractual obligations in the investment contract, applying the law as defined in the contract, which is rarely only international law.[29] As noted by the Ad Hoc Committee in *Vivendi I*: 'whether there has been a breach of the BIT and whether there has been a breach of contract are different questions. Each of these claims will be determined by reference to its own proper or applicable law – in the case of the BIT, by international law; in the case of the concession contract, by

[26] Salacuse, *The Law of Investment Treaties*, p. 381. [27] See, below, section 1.3.

[28] For a discussion, see *Compañiá de Aguas del Aconquija SA and Vivendi Universal (formerly Compagnie Générale des Eaux)* v. *The Argentine Republic*, ICSID Case No. ARB/97/3, Decision on Annulment, 3 July 2002, para. 98.

[29] See Dumberry, 'International Investment Contracts'.

the proper law of the contract.'[30] This principle was subsequently endorsed by several tribunals.[31] Thus, investment treaty arbitration concerns claims brought before an international investment tribunal for an alleged violation by the host state of the applicable investment treaty, which is principally the invocation by the foreign investor of the international responsibility of that state. The dispute concerns the responsibility of a state under public international law.

### *1.2.2 State responsibility under public international law*

It is not because foreign investors are granted the right to invoke the international responsibility of the state that such claims are by definition 'private law' claims. The mere fact that private rights are at stake in investment disputes does not suffice to disqualify these disputes as international disputes and instead label them as private or national disputes. The grant of an individual right of access to an arbitral tribunal does not as such modify the legal relations between the parties to the dispute, nor would the question of the international legal personality of foreign investors, either individuals or corporations.[32] In other words, if a treaty grants certain rights to individuals or corporations, including access to a dispute settlement mechanism, this does not transform the type of claim that is brought before that dispute settlement mechanism. The determinant factor is whether the obligation breached is an international legal obligation contained in an international legal instrument, even if that obligation has been contracted by states for the benefit of non-state entities, which is habitually the case in investment treaty arbitration. The involvement of a private actor does not alter the

[30] *Compañiá de Aguas del Aconquija SA and Vivendi Universal* v. *Argentina*, Decision on Annulment, para. 96.

[31] See, for instance, *Impregilo SpA* v. *Islamic Republic of Pakistan*, ICSID Case No. ARB/03/3, Decision on Jurisdiction of 22 April 2005, para. 210: 'a clear distinction exists between the responsibility of a State for the conduct of an entity that violates international law (e.g. a breach of Treaty), and the responsibility of a State for the conduct of an entity that breaches a municipal law contract (i.e. Impregilo's Contract Claims). As noted by the Ad Hoc Committee in its decision on annulment in *Compañia de Aguas del Aconquija and Vivendi Universal* v. *The Argentine Republic*, the international law rules on State responsibility and attribution apply to the former, but not the latter.'

[32] See De Brabandere, 'Pragmatism in International Law', pp. 342–59. For the opposite claim, however, see Patrick Dumberry and Erik Labelle-Eastaugh, 'Non-state Actors in International Investment Law: The Legal Personality of Corporations and NGOs in the Context of Investor–State Arbitration', in Jean d'Aspremont (ed.), *Participants in the International Legal System. Multiple Perspectives on Non-State Actors in International Law* (London: Routledge, 2011), pp. 360–71.

fundamental premise that treaty breaches by a state are governed by the principles applicable to the international responsibility of states.

As noted by the ILC in its Articles on the Responsibility of States for Internationally Wrongful Acts, the obligations of states may relate to 'any right, arising from the international responsibility of a State, which may accrue directly to any person or entity other than a State'.[33] The ILC further noted that the subject matter of the legal obligation concerned has no influence on the possibility of state responsibility for a breach of that obligation:

> The general scope of the articles extends not only to the conventional or other origin of the obligation breached but also to its subject matter. International awards and decisions specifying the conditions for the existence of an internationally wrongful act speak of the breach of an international obligation without placing any restriction on the subject matter of the obligation breached. Courts and tribunals have consistently affirmed the principle that there is no *a priori* limit to the subject matters on which States may assume international obligations.[34]

The characterization of an act as internationally wrongful is governed solely by general international law, while national law, and the characterization of an act as wrongful or lawful under that legal system does not affect the international wrongfulness of the act.[35] In its commentary to this specific Article, the ILC referred explicitly to international investment law, and noted that:

> the rule that the characterization of conduct as unlawful in international law cannot be affected by the characterization of the same act as lawful in internal law makes no exception for cases where rules of international law require a State to conform to the provisions of its internal law, for instance by applying to aliens the same legal treatment as to nationals.[36]

The same is true as far as the attribution of conduct is concerned.[37] Whether or not the conduct complained of is the conduct of a state acting in its 'governmental' or 'sovereign' capacity is of no relevance for

[33] See Article 33(2) and the accompanying commentary to that Article (para. 4), ILC Articles on the Responsibility of States', UN Doc. A/56/10.

[34] Commentary to Article 12, ILC Articles on the Responsibility of States, UN Doc. A/56/10, para. 9.

[35] *Ibid.*, Article 3.

[35] *Ibid.*, Commentary to Article 12, para. 9.

[36] *Ibid.*, Commentary to Article 3, para. 7.

[37] On this, see *Sergei Paushok, CJSC Golden East Co. and CJSC Vostokneftegaz Co.* v. *Mongolia*, UNCITRAL, Award on Jurisdiction and Liability, 28 April 2011, paras 576 ff.

the establishment of the international responsibility of that state.[38] The ILC in its commentary to Article 4, which governs the attribution of conduct of *organs of a state*, noted that:

> It is irrelevant for the purposes of attribution that the conduct of a State organ may be classified as 'commercial' or as *acta iure gestionis*. Of course, the breach by a State of a contract does not as such entail a breach of international law. Something further is required before international law becomes relevant, such as a denial of justice by the courts of the State in proceedings brought by the other contracting party. But the entry into or breach of a contract by a State organ is nonetheless an act of the State for the purposes of article 4, and it might in certain circumstances amount to an internationally wrongful act.[39]

From this principle one cannot, however, presume that every contract breach by the state engenders the international responsibility of the state, as is explicitly acknowledged by the ILC. Indeed, to paraphrase the ILC Commentary, 'something further is required before international law becomes relevant'. In other words, a contract breach, even though attributable to the state, engages the international responsibility of a state only to the extent that that breach also constitutes a breach of an international legal obligation. To consider that a state has breached its international treaty obligations will very often require that the state has taken certain measures or has acted in a sovereign capacity, namely, in a capacity that enables the state to breach the obligations contained in a treaty, a requirement which has been confirmed by multiple tribunals.[40] But the principle remains that the 'commercial' nature of the conduct of the state and its organs is, as a matter of principle, irrelevant to establish the international responsibility of a state.

### 1.2.3 *Investment contracts*

In practice foreign investors and host states will, in addition to the protection offered by the relevant investment treaty, sign one or more contracts in which the specifics of the investment will be detailed. This constitutes the second layer of obligations. This contract is very often concluded by the foreign investor and an agency or subdivision of a state.

[38] See also James Crawford, 'Treaty and Contract in Investment Arbitration', *Arbitration International*, 24(3) (2008): 351, 357.

[39] Commentary to Article 4, ILC Articles on the Responsibility of States, UN Doc. A/56/10, para. 6.

[40] For a recent example, see *Ambiente Ufficio SpA and others* v. *The Argentine Republic (formerly Giordano Alpi and others* v. *The Argentine Republic)*, ICSID Case No. ARB/08/9, Decision on Jurisdiction and Admissibility, 8 February 2013, paras 545 ff. See also, below, section 4.1.

Investment contracts are not regulated by international law,[41] since the presence of the foreign investor as a party to the contract makes it impossible to conclude an international legal instrument because they have no treaty-making capacity.

Despite the controversial question of the 'internationalization' of such contracts, which has triggered much attention in the past, the contract remains essentially a private law instrument.[42] The main reason to claim that such contracts are 'international(ized)' instruments resides principally in the fact that international law is applied to the contract rather than to domestic law. However, in the end, what counts is the applicable law clause contained in the contract, which in the majority of cases reveals that they are governed by domestic law, very often that of the host state, occasionally coupled with international law.[43] Contemporary investment contracts very rarely provide for the exclusive application of international law, which may be explained by the absence in general international law of rules specifically regulating the contractual legal relations between states and foreign investors.[44] In any event, even when international law applies jointly with domestic law, the former essentially functions in a corrective or complementary function.[45]

The question of whether the state has breached its international obligations towards the foreign investor, which is governed solely by the rules on state responsibility, is fundamentally different from state liability for breaches of the investment or concession contract.[46] In terms of attribution, for example, the state may not be liable under its domestic laws for the conduct of a separate legal entity, despite the fact that the acts of the latter may be attributable to the state under general international law.[47] Also, as explained in the previous section, a breach

[41] See, however, Weil, 'Droit international et contrat d'Etat', p. 562 and Mann, 'Theoretical Approach Towards the Law Governing Contracts Between States and Private Persons', pp. 564–5.

[42] See Weil, 'Droit international et contrat d'Etat', p. 562 ; Mann, 'Theoretical Approach Towards the Law Governing Contracts Between States and Private Persons', pp. 564–5; and Bernard Audit, 'L'arbitrage international et les contrats d'État: bilan et perspectives', in Centre d'étude et de recherche de droit international et de relations internationales, *L'arbitrage transnational et les contrats d'État* (Dordrecht: Martinus Nijhoff, 1987).

[43] Dumberry, 'International Investment Contracts', pp. 223 ff. [44] *Ibid.*, p. 224.

[45] See below, section 4.1.

[46] Crawford, 'Treaty and Contract in Investment Arbitration', p. 358.

[47] See *Compañiá de Aguas del Aconquija SA and Vivendi Universal* v. *Argentina*, ICSID Case No. ARB/97/3, Decision on Annulment, para. 96: 'in the case of a claim based on a treaty, international law rules of attribution apply, with the result that the state of Argentina is internationally responsible for the acts of its provincial authorities. By contrast, the

of a contract does not amount to a wrongful act under international law. This again is a consequence of the clear division between contract and international legal obligations. This distinction is, despite its complexity, paramount in delineating the jurisdiction of arbitral tribunals.

## 1.3 Distinguishing the contract and treaty levels in investment treaty arbitration

The relation between public international law and municipal law appears complex and has evolved substantially following the increase in international arbitral awards. Despite the relative clarity of the distinction between the contract and treaty levels of obligation in investment law, practice shows that the two levels may not always be clearly separable in the application of the rules to the specific dispute. Investment tribunals, sometimes as a consequence of the application of an 'umbrella clause', may be required to apply not only principles of public international law, but at the same time the municipal law of the host state or principles of private law, therefore creating a potential 'substantive overlap' between these two levels of obligation and protection in terms of applicable law, a question I will address in Chapter 4. The multiple levels of legal obligations also may result in a 'procedural overlap'. International investment tribunals may, in theory, be mandated to deal with contract claims as well as treaty claims, and the foreign investor will very often have different available dispute settlement fora in the contract and in the BIT.[48] Although in some instances the different levels are indeed difficult to discern, both levels should be clearly separated, in particular, in respect of the jurisdiction of arbitral tribunals. The vast majority of investment tribunals operating under the ICSID Convention are clearly treaty-based, and thus derive their jurisdiction from the applicable investment treaty. Then, the claim of the foreign investor is in principle a claim in respect of the violation of the treaty to which the respondent state is a party, and the tribunal is mandated to assess whether the state has respected its international obligations. In some instances, however, it has been argued that

state of Argentina is not liable for the performance of contracts entered into by Tucumán, which possesses separate legal personality under its own law and is responsible for the performance of its own contracts.'

48 See Yuval Shany, 'Notes and Comments. Contract Claims v. Treaty Claims: Mapping Conflicts Between ICSID Decisions on Multi-Sourced Investment Claims', *American Journal of International Law*, 99(4) (2005): 835.

investment treaties may also provide the basis for contract claims, notably when the dispute settlement clause in the treaty is broadly formulated, or when the treaty contains a so-called 'umbrella clause'. But even in those cases, differentiating contract claims from treaty claims is necessary to delimit the jurisdiction of arbitral tribunals.

Indeed, investment treaty arbitration is a specific type of mixed dispute settlement that, as every forum which settles international disputes, is limited by the compromissory clause in which states have expressed their consent to the jurisdiction of the arbitral tribunal. The scope of jurisdiction is defined and limited by the agreement of the states party to the treaty granting jurisdiction. The tribunal thus has no competence in matters that fall outside the mandate given to the tribunal by the parties.[49] The divide between the contract and treaty levels of obligations, and the accompanying dispute settlement clauses in the investment contract and the investment treaty, respectively, has, however, proven difficult in practice and has led to a long list of decisions from arbitral tribunals discussing the matter with some considerable variations. It is not the purpose here to discuss this question exhaustively. I will, rather, outline the main principles that are necessary to understand the main argument of this book.

### *1.3.1 Differentiating contract claims from treaty claims*

The fundamental distinction between the contract level and the treaty level of obligations, and the difference in jurisdictional basis of investment tribunals was famously and cogently explained by the Ad Hoc Committee in *Vivendi I*, briefly mentioned above.[50] The decision of the Committee in *Vivendi I* and the principles stated therein have proven to constitute the leading case on which many arbitral tribunals have subsequently relied.

The case concerned the operation of water and sewage systems by an Argentinian company *Compañiá de Aguas del Aconquija*, which was then controlled by the French company *Compagnie Générale des Eaux* (later on *Vivendi Universal*) in the Argentinian province of Tucamàn.[51] Article 16(4) of the Concession Contract provided that contractual disputes arising out of the contract were to be submitted to the exclusive jurisdiction of

[49] John Collier and Vaughan Lowe, *The Settlement of Disputes in International Law. Institutions and Procedures* (Oxford University Press, 1999), p. 227.

[50] *Compañiá de Aguas del Aconquija SA and Vivendi Universal* v. *Argentina*, Decision on Annulment. See also, above, section 1.2.

[51] For the relevant facts, see *ibid.*, paras 11 ff.

Tucumàn's Contentious Administrative Tribunals. Article 8 of the BIT between Argentina and France, on the other hand, provided for the submission of investment disputes, at the investor's option, to the domestic courts of the host state, or to arbitration under the ICSID Convention, or to an ad hoc tribunal pursuant to the UNCITRAL Arbitration Rules. In 1996, relying on Article 8 of the Argentina–France BIT, *Compagnie Générale des Eaux* filed a claim against Argentina before an ICSID Tribunal, without having pursued a claim before Tucumàn's Contentious Administrative Tribunals. The arbitral tribunal originally held, in respect of the claim related to the acts of Tucumàn Province which were considered attributable to Argentina in respect of the concession contract, that it had jurisdiction but that:

> because of the crucial connection in this case between the terms of the Concession Contract and these alleged violations of the BIT, the Argentine Republic cannot be held liable unless and until Claimants have, as Article 16.4 of the Concession Contract requires, asserted their rights in proceedings before the contentious administrative courts of Tucumàn and have been denied their rights, either procedurally or substantively.[52]

As far as the claim in respect of violations of the BIT was concerned, the Tribunal rejected the claim on the basis that 'the record of these proceedings does not provide a basis for holding that the Argentine Republic failed to respond to the situation in Tucumàn and the requests of the Claimants in accordance with the obligations of the Argentine government under the BIT'.[53] *Vivendi* subsequently filed a claim in annulment of the arbitral award.

The Ad Hoc Committee partly annulled the award. It confirmed the positive finding of jurisdiction, but reversed the Tribunal's decision not to examine the merits of the dispute on the following grounds:

> In a case where the essential basis of a claim brought before an international tribunal is a breach of contract, the tribunal will give effect to any valid choice of forum clause in the contract.
>
> … where 'the fundamental basis of the claim' is a treaty laying down an independent standard by which the conduct of the parties is to be judged, the existence of an exclusive jurisdiction clause in a contract between the claimant and the respondent state or one of its subdivisions cannot operate as a bar to the application of the treaty standard.

[52] *Compañiá de Aguas del Aconquija SA and Compagnie Générale des Eaux* v. *The Argentine Republic*, ICSID Case No. ARB/97/3, Award, 21 November 2000, para. 78.

[53] *Ibid.*, para. 92.

> . . . the Committee does not understand how, if there had been a breach of the BIT in the present case (a question of international law), the existence of Article 16(4) of the Concession Contract could have prevented its characterisation as such. A state cannot rely on an exclusive jurisdiction clause in a contract to avoid the characterisation of its conduct as internationally unlawful under a treaty.
>
> A treaty cause of action is not the same as a contractual cause of action; it requires a clear showing of conduct which is in the circumstances contrary to the relevant treaty standard. The availability of local courts ready and able to resolve specific issues independently may be a relevant circumstance in determining whether there has been a breach of international law (especially in relation to a standard such as that contained in Article 3). But it is not dispositive, and it does not preclude an international tribunal from considering the merits of the dispute.[54]

To distinguish treaty claims from contract claims, the Ad Hoc Committee in *Vivendi I* posited that the test to be applied is whether the 'essential basis' or 'fundamental basis' of the claim is contract- or treaty-based.[55] In applying this test, an arbitral tribunal will thus be able to define the legal foundation of the claim and so characterize the claim as treaty-based, contract-based or both, establish the proper defendant,[56] and determine the appropriate dispute settlement forum. An arbitral tribunal will then, in light of the relevant dispute settlement clauses, be able to establish (or not) its jurisdiction for either of these claims. The decision of the Ad Hoc Committee in *Vivendi I*, and its clear formulation of the differences between contract and treaty claims, has been followed and cited by a large number of other tribunals.[57]

[54] *Compañiá de Aguas del Aconquija SA and Vivendi Universal* v. *Argentina*, ICSID Case No. ARB/97/3, Decision on Annulment, paras 98, 101, 103 and 113.

[55] Whether or not tribunals should apply an objective test in the qualification of the legal foundation of the claim or, rather, rely on the characterization of the legal foundation of the claim by the claimant is a question that has divided arbitral tribunals and doctrine. It is not the purpose here, however, to discuss this question, which has been extensively analysed elsewhere. On this, see Douglas, *The International Law of Investment Treaty Claims*, pp. 263 ff. See also *Impregilo* v. *Pakistan*, ICSID Case No. ARB/03/3, paras 237–254.

[56] Douglas, *The International Law of Investment Treaty Claims*, p. 271.

[57] See, for example, *TSA Spectrum de Argentina SA* v. *The Argentine Republic*, ICSID Case No. ARB/05/5, Award, 19 December 2008; *Enron Corporation and Ponderosa Assets LP* v. *The Argentine Republic*, ICSID Case No. ARB/01/3, Decision on Jurisdiction, 14 January 2004; *Azurix Corp*. v. *The Argentine Republic*, ICSID Case No. ARB/01/12, Award on Jurisdiction, 8 December 2003; *CMS Gas Transmission Co*. v. *The Argentine Republic*, ICSID Case No. ARB/01/8, Decision on Jurisdiction, 17 July 2003; and *Salini Costruttori SpA and Italstrade SpA* v. *Morocco*, ICSID Case No. ARB/00/4, Decision on Jurisdiction, 23 July 2001.

As a consequence of this distinction, contract claims should, in principle, be brought before the contractually provided dispute settlement forum, while treaty claims may be brought before the dispute settlement forum provided for in the investment treaty. As recently noted by the Tribunal in *Abaclat* v. *Argentina*:

> It is in principle admitted that with respect to a BIT claim an arbitral tribunal has no jurisdiction where the claim at stake is a pure contract claim. This is because a BIT is not meant to correct or replace contractual remedies, and in particular it is not meant to serve as a substitute to judicial or arbitral proceedings arising from contract claims. Within the context of claims arising from a contractual relationship, jurisdiction in relation to BIT claims is in principle only given where, in addition to the alleged breach of contract, the Host State further breaches obligations it undertook under a relevant treaty. Pure contract claims must be brought before the competent organ, which derives its jurisdiction from the contract, and such organ be it a court or an arbitral tribunal can and must hear the claim in its entirety and decide thereon based on the contract only.[58]

This, of course, raises the question of whether and when breaches of contractual obligations also constitute breaches of the investment treaty.

### 1.3.2 *When does a breach of contract amount to a treaty breach?*

As well as the question of whether purely contract claims fall within the scope of the dispute settlement clause in a treaty, which I address later in this section, a violation of a contract does not *ipso facto* amount to a violation of international law. As noted by the Tribunal in *Duke Energy*: 'in and of itself the violation of a contract does not amount to the violation of a treaty. This is only natural since treaty and contract breaches are different things, responding to different tests, subject to different rules.'[59] As a consequence, not all contract breaches will automatically lead to a breach of a treaty standard. This does not mean that the conduct that amounts to a breach of the contract may not also constitute a breach of the treaty, and thus give rise to both a contract claim and a treaty claim, but this is not automatic.

There is a relatively well-established jurisprudence according to which a mere commercial breach of an investment contract does not amount to a breach of the investment treaty, and does not therefore

[58] *Abaclat and others (case formerly known as Giovanna a Beccara and others)* v. *The Argentine Republic*, ICSID Case No. ARB/07/5, Decision on Jurisdiction and Admissibility, 4 August 2011, para. 316.

[59] *Duke Energy Electroquil Partners and Electroquil SA* v. *Republic of Ecuador*, ICSID Case No. ARB/04/19, Award, 18 August 2008, para. 342.

trigger the dispute settlement clause of that treaty.[60] At the same time, one single act may constitute both a contract breach and a treaty breach. The Tribunal in *Impregilo* v. *Pakistan*, for instance, having found that the jurisdiction of the Tribunal did not extend to contract breaches to which an entity other than the state is a party, held that 'the fact that Article 9 of the BIT does not endow the Tribunal with jurisdiction to consider Impregilo's Contract Claims does not imply that the Tribunal has no jurisdiction to consider Treaty Claims against Pakistan which at the same time could constitute breaches of the Contracts'.[61] It further noted that 'the fact that a breach may give rise to a contract claim does not mean that it cannot also – and separately – give rise to a treaty claim. Even if the two perfectly coincide, they remain analytically distinct, and necessarily require different enquiries.'[62] In respect of the test to determine whether a claimant can allege a breach of a treaty when the claim also simultaneously gives rise to a contract claim, the Tribunal went on to hold that:

> in order that the alleged breach of contract may constitute a violation of the BIT, it must be the result of behaviour going beyond that which an ordinary contracting party could adopt. Only the State in the exercise of its sovereign authority ('*puissance publique*'), and not as a contracting party, may breach the obligations assumed under the BIT. In other words, the investment protection treaty only provides a remedy to the investor where the investor proves that the alleged damages were a consequence of the behaviour of the Host State acting in breach of the obligations it had assumed under the treaty.[63]

This line of reasoning has been followed by many tribunals.[64] The principle that a contract breach may only be brought before an international investment tribunal to the extent that it is proven that the conduct

[60] See also for a discussion Stephan W. Schill, 'Enabling Private Ordering: Function, Scope and Effect of Umbrella Clauses in International Investment Treaties', *Minnesota Journal of International Law*, 18(1) (2009): 32.

[61] *Impregilo* v. *Pakistan*, ICSID Case No. ARB/03/3, para. 219. [62] *Ibid*., para. 258.

[63] *Ibid*., para. 260 (internal footnotes omitted).

[64] The view that a contract breach may only be brought before an international investment tribunal to the extent that it is proven that the conduct complained of was not merely commercial or contractual in nature was further clarified by the tribunal in *Bayindir Insaat Turizm Ticaret Ve Sanayi AS* v. *Islamic Republic of Pakistan*, ICSID Case No. ARB/03/29, Decision on Jurisdiction, 14 November 2005, para. 183. The tribunal in *Hamester* v. *Ghana* also discussed extensively the invocation by the claimant of both treaty and contract claims and addressed the question of whether and how contract claims may be brought as treaty claims in an *obiter dictum* (*Gustav F. W. Hamester GmbH & Co. KG* v. *Republic of Ghana*, ICSID Case No. ARB/07/24, Award, 18 June 2010, paras 313 ff). See also *Abaclat* v. *Argentina*, ICSID Case No. ARB/07/5, Decision on Jurisdiction and Admissibility, 4 August 2011, paras 318 ff.

complained of was not merely commercial or contractual in nature was relatively broadly formulated by various tribunals. As far as international investment law is concerned, this is the logical consequence of the fact that the majority of the obligations contained in investment treaties can in effect be breached only by sovereign acts of states, having been developed to protect aliens from the sovereign acts of states. In other words, the state, when acting in a private or commercial capacity, will very often not be in a position to breach the obligations it has entered into in an investment treaty. That is also why the discussed decisions have highlighted the need for the state to act in a sovereign capacity in order for it to breach certain treaty provisions, such as those relating to expropriation.[65] This is in line with the general rationale of investment protection treaties, that is, to guarantee certain rights to foreign investors who are exposed to the sovereign conduct of the host state, and thereby minimize their exposure to the sovereign risk attached to investments in foreign states.[66] This question is directed at the *wrongfulness of the act* and is thus distinct from the question of attribution. In other words, although a certain conduct may be attributable to a state, such conduct would not, according to this case law, result in the international responsibility of the state if it has not acted in its sovereign capacity.[67]

It is consequently beyond doubt that international investment tribunals have jurisdiction over a claim if it is presented as a treaty claim and plausibly concerns violations of the relevant investment treaty. Conversely, domestic courts or other mechanisms, including arbitration under the ICSID Convention or otherwise[68] provided for in the concession contract or the national legislation of the host state, have jurisdiction over contract claims,[69] and, some argue, depending on the

[65] See, for instance, *Waste Management, Inc.* v. *The United Mexican States (No. 2)*, ICSID Case No. ARB(AF)/00/3, Final Award, 30 April 2004, para. 160.

[66] Douglas, *The International Law of Investment Treaty Claims*, p. 161.

[67] See *Hamester* v. *Ghana*, ICSID Case No. ARB/07/24, para. 143; *Sergei Paushok* v. *Mongolia*, UNCITRAL, Award on Jurisdiction and Liability, paras 574 ff; *Joy Mining Machinery Ltd* v. *Egypt*, ICSID Case No. ARB/03/11, Award on Jurisdiction, 6 August 2004, para. 72; *Noble Ventures, Inc.* v. *Romania*, ICSID Case No. ARB/01/11, Award, 12 October 2005, para. 82; and *Azurix Corp.* v. *The Argentine Republic*, ICSID Case No. ARB/01/12, Award, 14 July 2006, para. 315.

[68] See, for instance, *Perenco Ecuador Ltd* v. *Republic of Ecuador and Empresa Estatal Petróleos del Ecuador*, ICSID Case No. ARB/08/6, Decision on Jurisdiction, 30 June 2011, paras 125 ff.

[69] See, generally, Christoph Schreuer, 'Investment Treaty Arbitration and Jurisdiction over Contract Claims: The *Vivendi I* Case', in Todd Weiler (ed.), *International Investment*

circumstances and the wording of the clause, also have jurisdiction over breaches of an applicable investment treaty.[70]

In any event, all this implies that foreign investors, confronted with two possible dispute settlement methods, may choose to characterize the claim either as a contract claim or as a treaty claim and bring proceedings according to the contractual or treaty-based dispute settlement mechanism.[71] There is thus no procedural overlap - which does not mean that there is no link between the two procedures - since the conceptually distinct levels of obligations are assessed independently by separate dispute settlement mechanisms, either under public international law or under domestic law.

### 1.3.3 *'Umbrella clauses'*

The difference between the contract and the treaty levels is complicated by the inclusion in certain BITs of so-called 'umbrella-clauses'.[72] The outcome of such clauses is that a breach of a contractual obligation will simultaneously be a breach of a treaty obligation, with the result that in that case the investor gains access to the dispute settlement forum contained in the investment treaty. If no clear divide between the two levels of obligation existed, there would of course be no reason for 'umbrella clauses'. The existence of 'umbrella clauses' thus fortifies the idea that a clear and neat distinction between the contract and treaty levels not only exists, but should also be maintained.

Admittedly, in practice 'umbrella clauses' have a tendency to blur the division between contractual obligations and treaty obligations, since international investment tribunals, when confronted by such a clause, will need to investigate whether the state has breached its contractual obligations in order to determine whether there is a breach of the applicable investment treaty. In the event of an investment dispute brought before an international investment tribunal solely through the application of an 'umbrella clause', the analogy between investment treaty arbitration and other public international law dispute settlement

*Law and Arbitration. Leading Cases from the ICSID, NAFTA, Bilateral Treaties and Customary International Law* (London: Cameron May, 2005), pp. 281–323.

70 For a discussion, see Douglas, *The International Law of Investment Treaty Claims*, pp. 277–8.

71 See *SGS Société Générale de Surveillance SA* v. *Islamic Republic of Pakistan*, ICSID Case No. ARB/01/13, Decision of the Tribunal on Objections to Jurisdiction, 6 August 2003, para. 145.

72 See, for instance, Article 10(2) of the Swiss Model BIT: 'Each Contracting Party shall observe any obligation it has assumed with regard to investments in its territory by investors of the other Contracting Party.'

mechanisms or the public international law character of investment treaty arbitration may not be as clear.[73] However, the theoretical and concrete distinction between contract and treaty remains intact, since the international obligations contracted by the state – the obligation under the umbrella clause – is clearly an international legal obligation of the state under public international law, and a violation thereof entails the international responsibility of the state.

It is well known that the effect of 'umbrella clauses' has resulted in divergent and conflicting arbitral decisions.[74] It is not the purpose here to engage in an extensive discussion of this divergence.[75] It is nevertheless possible to distil certain common principles that apply to 'umbrella clauses', which reinforce the distinction between the contract and the treaty levels of obligations, and thus the public international law dimension of investment treaty arbitration.

First, as rightly pointed out by the Ad Hoc Committee in *CMS Gas* v. *Argentina*:

> the effect of the umbrella clause is not to transform the obligation which is relied on into something else; the content of the obligation is unaffected, as is its proper law. If this is so, it would appear that the parties to the obligation (i.e. the persons bound by it and entitled to rely on it) are likewise not changed because of the umbrella clause.[76]

[73] See Charles H. Brower II, 'The Function and Limits of Arbitration and Judicial Settlement under Private and Public International Law', *Duke Journal of Comparative and International Law*, 18(2) (2007/8): 259, 299.

[74] Ranging from the denial of any effect to 'umbrella clauses' (see, e.g., *SGS* v. *Pakistan*, ICSID Case No. ARB/01/13, Decision of the Tribunal on Objections to Jurisdiction, and *Joy Mining* v. *Egypt*, ICSID Case No. ARB/03/11), the effect of an automatic transformation of a contract violation into a treaty violation (see, e.g., *Eureko BV* v. *Republic of Poland*, Ad Hoc, Partial Award, 19 August 2005, including a strong dissent of Arbitrator Rajski on precisely this issue) to the transformation of a contract violation into a treaty violation provided that the contract does not contain any exclusive dispute settlement clause (see, e.g., *SGS Société Générale de Surveillance SA* v. *Republic of the Philippines*, ICSID Case No. ARB/02/6, Decision of the Tribunal on Objections to Jurisdiction, 29 January 2004).

[75] For a discussion, see Schill, 'Enabling Private Ordering', and Emmanuel Gaillard, 'Investment Treaty Arbitration and Jurisdiction over Contract Claims: The SGS Cases Considered', in Todd Weiler (ed.), *International Investment Law and Arbitration. Leading Cases from the ICSID, NAFTA, Bilateral Treaties and Customary International Law* (London: Cameron May, 2005), pp. 338–45. See for an extensive discussion of the various viewpoints: *Pan American Energy LLC and BP Argentina Exploration Co.* v. *The Argentine Republic*, ICSID Case No. ARB/03/13, Decision on Preliminary Objections, 27 July 2006.

[76] *CMS Gas Transmission Co.* v. *The Argentine Republic*, ICSID Case No. ARB/01/8, Decision on Annulment, 25 September 2007, para. 95.

It is, therefore, not completely accurate to posit that an 'umbrella clause' actually transforms a contract obligation into a treaty obligation.[77] Rather, the presence of such a clause merely implies that if a state breaches one of its contractual obligations, this at the same time constitutes a violation of the treaty obligation contained in the 'umbrella clause'. Both obligations nevertheless remain conceptually distinct. Secondly, the exact wording of the 'umbrella clause' will be determinant in analysing the effect the clause has on the 'elevation' of contract breaches to breaches of the investment treaty.

As a consequence of these principles, various tribunals have held that in order for a foreign investor to rely on an 'umbrella clause' for the purposes of establishing the jurisdiction of the arbitral tribunal for a treaty claim, the investment contract should include not only the claimant,[78] but also the state as a party.[79] Since 'umbrella clauses' very often state that the *contracting parties*, that is, the states party to the investment treaty, are under an obligation to respect any other obligations they have entered into in relation to investments made by investors of the other contracting party,[80] it is indeed correct to assume that when the concession contract was signed by a third party or a separate legal entity, the

[77] Cf. *Noble Ventures* v. *Romania*, ICSID Case No. ARB/01/11, para. 53: 'An umbrella clause is usually seen as transforming municipal law obligations into obligations directly cognizable in international law.'

[78] On this, see *Burlington Resources Inc.* v. *Republic of Ecuador (formerly Burlington Resources Inc. and others* v. *Republic of Ecuador and Empresa Estatal Petróleos del Ecuador (PetroEcuador))*, ICSID Case No. ARB/08/5, Decision on Liability, 14 December 2012, paras 200 ff.

[79] See, for instance, *Impregilo* v. *Pakistan*, ICSID Case No. ARB/03/3, para. 223: 'In the Tribunal's view, given that the Contracts were concluded by Impregilo with WAPDA, and not with Pakistan, Impregilo's reliance upon Article 3 of the BIT takes the matter no further.' A similar finding was made in *Hamester*: 'Applying the actual words of Article 9(2) of the BIT, the contractual obligations which the Claimant seeks to impose upon the ROG were not "assumed by it". Given that the umbrella clause in this BIT is specifically delimited by reference to obligations that have been "assumed by the State", the Tribunal sees no basis to ignore these words, and to extend the ambit of the provision to contractual obligations assumed by other separate entities' (*Hamester* v. *Ghana*, ICSID Case No. ARB/07/24, para. 347). See also *Limited Liability Co. Amto* v. *Ukraine*, SCC Case No. 080/2005, Final Award, 26 March 2008, para. 110. See also *Bureau Veritas, Inspection, Valuation, Assessment and Control BIVAC BV* v. *Paraguay*, ICSID Case No. ARB/07/9, Decision on Jurisdiction, 19 May 2009, para. 141, and *Bosh International, Inc. and B&P Ltd Foreign Investments Enterprise* v. *Ukraine*, ICSID Case No. ARB/08/11, Award, 25 October 2012, paras 241 ff, which provides a rather comprehensive overview of all relevant cases in this respect (para. 248).

[80] See, for instance, Article 7(2) of the German Model BIT: 'Each Contracting State shall fulfil any other obligations it may have entered into with regard to investments in its territory by investors of the other Contracting State.'

'umbrella clause' is not triggered.[81] Conversely, tribunals have also denied the application of the 'umbrella clause' to contracts that were signed by the respondent state, but with a subsidiary of the claimant.[82]

Certain tribunals have limited the application of the 'umbrella clause' to contract breaches committed by the state in the exercise of sovereign authority,[83] a position that has also been adopted by certain scholars,[84] and that is in conformity with the well-established jurisprudence in respect of whether and how international investment tribunals established under an investment treaty may consider contract claims, irrespective of the application of an 'umbrella clause', as was discussed in the previous paragraph. This position, however, has been criticized on the basis that 'umbrella clauses' from that perspective would add nothing more than what is already provided for by the treaty in terms of substantive protection, since the majority of the standards of protection require the conduct of the state acting in its sovereign capacity.[85] At the same time, it should be noted that, in view of the fact that the operation of an 'umbrella clause' results in a contract breach being at the same time a treaty breach, in the sense that the violation of the contract by a state amounts at the same time to a violation of the investment treaty, the relevant standards for the violation of a treaty should be met.[86]

[81] The relevant criterion here has been the subject of divergent decisions. For a discussion, see Crawford, 'Treaty and Contract in Investment Arbitration', pp. 367–8. See also *Hamester* v. *Ghana*, ICSID Case No. ARB/07/24, para. 347 (analysing whether the party to the concession contract is, under the municipal laws of the host state, a distinct and separate legal entity); *Noble Ventures* v. *Romania*, ICSID Case No. ARB/01/11, para. 68. See also *Eureko* v. *Poland*, Partial Award and Dissenting Opinion, paras 115–134; and *Bosh* v. *Ukraine*, ICSID Case No. ARB/08/11, para. 246 (holding that the relevant standard is whether the acts may be attributed to the state).

[82] See *Burlington* v. *Ecuador*, ICSID Case No. ARB/08/5; *Azurix* v. *Argentina*, ICSID Case No. ARB/01/12, Award, para. 384; *Siemens AG* v. *The Argentine Republic*, ICSID Case No. ARB/02/8, Award and Separate Opinion, 6 February 2007, para. 204; and *Hamester* v. *Ghana*, ICSID Case No. ARB/07/24, para. 346.

[83] See, for example, *Pan American Energy* v. *Argentina*, ICSID Case No. ARB/03/13, paras 108 ff; and *El Paso Energy Int'l Co.* v. *The Argentine Republic*, ICSID Case No. ARB/03/15, Decision on Jurisdiction, 27 April 2006, paras 79 ff.

[84] See, for example, Thomas W. Wälde, 'The "Umbrella Clause" in Investment Arbitration: A Comment on Original Intentions and Recent Cases', *Journal of World Investment & Trade*, 6(2) (2006): 183, 196: 'disputes over contracts that display merely commercial- and contract-law elements will not fall under international law; such disputes do not involve the power of government'.

[85] See, for instance, Schill, 'Enabling Private Ordering', p. 39.

[86] For a discussion, see Crawford, 'Treaty and Contract in Investment Arbitration', pp. 356 ff.

A different question is whether purely contract claims may be brought before an international investment tribunal based on the investment treaty only, independently of any umbrella clause, and the implications of this for the jurisdiction of the tribunal.

### 1.3.4 *Jurisdiction over contract claims and dispute settlement provisions in investment treaties*

As noted by Crawford, the Algiers Accords[87] setting up the Iran–US Claims Tribunal in reality constituted an international treaty which granted jurisdiction to an international arbitral tribunal over essentially contract claims.[88] The creation of the Iran–US Claims Tribunal has thus unambiguously shown the possibility in international law of establishing an international arbitral tribunal with jurisdiction over contract claims only. Because of the limited number of substantive provisions governing the *legal relations* between Iranian and US citizens and the United States and Iran, respectively, and the explicit provision of jurisdiction over contract claims, the Iran–US Claims Tribunal may, however, not be the best institution with which to compare investment treaty arbitration.[89]

[87] Declaration of the Democratic and Popular Republic of Algeria Concerning the Settlement of Claims by the Government of the United States of America and the Government of the Islamic Republic of Iran, *International Legal Materials*, 20 (1981): 223.

[88] See, generally, Crawford, 'Treaty and Contract in Investment Arbitration', p. 364.

[89] Moreover, one should add that the hybrid nature of the tribunal, being established by an international treaty and mandated mainly to settle outstanding contractual disputes may explain why there is a clear lack of consensus on the international or private character of the tribunal. Judge Brower has claimed, for instance, that it is an international institution (Charles N. Brower and Jason D. Brueschke, *The Iran–United States Claims Tribunal* (The Hague: Martinus Nijhoff, 1998), p. 16. See also Hazel Fox, 'States and the Undertaking to Arbitrate', *International and Comparative Law Quarterly*, 37(1) (1988): 1, 3. See, however, David Caron, 'The Nature of the Iran–United States Claims Tribunal and the Evolving Structure of International Dispute Resolution', *American Journal of International Law*, 84(1), (1990): 104, 106). On the claim that the Iran–United States Claims Tribunal is not a national, or an international, institution, but rather a denationalized institution, see William Lake and Jane Tucker Dana, 'Judicial Review of Awards of the Iran–United States Claims Tribunal: Are the Tribunal's Awards Dutch?' *Law & Policy in International Business*, 16 (1984): 755, 811. This debate is also expounded by the question of whether Dutch law applies as the *lex loci arbitri* or not, the tribunal being situated in the Netherlands. For the conclusion that Dutch law does not apply, see L. Hardenberg, 'The Awards of the Iran–United States Claims Tribunal Seen in Connection with the Law of the Netherlands', *International Business Lawyer*, 12 (1984): 337. For the contrary claim, see Albert-Jan van den Berg, 'Proposed Dutch Law on the Iran–United States Claims Settlement Declaration, A Reaction to Mr. Hardenberg's Article', *International Business Lawyer*, 12 (1984): 341.

In investment treaty arbitration, if the specific terms of the dispute settlement clause in an applicable BIT are explicit enough to encompass contract claims, it has been held that there is no reason to exclude purely contract claims from the jurisdiction of international investment tribunals.[90] Here again, the decision of the Annulment Committee in *Vivendi I* is very relevant. The Committee noted that:

> Article 8 [of the BIT] deals generally with disputes 'relating to investments made under this Agreement between one Contracting Party and an investor of the other Contracting Party'. It is those disputes which may be submitted, at the investor's option, either to national or international adjudication. Article 8 does not use a narrower formulation, requiring that the investor's claim allege a breach of the BIT itself. Read literally, the requirements for arbitral jurisdiction in Article 8 do not necessitate that the Claimant allege a breach of the BIT itself: it is sufficient that the dispute relate to an investment made under the BIT.[91]

A similar observation was made by the Tribunal in *SGS* v. *The Philippines*, which established jurisdiction over contract claims[92] essentially on the basis of the 'umbrella clause', but nevertheless posited that in view of the broad formulation of the dispute settlement provision of the applicable BIT, which referred to 'disputes with respect to investments' generally, investment tribunals may consider purely contract claims:

> Prima facie, Article VIII is an entirely general provision, allowing for submission of all investment disputes by the investor against the host State. The term 'disputes with respect to investments' ('différents relatifs à des investissements' in the French text) is not limited by reference to the legal classification of the claim that is made.[93]

The Tribunal, however, noted at the same time that 'the general provisions of BITs should not, unless clearly expressed to do so, override specific and exclusive dispute settlement arrangements made in the investment contract itself'.[94] Applied to the facts, the Tribunal conceded that the investment contract included an exclusive jurisdiction

[90] See Schreuer, 'Investment Treaty Arbitration and Jurisdiction over Contract Claims', p. 289.

[91] *Compañiá de Aguas del Aconquija SA and Vivendi Universal* v. *Argentina*, ICSID Case No. ARB/97/3, Decision on Annulment, para. 55.

[92] The tribunal in *Salini* v. *Morocco*, which chronologically preceded the Annulment Committee's decision in *Vivendi I*, adopted a similar approach (*Salini* v. *Morocco*, ICSID Case No. ARB/00/4, para. 59).

[93] *SGS* v. *The Philippines*, ICSID Case No. ARB/02/6, para. 132.

[94] *Ibid.*, para. 134. See also *Bosh* v. *Ukraine*, ICSID Case No. ARB/08/11, paras 251–258, in which the tribunal considered in an *obiter dictum* that, notwithstanding the application

clause, providing for the domestic courts of the host state, and thus declared the contract claim inadmissible:

The jurisdiction of the Tribunal is determined by the combination of the BIT and the ICSID Convention. It is, to say the least, doubtful that a private party can by contract waive rights or dispense with the performance of obligations imposed on the States parties to those treaties under international law. Although under modern international law, treaties may confer rights, substantive and procedural, on individuals, they will normally do so in order to achieve some public interest. Thus the question is not whether the Tribunal has jurisdiction: unless otherwise expressly provided, treaty jurisdiction is not abrogated by contract.[95]

Having confirmed jurisdiction over the *treaty claim*, and with the treaty claim essentially boiling down to the question of compliance with the investment contract, the Tribunal was faced with the existence of parallel proceedings, namely, the contractual dispute in the domestic courts of the home state, and the treaty-based proceedings before the ICSID Tribunal. The Tribunal eventually decided to stay the proceedings until the contract claim was settled in the domestic court of the Philippines.[96]

Although the principle of the distinct nature of the contract claim and the treaty-based claim does not hinder parallel proceedings before the dispute settlement mechanism provided for in the contract and in the investment treaty, the pragmatic solution adopted by the Tribunal in *SGS* v. *The Philippines* may on occasion prove effective, in particular, when the treaty claim is dependent upon the finding of a contract breach, over which the Tribunal has no jurisdiction. It should be noted, however, that several tribunals have confirmed that, despite

of the umbrella clause, contract claims should be determined in accordance with the applicable dispute settlement procedure provided for in the contract.

95 *Ibid.*, paras 154 ff.

96 *Ibid.*, para. 175. Next to criticism in scholarship on the decision to stay the proceedings, which according to one author 'results in the BIT tribunal having jurisdiction over an empty shell and depriving the BIT dispute resolution of any meaning' (Gaillard, 'Investment Treaty Arbitration and Jurisdiction over Contract Claims', p. 344), the majority of the tribunals that have been confronted with such an issue have decided to continue with the arbitral proceedings, based on the principled difference between the contract claim and the treaty-based claim. The facts of these later cases were, however, relatively different and may have justified a departure from the principles posted by the tribunal in *SGS* v. *The Philippines*. (See, e.g., *Impregilo* v. *Pakistan*, ICSID Case No. ARB/03/3, paras 289–290; *Bayindir* v. *Pakistan*, ICSID Case No. ARB/03/29, Decision on Jurisdiction, para. 270; and *Camuzzi International SA* v. *The Argentine Republic*, ICSID Case No. ARB/03/2, Decision on Objection to Jurisdiction, 11 May 2005, para. 91. See, however, for a positive appraisal of the decision to stay the proceedings, Douglas, *The International Law of Investment Treaty Claims*, pp. 3780 ff.)

the lack of jurisdiction for contract claims, they may assess contract breaches as a preliminary question.[97]

The relatively broad perspective on the jurisdiction of international investment tribunals, as exemplified by the *Vivendi I* and *SGS* v. *The Philippines* decisions, which consists in accepting the jurisdiction of investment tribunals for purely contract claims when the state is a party to the investment contract, seems, however, difficult to reconcile with the public international law character of investment treaty arbitration. As mentioned above, investment treaties can be considered to create rights for individuals, both substantive and procedural rights. The procedural right given to the foreign investor is given in the investment treaty through the explicit consent of the states, and, more importantly, in relation to the substantive provisions of the treaty. In other words, the procedural right of the foreign investor to initiate international arbitral proceedings against a contracting state, being based on a treaty, seems by necessary implication to be limited to cases in which a violation of the provisions of that treaty is invoked by the foreign investor. This is the logical outcome of the explicit and specific consent of states to the dispute settlement method in the investment treaty. It would, indeed, be relatively odd to accept that an investment treaty, which contains substantive protection standards for the treatment of foreign investors, would provide jurisdiction over investment disputes in cases where the tribunal would not even be called upon to rule on the violation of the substantive provisions of that treaty.[98] The arbitration clause is not autonomous – that is, detachable from the rest of the investment agreement – and applies only to disputes arising out of the other clauses of the agreement.[99]

In the event of a broadly formulated dispute settlement clause, awards have nevertheless shown a tendency to consider that the treaty dispute settlement clause equally targets purely contract claims. In a relatively recent decision, *SGS* v. *Paraguay*, the Tribunal noted in an *obiter dictum* that:

> Claimant has not asked this Tribunal to decide claims by SGS under the Contract for breach of that Contract. We note in passing that the Treaty's dispute resolution provisions are arguably broad enough that Claimant would have been

[97] See, for instance, *Bayindir* v. *Pakistan*, Decision on Jurisdiction, para. 270.

[98] See Gaillard, 'Investment Treaty Arbitration and Jurisdiction over Contract Claims', p. 336.

[99] Yannick Radi, 'The Application of the Most-Favoured-Nation Clause to the Dispute Settlement Provisions of Bilateral Investment Treaties: Domesticating the Trojan Horse', *European Journal of International Law*, 18(4) (2007): 757, 762.

> entitled to do so: Article 9 provides for the resolution of 'disputes with respect to investments between a Contracting Party and an investor of the other Contracting Party', and, as discussed in Section IV.A above, Article 9(2) contains Paraguay's consent to international arbitration of such a dispute. There is no qualification or limitation in this language on the types of 'disputes with respect to investments' that a Swiss investor may bring against the Republic of Paraguay. The ordinary meaning of Article 9 would appear to give this Tribunal jurisdiction to hear claims for violation of Claimant's rights under the Contract – surely a dispute 'with respect to' Claimant's investment – should Claimant have chosen to bring them before us. But Claimant has not done so.[100]

In the recent case *Philip Morris Brands* v. *Uruguay*, this was also accepted by the Tribunal on the broad formulation of the clause, as it had been by the respondent state that had nevertheless excluded domestic law claims.[101]

The most often invoked arguments to support the claim that an investment tribunal may hear purely contract claims based on the investment treaty only is that the dispute settlement clauses of BITs are, in those cases, broadly formulated, that there is a distinction with the relatively narrowly formulated interstate dispute settlement clauses, and the exclusion in the dispute settlement clauses of certain BITs and multilateral investment treaties, such as the NAFTA, of contract claims.[102] However, it is rather unpersuasive to consider that, because certain states have excluded this possibility in their investment treaties, those states that have not done so in their treaties intended to include purely contract claims in the jurisdiction of tribunal set up under the treaty. This does not necessarily mean that the states intended otherwise, but the absence of an explicit provision to this effect, and the inclusion of such provisions in other treaties, is not sufficient to ascertain the intent of the states to include purely contract claims in their consent to arbitrate. Moreover, if one accepts this line of reasoning, one could also argue that because certain states have included 'umbrella clauses' in their treaties, the rationale of which – depending of course on the exact wording of the clause – is basically to elevate contract violations

100 *SGS Société Générale de Surveillance SA* v. *Republic of Paraguay*, ICSID Case No. ARB/07/29, Decision on Jurisdiction, 12 February 2010, para. 129.

101 *Philip Morris Brands Sarl, Philip Morris Products SA and Abal Hermanos SA* v. *Oriental Republic of Uruguay (formerly FTR Holding SA, Philip Morris Products SA and Abal Hermanos SA* v. *Oriental Republic of Uruguay)*, ICSID Case No. ARB/10/7, Decision on Jurisdiction, 2 July 2013, paras 107 ff.

102 See *SGS* v. *The Philippines*, ICSID Case No. ARB/02/6, para. 132. See also Crawford, 'Treaty and Contract in Investment Arbitration', p. 361.

into treaty violations and thus to ensure that contract claims may be brought before an international investment tribunal,[103] contract claims were not intended to be brought before an international investment tribunal independent of a treaty claim in all treaties that do not contain an 'umbrella clause'.[104]

As second argument invoked in this respect is to contrast the broadly worded investor–state dispute settlement clause with the narrowly formulated *interstate* dispute clause, which, indeed, is very often limited to disputes relating to the interpretation or application of the treaty.[105] However, since the objective of both dispute settlement clauses is very different, namely, in the first case, to offer foreign investors the possibility of resorting to international arbitration to enforce the rights they have been granted under the treaty, and, in the second case, to enable the parties to the treaty to settle disputes in relation to the application and interpretation of the treaty provisions generally, it seems difficult to compare both clauses, let alone to draw any conclusions from this as to the scope of the investor–state dispute settlement clause.

More generally, it seems more accurate to focus on the characteristics of the instrument granting access to arbitration, and its objective, rather than on the mere formulation of the clause, since the exact wording of the clause may be a valid method of interpretation only if one takes into consideration the former. The dispute settlement clause makes sense only if the clause is not detached from the rest of the treaty - which has as its main objective not to provide access to arbitration to foreign investors generally, but to promote and protect foreign investment through the grant of substantive protection to these investors coupled with access to arbitration in case of a dispute in respect of those obligations. A more restrictive and prudent approach to the question of whether investment tribunals may hear purely contract claims based on a dispute settlement provision in an investment treaty was defended by the Tribunal in *SGS* v. *Pakistan*, which focused on the treaty cause of action rather than on the formulation of the dispute settlement clause only. The facts of this case were very similar to *SGS* v. *The Philippines*, at least with regard to the question of whether purely

[103] Gaillard, 'Investment Treaty Arbitration and Jurisdiction over Contract Claims', p. 345.
[104] For a similar reasoning, see *LESI SpA and Astaldi SpA* v. *People's Democratic Republic of Algeria*, ICSID Case No. ARB/05/3, Decision on Jurisdiction, 12 July 2006, para. 84.
[105] See Douglas, *The International Law of Investment Treaty Claims*, p. 239.

contract claims may be brought before an investment tribunal established under an investment treaty. The Tribunal in *SGS* v. *Pakistan*, contrary to the *SGS* v. *The Philippines* Tribunal, argued that:

> disputes arising from claims grounded on alleged violation of the BIT, and disputes arising from claims based wholly on supposed violations of the PSI Agreement, can both be described as 'disputes with respect to investments', the phrase used in Article 9 of the BIT. That phrase, however, while descriptive of the factual subject matter of the disputes, does not relate to the legal basis of the claims, or the cause of action asserted in the claims. In other words, from that description alone, without more, we believe that no implication necessarily arises that both BIT and purely contract claims are intended to be covered by the Contracting Parties in Article 9. Neither, accordingly, does an implication arise that the Article 9 dispute settlement mechanism would supersede and set at naught all otherwise valid non-ICSID forum selection clauses in all earlier agreements between Swiss investors and the Respondent. Thus, we do not see anything in Article 9 or in any other provision of the BIT that can be read as vesting this Tribunal with jurisdiction over claims resting *ex hypothesi* exclusively on contract.[106]

The Tribunal thus declined jurisdiction for contract claims that do not amount to or are presented as a breach of the applicable investment treaty.[107] Several tribunals have likewise upheld the principle that purely contract claims are not capable of being submitted to an international investment tribunal, based on the applicable investment treaty only, unless the breaches complained of simultaneously constitute a breach of the investment treaty.[108] The lack of jurisdiction over purely contract claims does not, of course, imply that a tribunal established under an investment treaty may not consider contract-related matters.[109]

Be that as it may, if one admits the possibility that purely contract claims may be submitted to the jurisdiction of a treaty-based tribunal outside the formal application of an 'umbrella clause', it is nevertheless generally accepted that the principle is subject to a few exceptions, such as the existence of a specific and exclusive dispute settlement clause in the concession contract, or where the concession contract has been

[106] *SGS* v. *Pakistan*, ICSID Case No. ARB/01/13, para. 161. [107] *Ibid.*, para. 162.

[108] See *Pan American Energy* v. *Argentina*, ICSID Case No. ARB/03/13, para. 91; *Consortium Groupement LESI-DIPENTA* v. *Algeria*, ICSID Case No. ARB/03/08, Award, 10 January 2005, para. 25; *LESI and Astaldi* v. *Algeria*, ICSID Case No. ARB/05/3, para. 84; and *El Paso Energy Int'l Co.* v. *The Argentine Republic*, ICSID Case No. ARB/03/15, Award, 31 October 2011, para. 129.

[109] See *Bayindir Insaat Turizm Ticaret Ve Sanayi AS* v. *Islamic Republic of Pakistan*, ICSID Case No. ARB/03/29, Award, 27 August 2009, para. 135.

concluded between the foreign investor and a third party or a separate entity that has a legal personality distinct from that of the state.[110]

## 1.4 The systemic distinction between investment treaty arbitration and international commercial arbitration

Having discussed the procedural question relating to the distinction between contract and treaty claims, it is important to briefly ponder over the differences that exist between the general procedure used in international commercial arbitration, and the procedure habitually employed in investment treaty arbitration. This section at the same time provides a summary of the previous sections in that, as a result, it establishes how investment treaty arbitration differs from the standard procedure in international commercial arbitration, and introduces many aspects that will be developed further in Part II of this book. I will here focus on the systemic differences between international commercial arbitration and investment treaty arbitration, rather than the procedural differences, which I will address in Part II.

The method used to settle international investment disputes is clearly modelled on the rules and principles of international commercial arbitration. International commercial arbitration and investment treaty arbitration thus share many common features. Many of these common features are, moreover, inherent to the very concept of arbitration. Thus, in both mechanisms, parties decide to bring a claim before a party-appointed panel of arbitrators and, in principle, define the applicable law and the procedural rules. In the case of ICSID arbitration, the latter is limited because the procedural rules are established under the ICSID Convention and the adopted rules of arbitration. Likewise, the conduct of the proceedings is influenced by the common principles of arbitral procedures, such as those governing the constitution of the tribunal, the challenge of arbitrators and the rules in respect of the rendering of the final award.

110 On the first exception, see Crawford, 'Treaty and Contract in Investment Arbitration', p. 365; *SGS* v. *The Philippines*, ICSID Case No. ARB/02/6; and *TSA* v. *Argentina*, ICSID Case No. ARB/05/5. On the second exception, see Crawford, *ibid.*, p. 364; *Salini* v. *Morocco*, ICSID Case No. ARB/00/4, para. 60; and *Impregilo* v. *Pakistan*, ICSID Case No. ARB/03/3, para. 188.

The types of dispute settled through international commercial arbitration and investment treaty arbitration are nevertheless distinguishable from many perspectives. Investment treaty arbitration, from the perspective of the types of dispute settled resembles more traditional interstate arbitration than commercial arbitration.[111] Investment treaty arbitration is, in fact, fundamentally different from international commercial arbitration, despite the use in both proceedings of common principles and concepts.[112] Many of the elements discussed hereafter are specific to arbitration under the ICSID Convention. However, since the majority of treaty-based investment disputes are nowadays settled through the ICSID Convention, reference to this specific dispute settlement forum and its specific features is appropriate.[113]

First, the subject matter of the disputes differs substantially in both types of arbitration. Investment treaty arbitration is not concerned generally with adjudication of private rights between two parties established under a contract, but rather with the exercise by the state of its sovereign powers.[114] As a consequence, the consent to arbitration differs considerably in both types of arbitration. In international commercial arbitration, the parties to the dispute decide to bypass the jurisdiction of the courts of one particular state through an agreement to arbitrate the dispute between the parties. It is the result of a private act of parties acting in their private capacity. States can, of course, consent to arbitration in a contract when they are acting in their private capacity. In such circumstances, the arbitration will generally follow the rules and principles of international commercial arbitration, the only specificity being the involvement of a state.[115] Investment contracts

111 See Brower II, 'The Function and Limits of Arbitration and Judicial Settlement under Private and Public International Law', p. 299.

112 See Van Harten and Loughlin, 'Investment Treaty Arbitration as a Species of Global Administrative Law', pp. 139–45.

113 By the end of 2012, the ICSID accounted for 61 per cent of the total number of known investment arbitrations; 26 per cent were conducted under the UNCITRAL Arbitration Rules; 5 per cent before the Arbitration Institute of the Stockholm Chamber of Commerce; the remaining cases were brought before other institutions, such as the International Chamber of Commerce (UNCTAD, 'Recent Developments in Investor–State Dispute Settlement (ISDS)', IIA Issue Notes, 2013/1 (May 2013), available at: http://unctad.org/en/PublicationsLibrary/webdiaepcb2013d3_en.pdf, accessed 20 August 2013.

114 See, generally, Van Harten, *Investment Treaty Arbitration and Public Law.*

115 See Jeremy Carver, 'The Strengths and Weaknesses of International Arbitration Involving a State as a Party: Practical Implications', *Arbitration International*, 1(2) (1985): 179.

concluded between the host state, or a subdivision thereof, and a foreign investor may include such consent to arbitrate. The state then is acting in its private capacity, and the arbitration will be similar to international commercial arbitration.[116] Contrary to this type of consent, consent to arbitration in investment treaty arbitration is given by states, generally in an investment treaty, and thus constitutes a sovereign act.[117] This consent, however, apart from the fact that it originates in the state acting in its sovereign capacity, is not an agreement to arbitrate one specific dispute between two parties, but rather constitutes an offer to arbitrate for the future investments in the territory of that state.[118] In doing so, the state exercises its competences to determine the way in which disputes relating to its sovereign activity on its territory can be settled, which is foreign to the consent expressed by private parties who, among themselves, agree to arbitrate one specific dispute as an alternative to national courts.[119] Although the foreign investor, by filing a request for arbitration of a dispute it has with the state, is considered to have accepted the 'offer to arbitrate', such agreement to arbitrate is founded on different principles than is the case in international commercial arbitration, since the basis of the tribunal's jurisdiction is of a different - public international law - nature.[120]

Secondly, the types of obligation at stake in international commercial and investment treaty arbitration differ substantially, as was explained in detail in the previous section. In international commercial arbitration, the dispute relates to the contractual obligations of two parties in their private capacities. Investment treaty arbitration, on the other hand, concerns the international responsibility of the state for breaches of its international obligations towards a foreign investor. Although occasionally investment treaty arbitration may also concern the legal obligations of the host state under the investment contract, the main objective of contemporary investment treaty arbitration is to assess whether or not the state has violated its obligations under the applicable investment treaty and other applicable rules and principles of international law.

[116] Van Harten and Loughlin, 'Investment Treaty Arbitration as a Species of Global Administrative Law', p. 143.
[117] Van Harten, *Investment Treaty Arbitration and Public Law*, pp. 63 ff.
[118] Van Harten and Loughlin, 'Investment Treaty Arbitration as a Species of Global Administrative Law', p. 143.
[119] *Ibid.*, p. 144. [120] Schill, 'Crafting the International Economic Order', p. 411.

Thirdly, from a procedural perspective, and as a consequence of the involvement of a state acting in its sovereign capacity, investment treaty arbitration is a supranational or a-national form of arbitration since it is completely detached from the laws of any particular state, including the state in which the arbitration takes place.[121] The home state of the investor is completely eliminated from the arbitral process,[122] as is the domestic legal system of the state in which the arbitration takes place. As recently noted by the Arbitral Tribunal in *Electrabel* v. *Hungary*:

> Under Article 26 ECT and Article 42 of the ICSID Convention, the Tribunal is required to apply the ECT and 'applicable rules and principles of international law'. In other words, this Tribunal is placed in a public international law context and not a national or regional context. Moreover, this ICSID arbitration does not have its seat or legal place of arbitration in Hungary or elsewhere in the European Union. Such an arbitral seat could trigger the application of the *lex loci arbitri* and give rise to the jurisdiction of the local courts in regard to the arbitral process, including challenges to the award. This ICSID arbitration is a dispute resolution mechanism governed exclusively by international law. As a result of the Tribunal's international status under the ECT and the ICSID Convention, several of the Commission's submissions cannot be taken into account in this arbitration, because they are based on a hierarchy of legal rules seen only from the perspective of an EU legal order applying within the EU, whereas this Tribunal is required to operate in the international legal framework of the ECT and the ICSID Convention, outside the European Union.[123]

This is true, however, only for investment treaty arbitration conducted under the ICSID Convention, which is completely supranational. Investment treaty arbitration conducted under the UNCITRAL Arbitration Rules, or under other mechanisms, such as arbitration through the facilities of International Chamber of Commerce (ICC), the London Court of International Arbitration (LCIA) or the facilities of the Stockholm Chamber of Commerce (SCC), still maintains a territorial link with the state of the seat of the arbitration. However, since the vast majority of international investment disputes are today settled through the facilities of the ICSID, one could easily argue that investment treaty arbitration is largely a fully de-nationalized dispute

[121] On this, see Santiago Montt, *State Liability in Investment Treaty Arbitration. Global Constitutional and Administrative Law in the BIT Generation* (Oxford: Hart, 2009), p. 135.

[122] *Ibid.*, p. 136.

[123] *Electrabel SA* v. *Republic of Hungary*, ICSID Case No. ARB/07/19, Decision on Jurisdiction, Applicable Law and Liability, 30 November 2012, para. 4.112.

settlement mechanism. In international commercial arbitration, on the contrary, and although the principle of autonomy of the parties remains the basic founding principle of the agreement to arbitration, national laws, in particular, the laws of the seat of the arbitration, and national courts retain a certain degree of relevance.[124]

Fourthly, although, of course, linked to the previous distinction made, the direct enforceability of awards differs fundamentally in both scenarios. Here again one should distinguish between ICSID arbitration and investment arbitration conducted outside the formal ICSID framework. It is true that national courts and tribunals have consistently held that awards of non-ICSID investment tribunals are reviewable as 'commercial' arbitral awards for the purposes of Article 1(3) of the New York Convention.[125] This is obviously not the case for awards of international investment tribunals operating under the ICSID Convention. One of the specific benefits of ICSID arbitration is that the awards can easily be recognized and enforced through the ICSID Convention, especially in comparison with the recognition and enforcement of foreign arbitral awards in domestic courts, and even compared with enforcement of arbitral awards under the New York Convention. This is essentially a consequence of the fact that investment treaty arbitration under the ICSID Convention has been fully 'internationalized' and detached from the control of the national courts and tribunals of states. Although it facilitates enforcement, the New York Convention contains several possibilities for review by domestic courts which are broader than the grounds of annulment provided for under the ICSID Convention.[126] Article 54(1) of the ICSID Convention indeed imposes an obligation on all states that are parties to the Convention to enforce an ICSID award 'as if it were a final judgment of a court in that State'.[127] There is no possibility of review by the national courts of the states in which enforcement is sought, which may be any state that is a party to the ICSID

[124] For a discussion of the various ways in which national courts and national laws may 'interfere' in the proceedings, see Nigel Blackaby, Constantine Partasides, Alan Redfern and Martin Hunter, *Redfern & Hunter on International Arbitration*, 5th edn (Oxford University Press, 2009), paras 7.01–7.64.

[125] Convention on the Recognition and Enforcement of Foreign Arbitral Awards, 10 June 1958, 330 UNTS 38 (1959) (hereafter 'the New York Convention'). For a discussion, see Campbell McLachlan, Laurence Shore and Matthew Weiniger, *International Investment Arbitration. Substantive Principles* (Oxford University Press, 2008), p. 65.

[126] See Edward Baldwin, Mark Kantor and Michael Nolan, 'Limits to Enforcement of ICSID Awards', *Journal of International Arbitration* 23(1) (2006): 1, 4–5.

[127] Article 54(1) of the ICSID Convention.

Convention where the respondent has assets. Although this is specific to ICSID arbitration, the a-national character of ICSID arbitration is a fundamental characteristic of, and is specific to, investment treaty arbitration. International investment arbitral awards under the ICSID Convention can be freely enforced with no judicial scrutiny in the state in which enforcement is sought.[128]

[128] See Articles 53 and 54 of the ICSID Convention.

# 2 The legal character of the direct access of foreign investors to investment treaty arbitration

A question that has puzzled doctrine, and more limitedly practice, since the very inception of investor access to investment treaty arbitration, and thus of the direct claims rights of foreign investors, is whether the foreign investor when bringing a claim before an investment tribunal is in fact exercising its own right, or a right derived from the right of its home state.[1] More broadly, the question can be asked whether the protection offered to foreign investors in modern investment treaties creates individual rights for the foreign investor.

Whether or not the investor who triggers the investor–state dispute settlement mechanism acts in its own right may seem important from a theoretical perspective, this question has not so far troubled practice too much. One should, however, not ignore the potentially important practical implications of the characterization of investor access to investment treaty arbitration either as 'direct' or 'derivative'. The characterization may indeed, for instance, determine the possibility of the foreign investor waiving the protection offered under the investment treaty, or may influence the possibility of domestic courts and tribunals engaging in the review of arbitral awards rendered by international investment tribunals outside the ICSID context.

Before entering into discussion of both approaches to the claims rights of foreign investors, it seems important to restate that a clear distinction between the substantive rights granted to private parties and the ability to bring a claim for the violation of these rights needs to be made. When certain treaties have granted rights to individuals, one needs to distinguish clearly between the substantive rights granted to

[1] See McLachlan *et al.*, *International Investment Arbitration*, pp. 61–2, and generally Douglas, 'The Hybrid Foundations of Investment Treaty Arbitration', pp. 151–290.

private parties and the ability to bring a claim for alleged violations of these rights, which does not automatically follow from the former. Both rights exist only as a consequence of the positive action of states, which traditionally reserve for themselves the right to bring claims against other states, even if this concerns the violation of an individual right.

Section 2.1 analyses, generally, the character of the rights granted to foreign investors under investment treaties, and distinguishes between substantive and procedural rights. Section 2.2 addresses the specific attributes of investor access to investment treaty arbitration, the question of whether such rights should be characterized as direct rights or as rights derived from the rights of states under public international law, and the implications of this classification.

## 2.1 The distinction between substantive and procedural rights

Under general international law, the grant of certain rights to individuals and corporations by international treaties concluded between two or more states is not exceptional and is generally accepted. As the ICJ noted in the *LaGrand* case, 'Article 36, paragraph 1 [of the Vienna Convention on Consular Relations], creates individual rights [for the national concerned], which ... may be invoked in this Court by the national State of the detained person.'[2] This principle further develops the more cautious approach adopted by the PCIJ in its Advisory Opinion in the *Jurisdiction of the Courts of Danzig* case, in which it noted that:

> it may be readily admitted that, according to a well-established principle of international law, the Beamtenabkommen, being an international agreement, cannot, as such, create direct rights and obligations for private individuals. But it cannot be disputed that the very object of an international agreement, according to the intention of the contracting Parties, may be the adoption by the Parties of some definite rules creating individual rights and enforceable by the national courts.[3]

The Vienna Convention on Consular Relations at stake in the cited *LaGrand* case, however, contains no direct claims rights for individuals,

[2] International Court of Justice, *LaGrand (Germany* v. *United States of America)*, Judgment, *ICJ Reports*, 2001, 466, p. 494, para. 77. This pronouncement was subsequently confirmed in the *Avena* case (International Court of Justice, *Avena and Other Mexican Nationals (Mexico* v. *United States of America)*, Judgment, *ICJ Reports*, 2004, 12, para. 40).

[3] Permanent Court of International Justice, *Jurisdiction of the Courts of Danzig*, Advisory Opinion, *PCIJ Reports*, Series B, No. 15 (1928), pp. 17–18.

but rather requires the intervention of the national state of the individuals to claim a violation of the Convention. The substantive rights granted to individuals by that treaty are rights originating from, and regulated by, international law, but do not encompass the right of individuals to enforce those rights directly against a state through an international dispute settlement mechanism. Also, the creation of individual rights by a treaty does not imply that a state is no longer in a position to initiate claims against another state for violations of these rights outside the formal context of diplomatic protection, as is made clear by the practice in relation to the Vienna Convention on Consular Relations.[4]

The practice in respect of certain human rights treaties, such as the European Convention on Human Rights (ECHR), supports these principles. Human rights treaties without doubt confer rights on individuals, although the *obligations* derived from the treaty remain interstate obligations. In other words, states take upon themselves to guarantee the respect of certain human rights of the individuals within their jurisdiction. Individuals are not a party to the treaty, and do not derive any international legal obligations from the treaty, but nevertheless may rely directly on the rights conferred to them by that treaty. The grant of individual rights in human rights treaties does not necessarily, or automatically, entail the capacity to bring a claim for a violation of that right before an international tribunal or court, traditionally reserved to the state of the nationality of the individual who has been the 'victim' of a violation of an international legal obligation of the state. Such direct claims rights are not inherent in the grant of individual rights, which is evidenced by the fact that to date, as far as human rights are concerned, the ECHR remains the exception rather than the rule, especially when compared with other regional human rights instruments such as the American Convention on Human Rights and the African Charter on Human and Peoples' Rights.[5] In the case of the ECHR, the beneficiaries

[4] Vienna Convention on Consular Relations, 24 April 1963, 596 UNTS 261. See ICJ, *LaGrand*, *ICJ Reports*, 2001, 466, p. 494, para. 77. This pronouncement also was subsequently confirmed in the *Avena* case (*ICJ Reports*, 2004, 12, para. 40).

[5] American Convention on Human Rights, 21 November 1969, 1144 UNTS 143; African Charter on Human and Peoples' Rights, 27 June 1981, 1520 UNTS 217. The main difference between human rights litigation and investment arbitration is that in international human rights litigation, the states that have accepted the direct claims rights of individuals have also principally accepted such a right for claims by their own nationals, while investment arbitration concerns only the claim brought by a foreign investor against a state other than the state of its nationality in which the investment was made. See Orrego Vicuña, *International Dispute Settlement in an Evolving Global Society*, p. 53.

of the rights are also granted the right to bring a claim directly against the state that has allegedly violated that right, but it is not a necessary corollary of the fact that individuals are given rights under these treaties.

Transposing these principles to investment treaty arbitration, it is clear that the obligations contracted by the states under international investment treaties are interstate obligations. States can incontestably contract obligations in an international legal instrument and thereby grant rights to non-state entities. It can thus be readily accepted that modern investment treaties do grant certain rights to foreign investors, but the legal obligations contracted by states remain international legal obligations.[6] Accordingly, in practice this means that foreign investors are the principal *beneficiaries* of the investment protection agreement, but they are not a *contracting party* to the agreement. The obligations essentially remain interstate obligations, but create rights for foreign investors. At the same time, the question of whether generally the treaty obligations are owed to the other contracting state or to the foreign investor directly will not make any difference in deciding a case. Indeed, as was pointed out by Crawford, investment treaty arbitration, when based on an alleged breach of a treaty obligation by the host state, concerns the international responsibility of that state, and it makes no difference whether the responsibility of the host state invoked by the foreign investor through its access to investment treaty arbitration is based on treaty obligations owed to the foreign investor directly or to the home state.[7]

The principles on the distinction between substantive and procedural rights also apply to investment treaty arbitration. The grant of substantive rights to foreign investors is fundamentally different from the access to investment treaty arbitration. The mere fact that contemporary investment treaties contain standards of treatment that create rights to investment protection does not in and of itself create a right to initiate a claim for alleged breaches of these rights directly against the host state. As cogently noted by Brigitte Stern in her Dissenting and Concurring Opinion in the *Impregilo* case:

> it is indeed not because a State has given its *consent to another State* to grant some substantive rights to the investors of that State that it automatically flows

[6] See also *Occidental Exploration and Production Co.* v. *The Republic of Ecuador*, LCIA Case No. UN3467 (US–Ecuador BIT), Judgment of the Court of Appeal regarding non-justiciability of challenge to arbitral award, 9 September 2005, para. 19; and Robert Jennings and Arthur Watts, *Oppenheim's International Law*, 9th edn (Oxford University Press, 1992), para. 375.

[7] See Crawford, 'Treaty and Contract in Investment Arbitration', p. 356.

from such a consent that the State also gives its *consent to the foreign investors* to allow the latter to sue the State directly in an international arbitration. For such a right to come into existence, a specific consent has to be given inside the treaty, and the State can shape this consent as it sees fit, in providing for the basic conditions under which such a consent is given, in other words, the conditions under which such an 'offer to arbitrate' is made to the foreign investors.[8]

This fundamental principle is an application of the general principle of international law that there is no automatic jurisdiction for any court or tribunal to settle international legal disputes. To quote again Brigitte Stern:

> It is of utmost importance not to forget that *no participant* in the international community, be it a State, an international organization, a physical or a legal person, has an inherent right of access to a jurisdictional recourse. Just as a State cannot sue another State, unless there is a specific consent to that effect, for example, through a declaration recognizing as compulsory the jurisdiction of the International Court of Justice, in the same manner, in the framework of BITs, investors are not capable of intervening on the international level against States for the recognition of their rights, unless States grant them such a right under conditions that they determine. An arbitral tribunal – just as the ICJ or any international court – does not have a general jurisdiction, it only has a '*compétence d'attribution*', which has to respect the limits provided for by the States.[9]

Investor access to investment treaty arbitration is, simply put, the withdrawal of the procedural barriers imposed by the rules on diplomatic protection, through the explicit consent by states that allow the foreign investor of one state to bring a claim directly against another state without the former state's intervention. This is confirmed by the fact that consent to arbitration is given by states in advance of the dispute, by the signature of treaties or by the adoption of legislation. The explicit consent of the individual or corporate investor is not required until the dispute has actually risen.

Based on these considerations, I will next address the question of whether the access to investment arbitration for violations of the investment treaty by the host state is to be considered as 'direct' or 'derivative' rights. This issue is most of all important to fully understand and grasp the influence of the public international law character of investment disputes in investment treaty arbitration.

8 *Impregilo SpA* v. *The Argentine Republic*, ICSID Case No. ARB/07/17, Concurring and Dissenting Opinion of Professor Brigitte Stern, 21 June 2011, para. 53 (emphasis in original).

9 *Ibid.*, para. 53.

## 2.2 The right of direct access to investment treaty arbitration

Whether or not the investor who initiates a claim against a host state, based on the consent to arbitration expressed by the latter and the home state of the investor in an investment treaty, acts in accordance with a direct right to this effect or is in fact exercising a right derived from the right of its home state is a relatively theoretical question. However, it may have certain important practical implications, since the characterization of this right either as 'direct' or 'derivative' may determine the possibility of the foreign investor waiving the protection offered under the investment treaty,[10] or it may influence the capacity of domestic courts and tribunals to engage in the review of arbitral awards rendered by international investment tribunals outside the ICSID system, as was the case in *Occidental*,[11] which I will discuss later in this section. In addition, the question of whether a state can rely on interstate countermeasures as a defence to international responsibility in investment treaty arbitration is essentially a consequence of the way in which investment treaty rights are categorized.[12]

### *2.2.1 The 'derivative rights' and 'direct rights' theories*

The 'direct right' theory essentially considers that a foreign investor is endowed directly with a right to make a claim against one of the states party to the treaty, by virtue of the investment protection treaty.[13] This right is granted to the foreign investor independently of the right of a state to act in diplomatic protection to invoke the responsibility of the host state. It is held that this right, being legally disconnected and not originating from the right of the home state of the foreign investor, gives foreign investors the capacity to waive this right of access to investment treaty arbitration.[14] The direct rights theory in respect of the right of action of foreign investors has been adopted by several

[10] See Newcombe and Paradell, *Law and Practice of Investment Treaties*, para. 10.19.

[11] *Occidental* v. *Ecuador*, LCIA Case No. UN3467.

[12] See *Archer Daniels Midland Co.* v. *Mexico*, ICSID Case No. ARB(AF)/04/05, Award, 21 November 2007, paras 178–179; and *Corn Products International Inc.* v. *The United Mexican States*, ICSID Case No. ARB(AF)/04/01, Decision on Responsibility, 15 January 2008, paras 161–179.

[13] Salacuse, *The Law of Investment Treaties*, p. 391.

[14] Jacomijn J. van Haersholte-van Hof and Anne K. Hoffmann, 'The Relationship between International Tribunals and Domestic Courts', in Peter Muchlinski, Federico Ortino and Christoph Schreuer (eds.), *The Oxford Handbook of International Investment Law* (Oxford University Press, 2008), pp. 1002–3.

investment tribunals, either explicitly or implicitly. In *Gas Natural* v. *Argentina*, for instance, the Tribunal noted that:

> The scheme of both the ICSID Convention and the bilateral investment treaties is that in this circumstance, the foreign investor acquires rights under the Convention and Treaty, including in particular the standing to initiate international arbitration.[15]

The direct rights theory was also explicitly adopted by the UK Court of Appeal in the *Occidental* case.[16] The case concerned the question of whether the courts and tribunals of the United Kingdom could 'enforce or interpret the terms of the Treaty, and ... adjudicate upon the transactions of foreign sovereign states'.[17] This could not have been possible, as *Occidental* submitted, if the rights invoked and the right of access were considered as rights of the state which were exercised by the foreign investor. The Court of Appeal noted first that:

> where a dispute arises out of or relates to a commercial agreement made with the investor, it would seem to us both artificial and wrong in principle to suggest that the investor is in reality pursuing a claim vested in his or its home State, and that the only improvement by comparison with the traditional State protection for investors is procedural.[18]

The court thus concluded that 'injured nationals or companies ... have a direct claim for their own benefit'.[19]

The 'derivative rights' theory, on the other hand, is based on the idea that the foreign investor is exercising a right derived from the right of its home state to initiate a claim against another state 'on behalf of' its national. More generally, the derivative rights theory holds that the obligations in the investment treaty are essentially interstate obligations, but that the enforcement of such obligations before an international arbitral tribunal is transferred to the foreign investor.[20] The derivative rights theory holds that the direct claims right of the foreign investor is an application of the right of a state to initiate claims against another state, and that the foreign investor is thus exercising the right of the state. It is based on the concept of diplomatic protection mentioned above, a procedure by which a state may bring a case against another state for alleged breaches by that state of the rights of the national of the former

[15] *Gas Natural* v. *Argentina*, ICSID Case No. ARB/03/10, para. 34.

[16] *Occidental* v. *Ecuador*, LCIA Case No. UN3467. [17] *Ibid.*, para. 11. [18] *Ibid.*, para. 17.

[19] *Ibid.*, para. 20.

[20] For a discussion, see McLachlan *et al.*, *International Investment Arbitration*, p. 61, and Douglas, *The International Law of Investment Treaty Claims*, p. 11.

state. Diplomatic protection traditionally implies that the state of the nationality of the foreign investor acts in its own right and seeks reparation for a violation of its own right.[21] At the same time, whether or not the *substantive* rights invoked in diplomatic protection and in investment treaty arbitration are direct rights of the state's nationals or not does not affect the character of the state's right to act in diplomatic protection, nor the investor's access to investment treaty arbitration, as explained in the previous section. Indeed, whether or not the state acting in diplomatic protection is taking up the rights of its nationals or not does not alter the fact that the right to exercise diplomatic protection and the right generally of a state to invoke the responsibility of another state is a right that belongs to the state only. It is precisely that right which is relevant in the 'direct rights versus derivative rights' debate, not the substantive rights which form the basis of a claim in diplomatic protection.

The derivative rights theory has been espoused by the Arbitral Tribunal in *Loewen* v. *United States*:[22]

> Rights of action under private law arise from personal obligations (albeit they may be owed by or to a State) brought into existence by domestic law and enforceable through domestic tribunals and courts. NAFTA claims have a quite different character, stemming from a corner of public international law in which, by treaty, the power of States under that law to take international measures for the correction of wrongs done to its nationals has been replaced by an ad hoc definition of certain kinds of wrong, coupled with specialist means of compensation. These means are both distinct from and exclusive of the remedies for wrongful acts under private law ... It is true that some aspects of the resolution of disputes arising in relation to private international commerce are imported into the NAFTA system via Article 1120.1(c), and that the handling of disputes within that system by professionals experienced in the handling of major international arbitrations has tended in practice to make a NAFTA arbitration look like the more familiar kind of process. But this apparent

[21] The theory that the state, in the context of diplomatic protection, is seeking redress for a violation of its own right has not been explicitly espoused by the International Law Commission in its recent Draft Articles on Diplomatic Protection, since it has left open the question of whether the state acts in its own right or is taking up the claim of its national: 'Draft article 1 is formulated in such a way as to leave open the question whether the State exercising diplomatic protection does so in its own right or that of its national – or both. It views diplomatic protection through the prism of State responsibility and emphasizes that it is a procedure for securing the responsibility of the State for injury to the national flowing from an internationally wrongful act' (Commentary to Article 1 of the Draft Articles on Diplomatic Protection, UN Doc. A/61/10, para. 5).

[22] *Loewen Group, Inc. and Raymond L. Loewen* v. *United States of America*, ICSID Case No. ARB (AF)/98/3, NAFTA, Award on Merits, 26 June 2003.

resemblance is misleading. The two forms of process, and the rights which they enforce, have nothing in common. There is no warrant for transferring rules derived from private law into a field of international law where claimants are permitted for convenience to enforce *what are in origin the rights of Party states*.[23]

A close look at the cited considerations of the *Loewen* Award reveals that the Tribunal clearly distinguished between the right of access to an international investment tribunal ('the form of process') and the substantive obligations contained in the treaty, such as the standards of protection ('the rights which [the forms of process] enforce'). The *Loewen* Tribunal essentially argued that the rights that a foreign investor seeks to enforce are 'in origin the rights of Party states', but that the foreign investor has been granted the right to enforce that right instead of the state. In doing so, the Tribunal did not decide that the right of action of foreign investors is derived from the right of the state to exercise diplomatic protection, but rather emphasized the public international law character and origin of these rights. The right of direct access to investment arbitration does not stem from a personal contractual relation regulated by private law, but rather originates from the consent of a state under an international legal instrument.[24]

In essence, the right of foreign investors to initiate arbitral proceedings is clearly a right of the investors, and it would be wrong to assert that the foreign investor is exercising a right to arbitration *on behalf of* the home state. This does not imply, however, that such a right is not derived from the right of the home state of the investor to initiate a claim against the host state. The obligations in the treaty are interstate obligations, but they create rights for foreign investors.

### 2.2.2 *Countering criticism of the 'derivative rights' theory*

As pointed out by several authors,[25] the derivative rights theory is problematic for several reasons, but the invoked reasons for the problems associated with the derivate rights theory may not be as fundamental as is often presented. Indeed, the 'direct right' versus 'derivate right' debate is often symptomatic of unwarranted analogies between the conditions governing diplomatic protection and investor access to

[23] *Ibid.* (emphasis added).

[24] This analysis is also shared by the UK Court of Appeal (*Occidental* v. *Ecuador*, LCIA Case No. UN3467, para. 22).

[25] See, for instance, McLachlan *et al.*, *International Investment Arbitration*, p. 64; Douglas, 'The Hybrid Foundations of Investment Treaty Arbitration', pp. 169–81; and Douglas, *The International Law of Investment Treaty Claims*, pp. 11–12.

investment treaty arbitration, and between investor access to investment treaty arbitration and the respective substantive rights that form the basis of the claim. Drawing analogies between the conditions under which a state can act in diplomatic protection and the conditions under which investors have been given access to investment treaty arbitration is misleading, since the objective of the latter is precisely to replace the former procedure. Certainly, the arguments usually invoked in this connection have certain merit, but they are not such as to undermine the derivative rights theory.

The first criticism is that the derivative rights theory is incompatible with the waiver of the direct access of the foreign investor to investment treaty arbitration, for, if the latter is only exercising a right of the state on behalf of the state, only the owner of that right, that is, the state, may validly make such waiver. However, as will be pointed out in the next section, it is not generally accepted that investors can in fact waive the rights they are granted under investment treaties, including the access to investment treaty arbitration.

Secondly, it is argued that the absence of any exhaustion of local remedies requirements in the majority of the BITs, coupled with the provision in Article 26 of the ICSID Convention that states need to explicitly require the exhaustion of local remedies in their consent to investment treaty arbitration, is incompatible with the derivative rights theory.[26] This argument precisely confuses a state's right to act in diplomatic protection, or generally to file a claim against another state for violations of certain treaty obligations, with the admissibility conditions of that right and the access to investment treaty arbitration. Diplomatic protection does not require *the state* to exhaust local remedies, which it could not practically do, but rather requires that the foreign investor first needs to seek redress of its *own right* in the domestic courts of the host state before the state may bring an international claim in diplomatic protection before an international court or tribunal. Because under the derivative rights theory the foreign investor is considered to be exercising rights derived from the right of the state, that is, the state's right to act in diplomatic protection, there is in fact no requirement of exhaustion of local remedies. Moreover, a state that claims violations by another state of treaty obligations outside the formal context of diplomatic protection, even when these obligations are owed to individuals, as is the case, for instance, with the Vienna

[26] For a discussion, see McLachlan *et al.*, *International Investment Arbitration*, p. 64

Convention on Consular Relations mentioned above, has no requirement to exhaust domestic remedies, since that claim is alien to the procedure of diplomatic protection. The exhaustion of local remedies requirement is an admissibility requirement for the exercise of the state's right to diplomatic protection; it does not affect the existence of the right of states to initiate claims as such. Furthermore, investment treaty arbitration is an alternative to diplomatic protection and the right of a state to initiate claims directly against another state for the violation of that state's obligations contained in an investment treaty. The foreign investor is in fact exercising a right that the state originally had under international law. The investor's right of access to investment treaty arbitration is surely not the direct exercise by that investor of the right of its home state to act in diplomatic protection, but this does not mean that the right of access is not derived or originates from that right. In other words, access to investment treaty arbitration is not the exercise by the investor of a state's right on the latter's behalf, but it is nevertheless derived from that right. As a consequence, the absence of any exhaustion of local requirements in the majority of the BITs and under the ICSID Convention is not incompatible with such a theory.

Thirdly, although it is correct that on several occasions the home state of the foreign investor has strongly opposed the submission of the claim by the foreign investor, which was, for example, the case in *Mondev International* v. *United States*[27] and *Gami* v. *Mexico*,[28] once a right of action has been given to the foreign investor, even though it originates from the right of the state, in advance and for a certain clearly delimited category of claims, it is up to the foreign investor to decide whether or not to exercise that right. The agreement or not of the home state with the initiation of the claim by the foreign investor, indeed, is no longer relevant once the investor has been given the right to exercise a right derived from that of the state, and has in fact exercised that right through the initiation of arbitral proceedings.

Fourthly, it is unquestionably also correct that the compensation awarded to a foreign investor is calculated not based on the injury caused to the state, but solely on the financial losses of the foreign investor, as will be discussed in Chapter 6.[29] This is, however, also the

[27] *Mondev International Ltd* v. *United States of America*, ICSID Case No. ARB(AF)/99/2, NAFTA, Award, 11 October 2002.

[28] *Gami Investments, Inc.* v. *The United Mexican States*, UNCITRAL, Final Award, 15 November 2004.

[29] See McLachlan *et al.*, *International Investment Arbitration*, p. 64.

case for claims pursued through the traditional diplomatic protection scheme. In the recent *Diallo* case before the ICJ, for instance, the court noted that the compensation due to Guinea for the injury flowing from the wrongful detention and expulsion of Mr Diallo, should include 'the resulting loss of his personal belongings'.[30] This is moreover an issue linked to the question of whose *substantive* rights are invoked through diplomatic protection, and not to the qualification of the direct or derivative character of the investor's procedural right of access to investment treaty arbitration.

Finally, whether or not a state can rely on interstate countermeasures as a defence to international responsibility in investment treaty arbitration is a consequence also of the way in which investment treaty rights are categorized. However, it is not because certain tribunals have denied the possibility to states of using countermeasures in order to deny the rights of foreign investors under investment treaties that this by definition implies that the derivative theory no longer holds.[31] Indeed, as was pointed out by the Tribunal in *Corn Products International Inc.* v. *Mexico*, the essence of the question is whether the foreign investor, when initiating arbitration under an investment treaty, acts in its own right – which the Tribunal acknowledged – or exercises a right of the state. It is clear, however, that the investor is not claiming on behalf of the state, but rather that the investor has rights that 'in origin' are rights of states, to paraphrase the Tribunal in *Loewen*.[32] It is only in the event that foreign investors have no rights, but merely interests, that states could resort to countermeasures in order to deny the rights of investors granted under investment treaties.[33]

From a theoretical perspective, there is certain value in the theory that foreign investors are in fact exercising a right derived from the state's right to initiate a claim against another state to invoke the responsibility of that state, either in its own right or through the procedure of diplomatic protection. The question is not to what extent the rules applicable to diplomatic protection are, or are not, similarly applicable to investor access to investment treaty arbitration, which forms the basis of the

[30] International Court of Justice, *Ahmadou Sadio Diallo (Republic of Guinea* v. *Democratic Republic of the Congo)*, Judgment, *ICJ Reports*, 2010, 639, para. 163.

[31] See *Corn Products* v. *Mexico*, ICSID Case No. ARB(AF)/04/01, paras 161–179.

[32] *Loewen* v. *United States*, ICSID Case No. ARB (AF)/98/3, para. 233. See also in relation to countermeasures *Archer Daniels Midland Co.* v. *Mexico*, ICSID Case No. ARB(AF)/04/05, paras 178–179.

[33] *Corn Products* v. *Mexico*, ICSID Case No. ARB(AF)/04/01, para. 176.

majority of the criticisms on the derivative right theory. The objective of this access is precisely the avoidance and circumvention of the cumbersome, lengthy and uncertain procedure of diplomatic protection and not the replacement of the state's right to exercise diplomatic protection with a foreign investor's hypothetical 'right to act in diplomatic protection'. The procedure of diplomatic protection is, simply put, replaced by the creation of a right of access for the foreign investor to international arbitration. This right is derived from the right of a state to invoke the responsibility of another state.

That is also why Article 26 of the ICSID Convention provides that the requirement of the exhaustion of local remedies is in principle excluded, but may nevertheless be required by a state when it expresses its consent to arbitration. This requirement is not the reintroduction of the admissibility requirements of diplomatic protection, but rather the addition of certain conditions to the consent of the states to the right of the foreign investor to initiate claims against the host state before an international arbitral tribunal. Article 27, in the same vein, provides that 'no Contracting State shall give diplomatic protection, or bring an international claim, in respect of a dispute which one of its nationals and another Contracting State shall have consented to submit or shall have submitted to arbitration under this Convention'. These provisions make clear that the direct access to investment arbitration is a substitute for the traditional system of diplomatic protection.

### *2.2.3 Waiver of access to investment treaty arbitration*

That foreign investors have the right to waive access to investment treaty arbitration is highly contested and, of course, depends on the theoretical premises on the characterization of such a right, which I just discussed. The derivative rights theory is certainly incompatible with the waiver of the access of the foreign investor to investment treaty arbitration, for, since the latter is exercising a right derived from a right of the state, only the owner of the original right, that is, the state, may validly make such waiver. The practice of arbitral tribunals so far has not been conclusive on this issue, and essentially leaves the answer to this question open. Before discussing this practice, two preliminary issues need to be considered.

First, under the ICSID Convention, when an investor accepts the offer to arbitrate by a state contained in an investment treaty, this in effect suspends the capacity of the state to act in diplomatic protection in relation to that specific dispute.[34] This, however, cannot be considered as implying the possibility of foreign investors waiving their right of access to investment treaty arbitration. Because states have signed the ICSID Convention, which contains the suspension of diplomatic protection in the event of a consent to arbitrate under that convention, it is the states that have in fact suspended their own right to act in diplomatic protection. This suspension is triggered only through the consent of foreign investors when instituting arbitral proceedings against a state under the ICSID Convention.

Secondly, the choice of the foreign investor to pursue litigation in domestic courts rather than before an arbitral tribunal, through a 'fork-in-the-road clause' for instance, cannot be equated with a waiver of the right of action, but rather constitutes a mere decision by the foreign investor not to exercise that right.[35]

The capacity of investors to waive the rights they are granted under investment treaties, including the access to investment treaty arbitration, is not generally accepted in the practice of tribunals. The Tribunal in *SGS* v. *The Philippines* unambiguously refuted such possibility:

> the jurisdiction of the Tribunal is determined by the combination of the BIT and the ICSID Convention. It is, to say the least, doubtful that a private party can by contract waive rights or dispense with the performance of obligations imposed on the States parties to those treaties under international law. Although under modern international law, treaties may confer rights, substantive and procedural, on individuals, they will normally do so in order to achieve some public interest. Thus the question is not whether the Tribunal has jurisdiction: unless otherwise expressly provided, treaty jurisdiction is not abrogated by contract.[36]

In *Eureko*, the Tribunal conversely noted that waivers of claims are in accordance with public international law.[37] However, that decision in

[34] Article 27 of the ICSID Convention. See also the ILC Commentary to Article 20 of the Articles on the Responsibility of States: 'Article 20 envisages only the consent of States to conduct otherwise in breach of an international obligation. International law may also take into account the consent of non-State entities such as corporations or private persons. The extent to which investors can waive the rules of diplomatic protection by agreement in advance has long been controversial, but under the Convention on the Settlement of Investment Disputes between States and Nationals of Other States (art. 27, para. 1), consent by an investor to arbitration under the Convention has the effect of suspending the right of diplomatic protection by the investor's national State' (UN Doc. A/56/10, para. 10).

[35] See, however, McLachlan *et al.*, *International Investment Arbitration*, p. 64, and Douglas, *The International Law of Investment Treaty Claims*, p. 27.

[36] *SGS* v. *The Philippines*, ICSID Case No. ARB/02/6, para. 154.

[37] *Eureko* v. *Poland*, Partial Award and Dissenting Opinion, paras 174–175.

essence revolved around the question of whether an agreement between the parties constituted a waiver. As a consequence, the question was not really to what extent investors can waive their rights under the investment protection agreement, but rather whether parties can settle cases through mutual agreement. This, according to the Tribunal, is in conformity with international law. However, and this is, of course, essentially a question of semantics, in the case of a settlement agreement, the parties do not waive their right as such, but rather waive their exercise of that right.

In *Aguas de Tunari* v. *Bolivia*, the Tribunal posited in an *obiter dictum* that investors could waive their access to investment treaty arbitration under the ICSID Convention, but it is unclear on which grounds the Tribunal came to this conclusion.[38]

A rather appealing alternative to the debate relating to the characterization of foreign investors' right of access, and by necessary implication the possibility of investors waiving their access, is to consider the broader intention of the state parties to investment treaties.[39] This perspective takes into consideration the public (international law) dimension of investment treaty arbitration. Since the objective of these treaties is not the settlement of private disputes between foreign investors and host states, but rather to 'strengthen economic relations', 'promote foreign investment' and the 'general development of States' economies', investor access to investment treaty arbitration needs to be seen as an element in the achievement of these objectives. Then, since access to investment treaty arbitration is also aimed at ensuring the respect of the treaty provisions to guarantee the attainment of these broader objectives, investors should not be able to waive these rights.[40] The presence and importance of interests other than those of the parties to the dispute is also confirmed by the fact that investment treaties usually contain, besides the possibility of investor–state dispute settlement, a specific compromissory clause for interstate dispute settlement to settle disputes between the states party to the investment treaty concerning the interpretation or application of the treaty.[41]

This view is in fact implicit in the reasoning of the Tribunal in *SGS* v. *The Philippines*, which I have cited earlier, and confirms also the public international law character of investment treaty arbitration. Investor

[38] *Aguas del Tunari SA* v. *Republic of Bolivia*, ICSID Case No. ARB/02/3, Decision on Respondent's Objections to Jurisdiction, 21 October 2005, para. 118.

[39] Salacuse, *The Law of Investment Treaties*, p. 391. [40] *Ibid.*

[41] See, for instance, Article 37 of the 2012 US Model BIT. See also Ole Spiermann, 'Individual Rights, State Interests and the Power to Waive ICSID Jurisdiction under Bilateral Investment Treaties', *Arbitration International*, 20(2) (2004): 179, 180.

access to investment treaty arbitration cannot be equated with a private dispute settlement mechanism, but rather forms part of a broader context, which is the investment protection treaty. That treaty, as noted earlier, does not have as its main objective providing foreign investors with direct access to arbitration or to regulate the private relations between host states and foreign investors. Rather, the obligations agreed on by states in the treaty have a broader objective, which is, generally, to promote foreign investment.

# PART II

# Procedural aspects and implications of the public international law character of investment treaty arbitration

# 3 The role, function and qualifications of arbitrators in investment treaty arbitration

The role, function and qualifications of the arbitrator in investment treaty arbitration differ to a certain extent from those of the arbitrator in international commercial arbitration, and in fact resemble more those of the arbitrator in interstate disputes or even of judges in international judicial procedures. At the same time, to say that arbitrators in investment treaty arbitration have an entirely different role and function than arbitrators in international commercial arbitration would be an overstatement. The arbitral function and the qualifications of arbitrators generally have many common features in investment treaty arbitration, interstate arbitration, international commercial arbitration or even national arbitration, because of the common principles applicable to any arbitral procedure. One should also keep in mind that the powers and duties of arbitrators differ substantially from judges in national judicial proceedings, since an arbitral tribunal, contrary to judges in national courts, derives its powers and duties from the consent of the parties.

Arbitral tribunals mandated to settle investment disputes share the main principles in respect of their powers and duties with other arbitral tribunals, but the involvement of a state in the proceedings, acting in its sovereign capacity, and the public international law dimension of investment disputes generally, as will be shown, justifies, and has resulted in, several deviations from the principles applicable in international commercial arbitration.

This chapter aims to describe and analyse the role, function and qualifications of arbitrators in investment treaty arbitration, and thereby make the distinction with international commercial arbitration in view of the special features of investment arbitration derived from the public international law character of investment treaty arbitration. This chapter is thus not concerned generally with providing an exhaustive description of the various rules applicable to the role, function and qualification of arbitrators, or with ethical considerations in the choice of arbitrators.[1] Rather, only those rules and issues that are relevant for the purposes of establishing the specificities of investment treaty arbitration will be discussed.

Section 3.1 will discuss the general and specific qualifications of arbitrators in investment treaty arbitration as required by the procedural rules of the main arbitral institutions that deal with investment disputes, in particular ICSID. Section 3.2 will analyse the specific rules that exist in respect of the independence and impartiality, and the challenge and disqualification of arbitrators. Section 3.3 will address the role of the arbitrator in relation to the legal reasoning of awards in investment treaty arbitration. Finally, this chapter will discuss the role and function of the international investment arbitrator regarding the application of the principle of *jura novit curia* and *proprio motu* inquiries.

## 3.1 The selection and qualifications of arbitrators in investment treaty arbitration

From a practical perspective, arbitrators in investment treaty arbitration have either a public international law background or a background in international commercial law and arbitration.[2] The perception of the precise function of the arbitrator will very much depend on the background of the arbitrator. While public international lawyers have a tendency to have more consideration, generally, of investment treaty arbitration's public international law foundation and character, lawyers with a background in international commercial arbitration habitually pay more attention to the private function of investment treaty arbitration, that is, the settlement of the dispute between the parties, and the private dimension of the legal relations between the disputing parties.[3] As a consequence, it is often suggested that commercial lawyers have a tendency to disregard the public dimension of investment treaty arbitration by equating investment treaty arbitration with

[1] See on this Jan Paulsson, 'Ethics, Elitism, Eligibility', *Journal of International Arbitration*, 14(4) (1997): 13, and David Hacking, 'Ethics, Elitism, Eligibility: A Response – What Happens if the Icelandic Arbitrator Falls Through the Ice?' *Journal of International Arbitration*, 15(4) (1998): 73.

[2] See Schill, 'Crafting the International Economic Order', pp. 406–7.

[3] *Ibid.*, p. 407. See also Roberts, 'Clash of Paradigms', pp. 61–2.

international commercial arbitration, while public international lawyers would have more consideration for the involvement of a state in the proceedings, and thus associate investment treaty arbitration more with public international law judicial settlement mechanisms and arbitration than with international commercial arbitration, from which investment treaty arbitration merely borrows the form and certain procedural rules.[4] Although a generalization of the differences between arbitrators in investment treaty arbitration in function of their public international law or international commercial arbitration background may not be fully in accordance with the practice,[5] one cannot ignore the fact that the legal background of arbitrators influences their opinion on the function of investment treaty arbitration.

### 3.1.1 *Selection and nationality of arbitrators*

It is a commonplace to consider that arbitration is only as good as the arbitrators.[6] The selection of the arbitrators is of high importance not only for the quality of the arbitral decision, but also, and perhaps more importantly, for what the parties may expect in respect of the substantive outcome of the decision.[7] This is, of course, inherent in the arbitral function generally, and the qualification requirements of arbitrators in investment treaty arbitration do not therefore differ substantially from arbitrators involved in international commercial arbitration. There are, however, several interesting features in the qualification requirements provided for in the ICSID Convention that are worth mentioning, because they clearly show the influence of the public

4 Schill, 'Crafting the International Economic Order', p. 408.

5 For instance, the claim that arbitrators with a public international law background would, in function of the public international law dimension of the dispute, be more favourable to 'developing the law' and ensuring consistency of arbitral jurisprudence, contrary to arbitrators with a background in international commercial law and arbitration (see Roberts, 'Clash of Paradigms', p. 62), is not entirely supported by practice. For a discussion, see Eric De Brabandere, 'Arbitral Decisions as a Source of International Investment Law', in Tarcisio Gazzini and Eric De Brabandere (eds.), *International Investment Law. Sources of Rights and Obligations* (Leiden: Martinus Nijhoff, 2012), pp. 245–88.

6 See, generally, Yves Derains and Laurent Levy (eds.), *Is Arbitration Only as Good as the Arbitrator? Status, Powers and Role of the Arbitrator* (Paris: ICC Institute of World Business Law, 2012).

7 Karl-Heinz Böckstiegel, 'The Role of the Arbitrators in Investment Treaty Arbitration', in Albert Jan van den Berg (ed.), *International Commercial Arbitration. Important Contemporary Questions*, ICCA Congress Series, 2002 London, vol. 11 (The Hague: Kluwer Law International, 2003), p. 368.

international law character of investment treaty arbitration on the arbitral procedure.

The selection procedure of the arbitrators in investment treaty arbitration is very similar to the method used in international commercial arbitration, the former being modelled on the latter as I explained in the first part of this book. Article 37 of the ICSID Convention, the most widely used dispute settlement forum for investment treaty arbitration, thus provides that a tribunal may consist of a sole arbitrator, or an uneven number of arbitrators appointed in accordance with the agreement of the parties, and that, in the absence of agreement, the tribunal will consist of three arbitrators: one arbitrator appointed by each party, and the third presiding arbitrator appointed by agreement of the parties.

Article 39 further requires that the majority of the arbitrators be nationals of states other than the contracting state party to the dispute and the contracting state whose national is a party to the dispute, except where each individual member of the tribunal has been appointed by agreement of the parties. Rule 1(3) of the ICSID Arbitration Rules further contains additional procedural rules in this respect and, *inter alia*, provides that the appointment by a party of an arbitrator who has the nationality of the home or host state requires the agreement of the other party. Such rules are generally absent in the standard rules of procedure in international commercial arbitration. Although nationality may be taken into account under those rules as well,[8] nationality of arbitrators tends to become an important factor only once the arbitration involves a state.[9]

[8] See, for instance, Article 13 of the ICC Rules of Arbitration: 'In confirming or appointing arbitrators, the Court shall consider the prospective arbitrator's *nationality*, residence and other relationships with the countries of which the parties or the other arbitrators are nationals . . . ' (emphasis added); and Article 6(7) of the UNCITRAL Arbitration Rules: 'The appointing authority shall have regard to such considerations as are likely to secure the appointment of an independent and impartial arbitrator and shall take into account *the advisability of appointing an arbitrator of a nationality other than the nationalities of the parties*' (emphasis added).

[9] For a discussion, see Omar E. García-Bolívar, 'Comparing Arbitrator Standards of Conduct in International Commercial, Trade and Investment Disputes', *Dispute Resolution Journal*, 60(4) (2005): 76; and Omar E. García-Bolívar, 'Comparing Arbitrator Standards of Conduct in International Commercial, Trade and Investment Disputes', in American Arbitration Association (ed.), *Handbook on International Arbitration Practice* (Huntington, NY: Juris, 2010), pp. 251–68. See also Ilhyung Lee, 'Practice and Predicament: The Nationality of the International Arbitrator (with Survey Results)', (2007) 31 *Fordham International Law Journal*, 603.

### *3.1.2 Qualification requirements of arbitrators*

As far as the qualifications of the arbitrators are concerned, Article 14 of the ICSID Convention requires that they need to be 'persons of high moral character and recognized competence in the fields of law, commerce, industry or finance, who may be relied upon to exercise independent judgment. Competence in the field of law shall be of particular importance in the case of persons on the Panel of Arbitrators.'

Because of the public international law foundation of investment treaty arbitration, arbitrators appointed in investment treaty arbitration should, as far as possible, not only be specialists in international arbitration, but also have specific competence in the field of public international law, in particular, the rules relating to treaty interpretation and the international responsibility of states.[10] While this requirement is not explicitly included in Article 14 of the ICSID Convention, essentially because at the time of the drafting and adoption of the ICSID Convention that dispute settlement forum was mainly crafted in view of contract-based investment disputes,[11] one may consider that with the advent of treaty-based investor–state arbitration specific competence in public international law, rather than just competence in international commercial arbitration, has become a relevant and determinant criterion in the selection and appointment of arbitrators in international investment tribunals.[12]

This is, for instance, reflected in NAFTA's Chapter Eleven Rules on the appointment of arbitrators. Article 1124(4) provides that the parties will establish a roster of presiding arbitrators, which need to meet 'the qualifications of the Convention and rules referred to in Article 1120 and *experienced in international law and investment matters*'.[13] The reason for this is rather obvious. Since international investment tribunals are principally required to investigate the international responsibility under public international law of the host state, and in doing so to analyse and apply the relevant primary obligations resting upon the state and the secondary rules relating to the interpretation of these obligations and the responsibility of states for internationally wrongful acts, it is reasonable to expect a specific knowledge of these areas of the law on the part of the arbitrators. There are, however, generally no such

[10] Böckstiegel, 'The Role of the Arbitrators in Investment Treaty Arbitration', p. 367.
[11] See Newcombe and Paradell, *Law and Practice of Investment Treaties*, para. 1.31.
[12] See also Schill, 'Crafting the International Economic Order', p. 421.
[13] Emphasis added.

specific requirements in BITs nor, as a matter of fact, in the ICSID Convention itself, NAFTA being rather exceptional in this respect. Some authors have also linked the competence in international law generally as a qualification requirement for arbitrators to the fact that international investment tribunals should be deemed to know and apply international law, as an application of the principle *jura novit curia*,[14] which I will discuss in section 3.4. At the same time, it should not be overlooked that a particular competence in, and knowledge of, arbitral procedure equally forms part of the qualification requirements of international arbitrators.

A second particular feature of the qualification requirements of arbitrators in investment treaty arbitration is contained in the second paragraph of Article 14 of the ICSID Convention. Interestingly, this paragraph requires the Chairman of the Administrative Council, in designating persons to serve on the panels, to 'pay due regard to the importance of assuring representation on the Panels of the principal legal systems of the world and of the main forms of economic activity'.[15] This provision is one that can be found regularly in the appointment procedures of judges at international courts and tribunals. Article 9 of the ICJ Statute thus provides that 'in the body as a whole the representation of the main forms of civilization and of the principal legal systems of the world should be assured'.[16]

Appointments by the ICSID Secretary-General indeed show a clear geographical spread. The ICSID-appointed panel members in 2013 counted two Western European, two North American (one US and one Mexican), two Asian, two African, one South American, and one New Zealand/Canadian arbitrator.[17] The very fact that such a requirement has been

[14] Jan Paulsson, 'International Arbitration and the Generation of Legal Norms: Treaty Arbitration and International Law', *Transnational Dispute Management*, 3(5) (2006): 14. Paulsson argues that: 'as the PCIJ put it in Brazilian Loans, an international tribunal "is deemed itself to know what law is", and this thought should be a sobering one to parties making appointments of arbitrators, and to arbitrators accepting appointment. There have indeed been some questionable decisions in investment arbitrations which suggest that the arbitrators had an insufficient grounding in international law.'

[15] The Chairman may, in addition to the designations of the panel members by the states, designate ten persons to both the Panel of Arbitrators and the Panel of Conciliators (Article 13(2) of the ICSID Convention).

[16] See also Article 2(2) of the ITLOS Statute: 'In the Tribunal as a whole the representation of the principal legal systems of the world and equitable geographical distribution shall be assured.'

[17] ICSID, Members of the Panels of Conciliators and Arbitrators, Doc. No. ICSID/10, available at: https://icsid.worldbank.org/ICSID/FrontServlet?requestType=ICSIDDocRH&actionVal=MembersofPannel, accessed 20 August 2013).

included in the ICSID Convention, although admittedly limited to the appointment by the Chairman and therefore not applicable to the party-appointed arbitrators or the presiding arbitrator in the event of agreement between the parties, is reminiscent of the public character of investment arbitration.

The rules of arbitration of the ICC or those of the SCC, for instance, contain only requirements, in the event of an appointment by the respective appointing authority of the institution, relating to nationality of the arbitrator and the nature of the dispute, with no reference to the representation of the various legal systems of the world.[18] Similarly, the UNCITRAL Arbitration Rules do not require any geographical representation, and merely focus on the nationality of the arbitrator appointed by the designated appointing authority.[19] This is a logical consequence of the purely private and contractual nature of international commercial arbitration, which does not require any representation of the various legal systems of the world, for the applicable law will essentially be the municipal laws of a state complemented by the relevant rules of private international law.

From a practical perspective, however, there is no substantial difference in respect of the geographical spread of arbitrators between investment treaty arbitration and international commercial arbitration. By mid-2013, arbitrators from eighty-six different nationalities had been appointed in ICSID arbitrations.[20] A similar geographical spread exists, for example, at the ICC.[21] However, when one looks at the geographical

[18] See, for instance, Article 13 of the ICC Rules of Arbitration: '1. In confirming or appointing arbitrators, the Court shall consider the prospective arbitrator's nationality, residence and other relationships with the countries of which the parties or the other arbitrators are nationals and the prospective arbitrator's availability and ability to conduct the arbitration in accordance with the Rules. The same shall apply where the Secretary General confirms arbitrators pursuant to Article 13(2).' Article 13(6) of the Rules of Arbitration of the Arbitration Institute of the SCC provides that: 'When appointing arbitrators, the Board shall consider the nature and circumstances of the dispute, the applicable law, the seat and language of the arbitration and the nationality of the parties.'

[19] See Article 6(7) of the UNCITRAL Arbitration Rules: 'The appointing authority shall have regard to such considerations as are likely to secure the appointment of an independent and impartial arbitrator and shall take into account the advisability of appointing an arbitrator of a nationality other than the nationalities of the parties.'

[20] ICSID, *ICSID Caseload – Statistics*, Issue 2013-2, Chart 14: State of Nationality of Arbitrators, Conciliators and ad hoc Committee Members Appointed in Cases Registered under the ICSID Convention and Additional Facility Rules, p. 20.

[21] In 2012, arbitrators of seventy-six nationalities were appointed or confirmed under the ICC Rules, 'Statistics – ICC Arbitration in 2012', available at: www.iccwbo.org/Products-and-Services/Arbitration-and-ADR/Arbitration/Introduction-to-ICC-Arbitration/Statistics, accessed 20 August 2013.

distribution of the arbitrators appointed by the parties, and arbitrators and ad hoc committee members appointed by ICSID, clear differences appear.[22] Arbitrators and ad hoc committee members from Eastern Europe/Central Asia, south and east Asia and the Pacific, sub-Saharan Africa, and Central America and the Caribbean are proportionally appointed more often by the ICSID than by the parties. North American arbitrators and ad hoc committee members are proportionally appointed more often by the parties than by the ICSID. Arbitrators and ad hoc committee members from Western Europe, the Middle East and North Africa, and South America are equally represented as both party-appointed and ICSID-appointed arbitrators. The parties, of course, retain an entirely discretionary power to appoint arbitrators without taking into consideration geographic elements. These statistics, however, show that the ICSID, despite not being under an explicit obligation to do so since the obligation to 'pay due regard to the importance of assuring representation on the Panels of the principal legal systems of the world and of the main forms of economic activity' only applies to arbitrators appointed by the ICSID Secretary-General to the panel of arbitrators, does in fact appoint arbitrators and ad hoc committee members according to a more equal geographical spread. The public international law character of investment treaty arbitration, reflected in Article 14 of the ICSID Convention, may well explain this admittedly limited geographical discrepancy between party-appointed and ICSID-appointed arbitrators.

## 3.2 Independence and impartiality of arbitrators

The independence and impartiality of international arbitrators is a fundamental principle of arbitral procedure.[23] Independence and impartiality, although often taken as forming one concept, in fact have different understandings. Independence relates to the absence of any relation between an arbitrator and one of the parties that may influence the arbitrator's decision, and is an *objective* standard. Impartiality, on the other hand, is *subjective* and implies the absence of actual, or an appearance of, bias or predisposition of an arbitrator

[22] ICSID, *ICSID Caseload – Statistics*, Issue 2013-2, Chart 13: Arbitrators, Conciliators and ad hoc Committee Members Appointed in Cases Registered under the ICSID Convention and Additional Facility Rules – Distribution of Appointments by ICSID and by the Parties (or Party-appointed Arbitrators) by Geographic Region, p. 19.

[23] Blackaby *et al.*, *Redfern & Hunter on International Arbitration*, para. 4.72.

towards the parties or the substance of the dispute.[24] Independence and impartiality are similar to the notions of 'party preference' and 'outcome preference', respectively, which are widely used in international commercial arbitration.[25]

### *3.2.1 Independence and impartiality requirements in investment treaty arbitration*

Article 14 of the ICSID Convention contains the basic rule in respect of the independence and impartiality of arbitrators: 'persons designated to serve on the Panels shall be persons of high moral character and recognized competence in the fields of law, commerce, industry or finance, who may be relied upon to exercise independent judgment'. Arbitrators, either party-appointed or appointed by the chairman, need thus to possess three essential qualities: be of 'high moral character'; have the necessary competence; and be independent. Although Article 14 does not explicitly contain the requirement of 'impartiality', even though the Spanish official text refers to impartiality rather than independence,[26] it is generally accepted that Article 14 requires arbitrators to be both independent and impartial.[27]

As far as challenge of arbitrators and members of ad hoc committees is concerned, Article 57 of the ICSID Convention provides that a party to the dispute may request that the commission or tribunal disqualify a member 'on account of any fact indicating a manifest lack of the qualities required by paragraph (1) of Article 14'.[28] The ICSID Convention thus imposes a relatively heavy burden on a party that seeks to challenge

[24] *Ibid.*, para. 4.74

[25] Sam Lutrell, 'Bias Challenges in Investor–State Arbitration: Lessons from International Commercial Arbitration', in Chester Brown and Kate Miles (eds.), *Evolution in Investment Treaty Law and Arbitration* (Cambridge University Press, 2011), pp. 448–9.

[26] For a discussion of this, see Gabriel Bottini, 'Should Arbitrators Live on Mars? Challenge of Arbitrators in Investment Arbitration', *Suffolk Transnational Law Review* 32(2) (2009): 341.

[27] See the Joint decisions in *Suez, Sociedad General de Aguas de Barcelona SA and InterAguas Servicios Integrales del Agua SA* v. *The Argentine Republic*, ICSID Case No. ARB/03/17, *Suez, Sociedad General de Aguas de Barcelona SA and Vivendi Universal SA* v. *The Argentine Republic*, ICSID Case No. ARB/03/19, and *AWG Group Ltd* v. *The Argentine Republic*, UNCITRAL, Decision on the Proposal for the Disqualification of a Member of the Arbitral Tribunal, 22 October 2007, and the joint decisions in the same cases: Decision on a Second Proposal for the Disqualification of a Member of the Arbitral Tribunal, 12 May 2008, para. 27.

[28] The ICSID Convention uses a system whereby the challenge by a party of an arbitrator or an ad hoc committee member will be decided by the remaining arbitrators or members of the ad hoc committee (Article 58 of the ICSID Convention).

an arbitrator because of the use of the word 'manifest'.[29] In that respect, the Tribunal in *Suez* noted that: 'it is important to emphasize that the language of Article 57 places a heavy burden of proof . . . to establish facts that make it obvious and highly probable, *not just possible*, that [the arbitrator] is a person who may not be relied upon to exercise independent and impartial judgment'.[30] In effect, the word 'manifest' imposes an 'objective' instead of a 'subjective' test to determine the lack of independence and impartiality of arbitrators.[31]

Other arbitration rules habitually refer only to the 'justifiable doubts' standard in their rules on the challenge of arbitrators, and do not usually require a 'manifest' lack of independence and impartiality. Article 12(1) of the UNCITRAL Arbitration Rules, for instance, provides the possibility to challenge an arbitrator 'if circumstances exist that give rise to justifiable doubts as to the arbitrator's impartiality or independence'. Similarly, the ICC Rules of Arbitration provide for the challenge of arbitrators 'for an alleged lack of impartiality or independence, or otherwise'.[32] The majority of the non-ICSID rules simultaneously provide for a duty of disclosure, both at the outset and during the proceedings.[33] The ICSID Convention conversely requires arbitrators to sign a declaration that, in its last paragraph added in 2006, contains a disclosure obligation, which is extended to the entire duration of the arbitral proceedings.[34]

[29] For a discussion of relevant case law in this respect, see Schreuer *et al.*, *The ICSID Convention*, p. 1201, paras 15 ff.

[30] *Suez, Sociedad General de Aguas de Barcelona SA* v. *The Argentine Republic*, ICSID Cases Nos ARB/03/17 and ARB/03/19, Decision on Second Proposal for Disqualification, 12 May 2008, para. 29 (emphasis in the original text).

[31] Blackaby *et al.*, *Redfern & Hunter on International Arbitration*, para. 4.98.

[32] See also Article 15(1) of the SCC Rules of Arbitration: 'A party may challenge any arbitrator if circumstances exist which give rise to justifiable doubts as to the arbitrator's impartiality or independence or if he/she does not possess qualifications agreed by the parties. A party may challenge an arbitrator whom it has appointed or in whose appointment it has participated, only for reasons of which it becomes aware after the appointment was made.'

[33] See, for instance, Article 10.3 of the LCIA Rules, Article 10 of the UNCITRAL Rules and Article 14(2) of the SCC Rules.

[34] The declaration is contained in Rule 6 of the ICSID Arbitration Rules: 'To the best of my knowledge there is no reason why I should not serve on the Arbitral Tribunal constituted by the International Centre for Settlement of Investment Disputes with respect to a dispute between — and —. I shall keep confidential all information coming to my knowledge as a result of my participation in this proceeding, as well as the contents of any award made by the Tribunal. I shall judge fairly as between the parties, according to the applicable law, and shall not accept any instruction or compensation with regard to the proceeding from any source except as provided in the Convention on the Settlement of Investment Disputes between States and Nationals of Other States

These rules in and of themselves do not show any substantial difference in requirements of independence and impartiality between investment treaty arbitration and international commercial arbitration. The independence and impartiality requirements used in investment treaty arbitration and in international commercial arbitration are very similar,[35] with the exception of the high threshold required to challenge arbitrators in the case of ICSID arbitration. However, in practice, major differences do appear as a consequence of investment treaty arbitration's public international foundation.

### 3.2.2 *Specific concerns of arbitral independence and impartiality in investment treaty arbitration*

Special consideration should be given to the independence and impartiality of arbitrators in investment treaty arbitration, because of certain specific features that are either directly or indirectly the consequence of the public international law dimension of investment treaty arbitration. These features entail a need to differentiate the challenges posed by the independence and impartiality requirement in investment treaty arbitration from international commercial arbitration. As noted by one author, 'the ethical hazards of the two disciplines [international commercial arbitration and investment treaty arbitration] are not shared, especially in the area of merits prejudgment'.[36]

First, investment treaty disputes usually concern relatively similar applicable laws, and even have a relative similarity in their factual circumstances. Contrary to international commercial arbitration, where the legal circumstances of the cases usually have little likeness, in particular, in view of the fact that the applicable law typically consists of municipal law possibly complemented by relevant rules of private international law, investment treaty arbitration, as was pointed out in Part I, requires the application of recurring principles of public

and in the Regulations and Rules made pursuant thereto. Attached is a statement of (a) my past and present professional, business and other relationships (if any) with the parties and (b) any other circumstance that might cause my reliability for independent judgment to be questioned by a party. I acknowledge that by signing this declaration, I assume a continuing obligation promptly to notify the Secretary-General of the Centre of any such relationship or circumstance that subsequently arises during this proceeding.'

35 See also Noah Rubins and Bernhard Lauterburg, 'Independence, Impartiality and Duty of Disclosure in Investment Arbitration', in Christina Knahr, Christian Koller, Walter Rechberger and August Reinisch (eds.), *Investment and Commercial Arbitration – Similarities and Divergences* (Utrecht: Eleven International Publishing, 2010), p. 158.

36 Lutrell, 'Bias Challenges in Investor–State Arbitration', p. 481.

international law, and is characterized by similarly worded legal instruments, which are applied in the majority of international investment disputes.[37]

Secondly, awards of international investment tribunals are habitually made public, at least under the ICSID Convention, as will be discussed in Chapter 5. As a consequence, it becomes relatively easy to identify the conception of arbitrators in respect of certain rules of international investment law. This reality, coupled with the *de facto* importance of the use of, and references to, precedents, which has become a widespread phenomenon in investment treaty arbitration[38] implies that 'issue conflicts' in investment treaty arbitration are relatively different from those that may arise in international commercial arbitration.[39]

Thirdly, under Article 54(1) of the ICSID Convention, states are required to enforce an ICSID award 'as if it were a final judgment of a court in that State', with no possibility of review by the national courts of the states in which enforcement is sought. Because of this feature, bias challenges may not be brought at the enforcement stage, contrary to international commercial arbitration.[40] Lack of independence and impartiality is also not possible as a claim in annulment under the ICSID Convention, with the exception of cases of improper constitution of the tribunal or corruption.[41] As a consequence, particular attention should be given to the independence and impartiality rules before and during the proceedings.

Finally, the need to ensure the legitimacy of the arbitral proceedings is paramount because of the public international law dimension of investment treaty arbitration.[42] For the legitimacy of the proceedings, and this is, of course, even more important because of the potential effects of such decisions on the general public, any appearance of bias or lack of independence should be strictly avoided. This idea was implicit in the reasoning of the Tribunal's ruling in *Hrvatska Elektroprivreda* v.

37 Thomas Buergenthal, 'The Proliferation of Disputes, Dispute Settlement Procedures and Respect for the Rule of Law', *Arbitration International*, 22(4) (2006): 495, 498; and Philippe Sands, 'Conflict and Conflicts in Investment Treaty Arbitration: Ethical Standards for Counsel', in Chester Brown and Kate Miles (eds.), *Evolution in Investment Treaty Law and Arbitration* (Cambridge University Press, 2011), p. 24.

38 See, generally, De Brabandere, 'Arbitral Decisions as a Source of International Investment Law'.

39 Lutrell, 'Bias Challenges in Investor–State Arbitration', p. 479.

40 *Ibid.*, p. 456.

41 Article 52(a) and (c) of the ICSID Convention.

42 See also Sands, 'Conflict and Conflicts in Investment Treaty Arbitration', pp. 22–4.

*Slovenia*,[43] which concerned the challenge made to counsel. Challenge of counsel is not covered by the rules on independence and impartiality. Despite this, and although the challenge was made by the claimant, the principles applied by the Tribunal are highly relevant. In this case, the claimant challenged the participation of Mr David Mildon QC of Essex Court Chambers as counsel, who was added in a later stage of the proceedings on the list of attendees at the hearing, because the president of the Tribunal was a door tenant at Essex Court Chambers. Besides relying on the powers of arbitral tribunals to decide questions of procedure not dealt with in the ICSID Convention, the Tribunal considered that 'as a judicial formation governed by public international law, the Tribunal has an inherent power to take measures to preserve the integrity of its proceedings'.[44] The Tribunal ruled that Mr David Mildon QC could not act as counsel in the proceedings. The reference here to the public international character of the proceedings is interesting since the tribunal derives from this the need to preserve the integrity of the proceedings. Indeed, the general confidence of the public in the outcome of the procedure is without doubt guaranteed only if it ensured that the arbitral proceedings were legitimate and that the dispute was decided by an independent and impartial arbitral tribunal.

These specificities of investment treaty arbitration give rise to particular problems. First, because of the public availability of the awards, and the *de facto* importance of precedents, one could have justifiable doubts when individuals act as counsel in one case, while at the same time being appointed as, or generally acting as, arbitrators in other investment law cases, or vice versa. This is generally referred to as 'issue conflicts'[45] or, as one author puts it, a 'role/issue conflict' because the conflict is more between the roles of individuals than the issues at stake in the arbitral proceedings.[46] Under those circumstances, arbitrators may be tempted to decide an issue in a way that could benefit a position adopted by that same arbitrator acting as counsel in another investment

[43] *Hrvatska Elektroprivreda dd.* v. *The Republic of Slovenia*, ICSID Case No. ARB/05/24, tribunal's ruling regarding the participation of David Mildon QC in further stages of the proceedings, 6 May 2008. For a discussion of this case in relation to independence and impartiality, see Sands, 'Conflict and Conflicts in Investment Treaty Arbitration', p. 31. See also *Rompetrol Group NV* v. *Romania*, ICSID Case No. ARB/06/3, Decision on the Participation of a Counsel, 14 January 2010.

[44] *Hrvatska Elektroprivreda* v. *Slovenia*, ICSID Case No. ARB/05/24, para. 33.

[45] See Blackaby *et al.*, *Redfern & Hunter on International Arbitration*, para. 4.125.

[46] Lutrell, 'Bias Challenges in Investor–State Arbitration', p. 479.

dispute. A challenge on this particular ground has been upheld in *Blue Bank International* v. *Venezuela*.[47] More generally, it has been suggested that arbitrators and counsel should be required to decide to be either arbitrator or counsel, at least for a certain period of time,[48] which certain professionals have also done.[49] Practice has shown, however, that the remaining arbitrators, or the appointing authority, when confronted with such questions when dealing with a claim of disqualification of an arbitrator or a member of an ad hoc committee, only very rarely uphold the challenge.[50]

The second consideration is related to the previous one and concerns the issue of 'repeat arbitrators'. This phenomenon denotes the case where arbitrators are appointed by the same party or the same law firm in different disputes.[51] The ICSID Convention and the arbitration rules of the other major arbitration institutions do not usually address the issue of repeat arbitrators. The matter simply falls under the general

47 *Blue Bank International & Trust (Barbados) Ltd* v. *Bolivarian Republic of Venezuela*, ICSID Case No. ARB 12/20, Decision on the Parties' Proposals to Disqualify a Majority of the Tribunal, 12 November 2013. See also Buergenthal, 'The Proliferation of Disputes', p. 498, and Schill, 'Crafting the International Economic Order', pp. 419–20.

48 Buergenthal, 'The Proliferation of Disputes', p. 498.

49 See, for example, Sands, 'Conflict and Conflicts in Investment Treaty Arbitration', p. 21.

50 See, however, for decisions where the challenge was upheld, the decision of ICSID's Deputy Secretary-General in *Vito G. Gallo* v. *Canada* in which the arbitrator in question was obligated to choose to pursue his appointment as arbitrator or as a counsel: *Vito G. Gallo* v. *Canada*, UNCITRAL, NAFTA, Decision on the Challenge to Mr J. Christopher Thomas QC, 14 October 2009. See also *ICS Inspection and Control Services Ltd* v. *The Argentina Republic*, UNCITRAL, PCA Case No. 2010-9, Decision on Challenge to Arbitrator, 17 December 2009, and the decision of the District Court of The Hague, which, in a PCA-administered investment arbitration conducted under the UNCITRAL Arbitration Rules, emphasized the incompatibility of arbitrator Emmanuel Gaillard as arbitrator in the procedure and his role as counsel in another case which raised similar questions to the *Telekom Malaysia* case where he was appointed as arbitrator. The District Court decided that the arbitrator should resign as counsel in the other dispute within ten days. The tribunal itself and the PCA Secretary-General had previously rejected the challenges (*Telekom Malaysia Berhad* v. *Republic of Ghana*, District Court of The Hague, Civil Law Section, Challenge No. 13/2004, Petition No. HA/RK2004/667, Decision, 18 October 2004). For a discussion, see Judith Levine, 'Dealing with Arbitrator "Issue Conflicts" in International Arbitration', *Dispute Resolution Journal*, 61(1) (2006): 60; and Sands, 'Conflict and Conflicts in Investment Treaty Arbitration', p. 29. See also *Blue Bank International* v. *Venezuela*, ICSID Case No. ARB 12/20, where the chairman of the ICSID Administrative Council upheld the challenge of an arbitrator based on the fact that the law firm, of which the arbitrator was a partner, represented the claimant in a case against the same respondent, which moreover concerned similar issues (paras 66–69).

51 See, generally, Houchi Kuo, 'The Issue of Repeat Arbitrators: Is it a Problem and How Should the Arbitration Institutions Respond?' *Contemporary Asia Arbitration Journal*, 4(2) (2011): 247.

rules relating to the independence and impartiality of arbitrators.[52] The reason why certain arbitrators are, or have been, repeatedly appointed by the same party, or even category of parties – foreign investors or states – is that, because of the publicly available knowledge of the position of the arbitrator in previous cases, appointing parties may wish to designate an arbitrator who is likely to decide the case in favour of the appointing party. This as such may not necessarily be *ipso facto* a problem of independence and impartiality, and may also be prompted and necessitated by the limited number of persons who are willing to and are capable of sitting as arbitrators.[53] At the same time, some authors, however, consider 'repeat arbitrators' to be a problem because, taking into account the repetitive appointments by one party, the arbitrator could be considered to be no longer independent because a form of financial dependence to the appointing party has been created.[54] These conflicting views on the issue of 'repeat arbitrators' may explain why the issue has not been explicitly regulated by either the ICSID Convention and Arbitration Rules or by the rules of arbitration of the other main arbitration institutions. The International Bar Association (IBA) Guidelines on Conflicts of Interest in International Arbitration, which do not constitute a binding or compulsory instrument, however, do mention this specific issue. The so-called 'orange list' contains several situations, which, according to the Guidelines: '(depending on the facts of a given case) in the eyes of the parties may give rise to justifiable doubts as to the arbitrator's impartiality or independence'.[55] The 'orange list', *inter alia*, targets the situation in which 'the arbitrator has within the past three years been appointed as arbitrator on two or more occasions by one of the parties or an affiliate of one of the parties'.[56] The mere fact that it is an 'orange list' proves that the issue is not as clear-cut as it might seem. It is probably judicious to leave the matter to the general rules on the independence and impartiality of arbitrators, and trust the judgement of the person(s) in charge of the challenge, without inferring any *ipso facto* consequences

[52] IBA Guidelines on Conflicts of Interest in International Arbitration, approved on 22 May 2004 by the Council of the International Bar Association, available at: www.ibanet.org/Publications/publications_IBA_guides_and_free_materials.aspx#conflictsofinterest, accessed 16 April 2012.

[53] For a discussion, see Kuo, 'The Issue of Repeat Arbitrators', p. 253.

[54] See, generally, Alan Scott Rau, 'On Integrity in Private Judging', *Arbitration International*, 14(2) (1998): 115.

[55] IBA Guidelines on Conflicts of Interest in International Arbitration, Part II: Practical Application of the General Standards, para. 3.

[56] *Ibid.*, para. 3.1.3.

from the repeated appointment of one arbitrator by the same party or law firm. ICSID tribunals generally have adopted this approach, and have confirmed their autonomy in applying the general rules on the independence and impartiality of arbitrators while taking the IBA Guidelines into consideration. In *Tidewater* v. *Venezuela*,[57] for example, the remaining members of the Tribunal noted that 'the ICSID Convention mandates a general standard for disqualification which differs from the "*justifiable doubts*" test formulated in the IBA Guidelines. Further, and in any event, the circumstances relied upon in the Proposal for Disqualification all fall within the "Orange List" in the IBA Guidelines, to the extent that they fall within the Guidelines at all.'[58] The Tribunal noted that 'repeat appointments may be as much the *result* of the arbitrator's independence and impartiality as an indication of justifiable doubts about it',[59] and 'the mere fact of holding three other arbitral appointments by the same party does not, without more, indicate a manifest lack of independence or impartiality'.[60]

While the standards applicable to the independence and impartiality requirements of arbitrators in investment treaty arbitration are not fundamentally different from those applicable in international commercial arbitration, with the exception of the 'manifest' standard in the ICSID Rules, the situations that may lead to challenges of arbitrators are clearly dissimilar. The specific features of investment treaty arbitration, resulting from its public international law dimension and of the public interest involved in international investment disputes, has indeed resulted in challenges of arbitrators in situations also present, but more uncommon, in international commercial arbitration, such as 'issue/role conflicts' and 'repeat arbitrators'. However, all in all, ICSID case law shows that challenges are only rarely upheld.[61] This may, however, be more a consequence of the higher threshold for challenges contained in the ICSID Rules than of the limited importance of arbitral independence and impartiality of arbitrators in investment treaty arbitration. At the same time, and this clearly shows the inherent tensions in the system, arbitration is based on the idea that parties choose the arbitrators that have to decide the dispute. An overly broad regulation

[57] *Tidewater Inc., Tidewater Investment Srl, Tidewater Caribe CA, Twenty Grand Offshore LLC, Point Marine LLC, Twenty Grand Marine Service LLC, Jackson Marine LLC and Zapata Gulf Marine Operators LLC* v. *The Bolivarian Republic of Venezuela*, ICSID Case No. ARB/10/5, Decision on Claimants' Proposal to Disqualify Professor Brigitte Stern, Arbitrator, 23 December 2010.

[58] *Ibid.*, para. 43. [59] *Ibid.*, para. 61. [60] *Ibid.*, para. 64.

[61] For an overview, see Lutrell, 'Bias Challenges in Investor–State Arbitration', pp. 462–81.

of the qualifications of arbitrators may thus be contrary to the flexibility offered by arbitration.

## 3.3 Legal reasoning of awards in investment treaty arbitration

One of the main consequences that appear as a result of the legal background of arbitrators in investment treaty arbitration will lie in the reasoning of arbitral decisions.[62] I will not engage in an empirical analysis of the numerous decisions and the influence of the legal expertise of arbitrators on the legal reasoning of the tribunal. The objective here is to show how the public international law character of investment treaty arbitration and international investment disputes directly or indirectly influences the requirements of legal reasoning of arbitral awards. This not only impacts the level of reasoning required in investment treaty arbitration generally, but also the use of previous arbitral awards as *de facto* precedents.

### *3.3.1 The obligation to render a reasoned award*

The obligation of arbitral tribunals to render a reasoned award is contained in Article 48(3) of the ICSID Convention: 'the award shall deal with every question submitted to the Tribunal, and shall state the reasons upon which it is based'. The requirement is reiterated in Rule 47(1)(i) of the ICSID Arbitration Rules. Article 34(3) of the UNCITRAL Arbitration rules likewise provides an obligation to render a reasoned award, unless, of course, the parties have decided otherwise. The majority of the arbitration rules in international commercial arbitration similarly provide for the obligation to render a reasoned award.[63]

It is important to point out, however, that under the ICSID Convention, the obligation to render a reasoned award may not be waived by the parties. An analysis of the drafting history of the ICSID Convention has shown that a preliminary draft of the Articles providing for the obligation to render a reasoned decision initially included the possibility of the parties to exempt the tribunal from this obligation.[64] The final version

62 See, generally, Schill, 'Crafting the International Economic Order', p. 406.
63 Blackaby *et al.*, *Redfern & Hunter on International Arbitration*, paras 9.119–9.124.
64 For a discussion of this, see Guillermo Aguilar Alvarez and W. Michael Reisman, 'How Well are Investment Awards Reasoned?', in Guillermo Aguilar Alvarez and W. Michael Reisman (eds.), *The Reasons Requirement in International Investment Arbitration: Critical Case Studies* (Leiden: Martinus Nijhoff, 2008), p. 2.

adopted by the state parties, however, suppressed the possibility of waiver, and thus turned the obligation to state the reasons into a mandatory provision from which the parties to the dispute cannot derogate.[65] This is not the case under the UNCITRAL Arbitration Rules, which contain the possibility for the parties to agree otherwise.[66] Similar provisions are also included in the Rules of Arbitration of the LCIA[67] and those of the SCC.[68] The Arbitration Rules of the ICC, however, do require an obligation to state reasons, without any possibility of waiver by the parties,[69] not only because it is in accordance with modern arbitral practice, but, more importantly, to allow scrutiny by the International Court of Arbitration, a specific feature of arbitration under the auspices of the ICC.[70]

The fact that parties cannot deviate from this requirement under the ICSID Convention is consistent with the public international law dimension of the procedure, but also with modern arbitral practice in international law. Moreover, in the ICSID system a failure to state the reasons can amount to an annulment of the decision, which reinforces the fundamental character of the obligation to state the reasons on which the award is based.[71] Outside the ICSID context, the possibility of having awards of international arbitral tribunals annulled for a failure to state the reasons, provided, of course, that the parties have not dispensed the tribunal from this requirement if such exemption is possible under the applicable rules of procedure, reflects a general principle of international law.[72]

65 *Ibid.*

66 Article 43(3) of the UNICTRAL Arbitration Rules: 'The arbitral tribunal shall state the reasons upon which the award is based, unless the parties have agreed that no reasons are to be given.'

67 Rule 26.1 of the LCIA Arbitration Rules: 'The Arbitral Tribunal shall make its award in writing and, unless all parties agree in writing otherwise, shall state the reasons upon which its award is based.'

68 Article 36 of the SCC Arbitration Rules: 'The Arbitral Tribunal shall make its award in writing, and, unless otherwise agreed by the parties, parties shall state the reasons upon which the award is based.'

69 Article 31(2) of the ICC Arbitration Rules.

70 Yves Derains and Eric A. Schwartz, *A Guide to the ICC Rules of Arbitration* (The Hague: Kluwer Law International, 2005), p. 309.

71 Article 52(1)(e) of the ICSID Convention.

72 For a discussion outside the context of investment arbitration, see International Court of Justice, *Arbitral Award of 31 July 1989 (Guinea-Bissau* v. *Senegal)*, Judgment, *ICJ Reports*, 1991, 53. See, generally, Shabtai Rosenne, *Interpretation, Revision and Other Recourse from International Judgments and Awards* (Leiden: Martinus Nijhoff, 2007).

### *3.3.2 The extended level of reasoning required in investment treaty arbitration*

There are many reasons underlying the obligation to render a reasoned award.[73] Essentially, the requirement of a reasoned award is the logical consequence of the fact that the parties have chosen a *legal* method of dispute settlement, based on the application of law, rather than on principles of equity (*ex aequo et bono*). Tribunals thus have the obligation to render an award based on the rational application of the law, rather than on their own views of justice.[74] The majority of ICSID ad hoc committees have followed the principle that the requirement of a reasoned award entails an obligation for the tribunal to state reasons in order to enable the reader to understand how the tribunal came to its conclusion.[75] The requirement to render a reasoned award equally contains an obligation to render an award based on the law as defined by the parties and/or the applicable procedural rules.

Beyond the general reasons behind the need for a reasoned award in arbitration generally, the involvement of a state in the proceedings in investment treaty arbitration and the public international law character of investment treaty arbitration generally imply a greater need for rendering a reasoned award and a higher threshold for the reasons requirement than is the case in international commercial arbitration.[76] This idea is very well reflected in the decision of the Tribunal in *Glamis* v. *United States*:

> All tribunals are to provide reasons for their awards and this requirement is owed to private and public authorities alike. In the Tribunal's view, however, it is particularly important that the State Parties receive reasons that are detailed and persuasive for three reasons. First, States are complex organizations

[73] See, generally, Thomas Bingham, 'Reasons and Reasons and Reasons: Differences Between a Court Judgment and an Arbitral Award', *Arbitration International*, 4(2) (1988): 141; Pierre Lalive, 'On the Reasoning of International Arbitral Awards', *Journal of International Dispute Settlement*, 1(1) (2010): 55; and Toby Landau, 'Reasons for Reasons: The Tribunal's Duty in Investor–State Arbitration', in A. J. van den Berg (ed.), *ICCA Congress Series No. 8 14 Dublin Conference, 2008* (The Hague: Kluwer Law International 2009), p. 199.

[74] Landau, 'Reasons for Reasons', pp. 188 and 190.

[75] For a discussion, see Tai-Heng Cheng and Robert Trisotto, 'Reasons and Reasoning in Investment Treaty Arbitration', *Suffolk Transnational Law Review*, 32(2) (2009): 409.

[76] See Landau, 'Reasons for Reasons', pp. 195–7, and Federico Ortino, 'Legal Reasoning of International Investment Tribunals: A Typology of Egregious Failures', *Journal of International Dispute Settlement*, 3(1) (2012): 31.

composed of multiple branches of government that interact with the people of the State. An award adverse to a State requires compliance with the particular award and such compliance politically may require both governmental and public faith in the integrity of the process of arbitration. Second, while a corporate participant in arbitration may withdraw from utilizing arbitration in the future or from doing business in a particular country, the three NAFTA State Parties have made an indefinite commitment to the deepening of their economic relations. In this sense, not only compliance with a particular award, but the long-term maintenance of this commitment requires both governmental and public faith in the integrity of the process of arbitration. Third, a minimum level of faith in the system is maintained by the mechanism for the possible annulment of awards. However, the time and expense of such annulments are to be avoided. The detailing of reasons may not avoid the initiation of an annulment procedure, but it is hoped that such reasons will aid the reviewing body in a prompt resolution of such motions.[77]

It is, indeed, beyond doubt that awards of international investment tribunals, being concerned with public international law disputes relating to the exercise by the state of its sovereign regulatory powers, may have a major long-term impact on the state's economic and financial stability, and on its foreign investment policy.[78] As a consequence, as is the case in general public law litigation as well, one can certainly agree with the proposition that the nationals of the host state are legitimately entitled to know and understand the reasons underlying the decision of the arbitral tribunal.[79]

Especially the first two reasons invoked by the *Glamis* Tribunal to support the argument for the importance of reasoning in investment treaty arbitration are interesting for the purposes of this analysis, since they explicitly relate to the public international law character of international investment disputes. These two reasons are related to the public availability of the awards, contrary to international commercial arbitration, which is, as noted before, usually conducted in a confidential way. The *Glamis* Tribunal's reasons essentially boil down to arguing that the involvement of a state in the arbitral proceedings, in relation to acts performed in the exercise of its sovereign authority, brings a public dimension to the arbitral proceedings, which in turn requires both governmental and public faith in the legitimacy and validity of the arbitral process. Although faith in the legitimacy of the arbitral

77 *Glamis Gold Ltd* v. *United States of America*, UNCITRAL, Final Award, 8 June 2009, para. 8 (internal footnotes omitted).
78 Aguilar Alvarez and Reisman, 'How Well are Investment Awards Reasoned?' p. 2.
79 *Ibid.*

process undoubtedly constitutes a fundamental prerequisite for the sustainability of arbitration as a dispute method generally, in particular, for the parties to the dispute, one can easily side with the *Glamis* Tribunal's consideration that international investment disputes require a general confidence and faith in the legitimacy and validity of the arbitral procedure by entities and individuals *beyond the parties to the dispute*. As was also pointed out by Kingsbury and Schill:

> the reasoning should nonetheless be transparent and accessible not only from the point of view of the parties to the proceeding, but to the tribunals' wider audience, including non-participating States, the investment community at large and those groups that may be impacted by specific decisions in the context of foreign investment activities.[80]

Here again, the difference with international commercial arbitration and the types of dispute settled though that mechanism becomes apparent. In the latter proceedings, the reach of the arbitral awards only rarely exceeds the parties to the dispute, since the dispute is essentially limited to the contractual relations between two entities that have a private contractual relation. Conversely, awards of arbitral tribunals in investment treaty arbitration have a much broader influence than the mere parties to the dispute. In line with the rationale behind the obligation to render a reasoned award, the award should contain the reasons in order to enable the wider audience of the award to understand the awards.[81]

### 3.3.3 *Precedents and* 'jurisprudence constante'

The question of whether international investment tribunals, because of the specificity of investment treaty arbitration, have a particular role to play in the development of a consistent and coherent international body of law lies at the heart of the tension that exists between the

[80] Benedict Kingsbury and Stephan W. Schill, 'Investor-State Arbitration as Governance: Fair and Equitable Treatment, Proportionality and the Emerging Global Administrative Law', *IILJ Working Paper 2009/6*, Global Administrative Law Series, available at: http://lsr.nellco.org/nyu_plltwp/146, p. 45, accessed 19 April 2012.

[81] Next to the public character of investment treaty arbitration it has also been pointed out that the system as such of investment treaty arbitration implies a greater need for reasoned awards. One could argue that because of the broad open-textured standards of investment protection in investment treaties, the power given to the arbitrators should be exercised with great clarity, and thus calls for an increased attention to the legal reasoning of the arbitral tribunal. Also, the absence of an appeals mechanism and a general system of review of the *quality* of the reasons contained in arbitral decisions warrants a higher requirement for the arbitral tribunal to state the reasons on which the award is based. See Landau, 'Reasons for Reasons', pp. 195–7.

dispute settlement method used, namely, international arbitration, and the public international law character of international investment disputes.[82] It is argued here that international arbitration, being an ad hoc dispute settlement mechanism, does not permit the transposition of the rules in respect of precedent applicable to domestic public law litigation. As noted already in the Introduction, the choice of arbitration as a dispute settlement mechanism comes with certain intrinsic concepts and principles which may not be deviated from without the risk of denaturing the very essence of international arbitration.

As noted by Judge Shahabuddeen in his seminal work on the role of precedent in the work of the ICJ,[83] precedent can, put simply, operate in three ways: (1) judicial and arbitral precedents may be considered by a judge or arbitrator as part of the legal materials available to ascertain the law while not being obliged to follow previous rulings or awards; (2) a judge or arbitrator may be obliged to decide a case in the same way as a previous case, unless there are good reasons to deviate from previous cases; and (3), a judge or arbitrator may be obliged to decide a case in the same way as previous cases even if there are good reasons not to, which is usually referred to as 'binding precedent' or '*stare decisis*'.[84] International law largely follows the civil law system in that there is no rule that would oblige a court or tribunal to follow decisions made by an earlier court or tribunal, or by earlier decisions of the same court or tribunal, as discussed above. A related – and in investment treaty arbitration frequently invoked – notion is that of '*jurisprudence constante*'. *Jurisprudence constante* is often used in civil law systems to denote a series of cases on similar issues that form a uniform and consistent interpretation or application of a certain rule.[85] In that sense, the value of previous case law resides in the *de facto* rather than *de jure* – which would be the case in the event of 'binding precedents' or '*stare decisis*' – recognition of a certain 'persuasive authority'.[86]

[82] See, generally, De Brabandere, 'Arbitral Decisions as a Source of International Investment Law'.

[83] Mohamed Shahabuddeen, *Precedent in the World Court* (Cambridge University Press, 1996), p. 1.

[84] *Ibid.*, p. 9.

[85] See, generally, Robert L. Henry, '*Jurisprudence Constante* and *Stare Decisis* Contrasted' *American Bar Association Journal*, 15(1) (1929): 11, 11–13, and Vincy Fon and Francesco Parisi, 'Judicial Precedents in Civil Law Systems: A Dynamic Analysis', *International Review of Law and Economics*, 26(4) (2006): 519.

[86] Albert Tate Jr., 'Techniques of Judicial Interpretation in Louisiana', *Louisiana Law Review*, 22(4) (1962): 727, 743.

There is no doubt that there is no binding precedent in investment treaty arbitration, as much as there is no such rule in general international law. This fundamental principle is included in Article 53(1) of the ICSID Convention, which provides that the award rendered by the arbitral tribunal is binding upon the parties, thus implicitly excluding any precedential value to awards rendered under the ICSID Convention.[87] There is, moreover, nothing in the *travaux préparatoires* that would indicate the application of the doctrine of *stare decisis* to investment arbitration.[88] The Arbitral Tribunal in *SGS* v. *The Philippines* nevertheless raised doubts as to whether the wording of Article 53(1) of the ICSID can be read as implying the absence of any precedential value to arbitral awards: 'the ICSID Convention provides only that awards rendered under it are "binding on the parties" (Article 53(1)), a provision which might be regarded as directed to the *res judicata* effect of awards rather than their impact as precedents in later cases'.[89] At the same time, the Tribunal in that case confirmed that 'there is no doctrine of precedent in international law, if by precedent is meant a rule of the binding effect of a single decision'.[90] A specific rule on the absence of precedential value to previous case law is contained in Article 1136 of the NAFTA, which states that 'an award made by a Tribunal shall have no binding force except between the disputing parties and in respect of the particular case'.

One could argue that the public function of investment treaty arbitration warrants the development of a consistent body of law, in order, *inter alia*, to ensure predictability and stability in international legal relations between host states and foreign investors. The absence of binding precedent in international investment law would, according to certain scholars, undermine the consistency of international investment law,[91] and the need for legal predictability in international business transactions.[92] Other authors have argued that the current system

[87] See also Christoph Schreuer and Matthew Weiniger, 'A Doctrine of Precedent?' in Peter Muchlinski, Frederico Ortino and Christoph Schreuer (eds.), *The Oxford Handbook of International Investment Law* (Oxford University Press, 2008), p. 1189; and Schreuer *et al.*, *The ICSID Convention*, p. 1101.

[88] Schreuer *et al.*, *The ICSID Convention*, p. 1101.

[89] *SGS* v. *The Philippines*, ICSID Case No. ARB/02/6, para. 97 (internal footnotes omitted).

[90] *Ibid.* (internal footnotes omitted).

[91] Ian Laird and Rebecca Askew, 'Finality versus Consistency: Does Investor-State Arbitration Need an Appellate System', *Journal of Appellate Practice and Process*, 7(2) (2005): 285, 285.

[92] Frank Spoorenberg and Jorge E. Viñuales, 'Conflicting Decisions in International Arbitration', *Law and Practice of International Courts and Tribunals*, 8(1) (2009): 91, 92.

of the *de facto* and unfettered use of precedent is not suitable in investment treaty arbitration, and have instead argued for an application of *jurisprudence constante*.[93] Some tribunals have even gone further by arguing that tribunals have a duty to contribute to the harmonization of international law. In *Saipem* v. *Bangladesh*, for example, the Tribunal, although adhering to the principle that 'it is not bound by previous decisions',[94] noted that:

> it must pay due consideration to earlier decisions of international tribunals. It believes that, subject to compelling contrary grounds, it has a duty to adopt solutions established in a series of consistent cases. It also believes that, subject to the specifics of a given treaty and of the circumstances of the actual case, it has a duty to seek to contribute to the harmonious development of investment law and thereby to meet the legitimate expectations of the community of States and investors towards certainty of the rule of law.[95]

The idea is thus that the development of a *jurisprudence constante* would be necessary 'to foster consistency', especially in those areas of the law which are not yet well developed.[96]

The specific characteristics of arbitration, however, preclude any form of use of binding precedent or *jurisprudence constante*. Indeed, although I agree as a matter of principle that coherence would as such be a welcome development for international investment law, as it is for general international law or any legal system for that matter, any obligation for arbitral tribunals resulting from such idea would run counter to the very nature of arbitral procedures. In other words, here, the specificity of investment treaty arbitration does not permit an adaptation of the rules applicable to the arbitral procedure, without denaturing the very essence of arbitration. Differentiating investment treaty arbitration from international commercial arbitration in support of the need of a *jurisprudence constante* is unwarranted. First, the type of disputes submitted to an arbitral tribunal in investment treaty

93 Andrea K. Bjorklund, 'Investment Treaty Arbitral Decisions as *Jurisprudence Constante*', in Colin B. Picker, Isabella D. Bunn and Douglas W. Arner (eds.), *International Economic Law: The State and Future of the Discipline* (Oxford: Hart, 2008), pp. 270 ff. See, however, Marie-Louise M. Rodgers, 'Bilateral Investment Treaties and Arbitration: An Argument and a Proposal for the ICSID's Implementation of a System of Binding Precedent', *Transnational Dispute Management*, 5(3) (2008): 5–6.

94 *Saipem* v. *People's Republic of Bangladesh*, ICSID Case No. ARB/05/7, Award, 30 June 2009, para. 90.

95 *Ibid.*, para. 90.

96 Gabrielle Kaufmann-Kohler, 'Arbitral Precedent: Dream, Necessity or Excuse?' *Arbitration International*, 23(3) (2007): 357, 377.

arbitration does not permit deviation from the fundamental principle that arbitral tribunals are bound by the applicable law as defined by the parties or, in the case of investment treaty arbitration, by the ICSID Convention. The law applicable to investment treaty arbitration does not include previous decisions, unless parties explicitly provide so. Secondly, the absence of binding precedent and *jurisprudence constante* in investment treaty arbitration is in reality not contrary to the public international law character of investment treaty arbitration. First of all, there is neither binding precedent nor obligation to form a *jurisprudence constante* in general international law. In addition, the presence of a state in investment treaty arbitration, the fact that a state's responsibility under international law is at stake, and the public interest does not imply that investment treaty arbitration needs to function with a system of binding precedent or *jurisprudence constante*. In fact, both binding precedent and *jurisprudence constante* would contravene the consent of states, including in relation to the applicable law. As said, the fact that states have chosen international arbitration as a dispute settlement method needs to be respected, and this implies that each case will be examined *de novo* based on the specific factual and legal circumstances of the case.

More generally, compared with standing judicial bodies or centralized dispute settlement mechanisms, investment treaty arbitration does not have centralized standing adjudicatory bodies, and has certain specific features that accentuate the impropriety of considering previous decisions as a source of law, that is, as having a binding character.

First, investment treaty arbitration is a decentralized ad hoc legal system of dispute settlement. When compared with other dispute settlement bodies, such as the system established under the World Trade Organization (WTO) Dispute Settlement Understanding, which also functions with ad hoc panels but has an appeals mechanism, the WTO Appellate Body, the concept of binding precedent seems even more unsuitable since it lacks a hierarchical structure. *Stare decisis* and *jurisprudence constante* very often presuppose a hierarchical system of courts and tribunals, as is the case in various national legal systems.[97] Investment tribunals cannot be expected to act as national courts in hierarchical vertical legal systems which function with rules on

[97] See Catherine Kessedjian, 'To Give or Not to Give Precedential Value to Investment Arbitration Awards', in Catherine A. Rogers and Roger P. Alford (eds.), *The Future of Investment Arbitration* (Oxford University Press, 2009), p. 63.

binding precedent or *jurisprudence constante*.[98] The very fact that states have chosen to establish a horizontal system of ad hoc arbitration with no appellate mechanism by necessary implication results in a system whereby each arbitral tribunal assesses the case without any obligation to consider or apply previous case law. As the Arbitral Tribunal in *SGS* v. *The Philippines* noted, 'there is no hierarchy of international tribunals, and even if there were, there is no good reason for allowing the first tribunal in time to resolve issues for all later tribunals'.[99]

Secondly, investment treaty arbitration is substantially different from permanent international courts and tribunals, mainly because the international arbitral tribunal is created only to resolve one specific dispute between two parties and its composition thus differs from one case to another. Although one could expect arbitral tribunals to decide similar issues in the same way, the fact that it is an ad hoc tribunal, instead of a standing body, weakens the expectation of 'consistency', and thus the application of any form of binding precedent. There is, so to speak, no interconnection between the various investment tribunals which operate independently of one another aside from the similarity in the object of the dispute and the procedural rules.

Thirdly, although publication has become the standard for investment decisions rendered by arbitral tribunals operating under the ICSID Convention, this is not the case for arbitration conducted under other rules. As a consequence, not all arbitrators have knowledge of all decisions previously rendered in investment disputes.[100] The publication of arbitral awards, of course, encourages the references to precedents as a source of inspiration.[101] This is not a problem *in se*, and in fact is a welcome development. However, the reference to precedents in that scenario is not the equivalent of using precedents as a source of law by treating these as binding, or the equivalent of considering it a duty of the arbitral tribunal to contribute to the development of a consistent body of laws.

The main reason for, and benefit of, the absence of binding precedent in investment treaty arbitration is that the parties are assured that their case will be examined in full based on the specific factual circumstances of the case, the law applicable to that dispute and the legal arguments

98 Schreuer and Weiniger, 'A Doctrine of Precedent?', p. 1189.

99 *SGS* v. *The Philippines*, ICSID Case No. ARB/02/6, para. 97 (internal footnotes omitted).

100 See also Gilbert Guillaume, 'The Use of Precedent by International Judges and Arbitrator', *Journal of International Dispute Settlement*, 2(1) (2011): 5, 14.

101 See De Brabandere, 'Arbitral Decisions as a Source of International Investment Law'.

presented by the parties. One of the members of the Ad Hoc Committee in *Vivendi II* noted in an additional opinion that:

> It may be recalled that in international law, there has never been a rule of binding precedent and this is so for very good reasons ... the Arbitral Tribunals and ad hoc Committees ... must find the law based on the facts as they present themselves to them. This does not, of course, rule out that earlier cases may have persuasive value but it is for the relevant Tribunal or ad hoc Committee to decide in each instance, taking into account the submissions of the parties.[102]

Many tribunals thus have confirmed the independence of arbitral tribunals, even in cases presenting very similar facts and circumstances.[103]

## 3.4 Party autonomy and the powers of the arbitral tribunals

That consent is the basis of investment treaty arbitration and the tribunal's jurisdiction is uncontested. As a consequence, generally, the consent of the parties to the investment treaty regarding certain procedural aspects of the arbitral proceedings must be taken into account by the arbitral tribunal, the latter's powers being founded on that legal instrument.

The autonomy of the parties, generally, in international arbitration forms one of the fundamental cornerstones of the proceedings before the arbitral tribunal. Because of the similarities between investment treaty arbitration and public law litigation, some authors have nevertheless considered the principle of party autonomy to be unwarranted.[104] That the equality of arms principle governing international commercial arbitration should not be similarly applied to investment treaty arbitration, which should allegedly, according to the opposing public law or public international law approach, give certain privileges

[102] *Compañía de Aguas del Aconquija SA and Vivendi Universal SA* v. *The Argentine Republic*, ICSID Case No. ARB/97/3, Decision on the Argentine Republic's Request for Annulment of the Award rendered on 20 August 2007, 10 August 2010, Additional Opinion of Professor J. H. Dalhuisen under Article 48(4) of the ICSID Convention, paras 16 and 18.

[103] In the *LESI and Astaldi* case, for example, which had similar facts and legal arguments and which were heard by an identically composed arbitral tribunal, the tribunal rightly confirmed that: 'En dépit du fait que le présent Tribunal arbitral est composé des mêmes personnes que celles qui formaient le premier, il n'est pas lié par les positions qui ont été prises sur les objections que la Défenderesse a formées, en des termes parfois identiques, à l'encontre de la compétence du Tribunal arbitral et de la recevabilité de la demande' (*LESI and Astaldi* v. *Algeria*, ICSID Case No. ARB/05/3, para. 56).

[104] Van Harten, *Investment Treaty Arbitration and Public Law*, pp. 130 ff.

and deference to the state, is erroneous.[105] There is indeed no 'clash' between them, since the equality of arms is a fundamental principle of arbitral procedure in public international law, as it is in international commercial arbitration.[106] Party autonomy is also present in international judicial proceedings, although not in a pure form.[107]

However, party autonomy – by which I mean the *parties to the dispute* – in investment treaty arbitration has less impact on the conduct of the proceedings than is usually the case in international commercial arbitration. First, being founded in public international law, investment tribunals and arbitrators are subjected to some specific principles imported from public international law litigation, such as the principle of *jura novit curia*. Secondly, the flexibility given to arbitrators in their discretionary power in the conduct of the proceedings allows for the taking into consideration of the public international law character of investment treaty arbitration. Such may be the case in particular in respect of the level of 'proactivity' of international arbitrators in fact-finding or in respect of the admission of *amicus curiae* briefs, as will be discussed in Chapter 5.

Before turning to these elements, I should point out for the sake of completeness that in the case of investment treaty arbitration conducted under the ICSID Convention, the parties are bound by the procedural rules established under the Convention.[108] The Convention contains mandatory provisions from which the parties cannot derogate. Parties can, however, deviate from certain principles contained in the ICSID Arbitration Rules, in particular when the ICSID Convention or Rules of Arbitration explicitly allow parties to derogate from a certain

[105] For a discussion, see Thomas Wälde, 'Procedural Challenges in Investment Arbitration Under the Shadow of the Dual Role of the State: Asymmetries and Tribunal's Duty to Ensure, Proactively, the Equality of Arms', *Arbitration International*, 26(1) (2010): 3. Wälde nevertheless concludes that in both instances equality of arms should prevail.

[106] For a discussion, see Eric De Brabandere, 'Individuals in Advisory Proceedings Before the International Court of Justice: Equality of the Parties and the Court's Discretionary Authority', *Law and Practice of International Courts and Tribunals*, 11(2) (2012): 253.

[107] See Stephan Wittich, 'The Limits of Party Autonomy in Investment Arbitration', in Christina Knahr, Christian Koller, Walter Rechberger and August Reinisch (eds.), *Investment and Commercial Arbitration. Similarities and Divergences* (Utrecht: Eleven International, 2010), pp. 50 ff.

[108] Article 44 of the ICSID Convention: 'Any arbitration proceeding shall be conducted in accordance with the provisions of this Section . . .'

rule.[109] Among the mandatory Articles, one finds those related to the powers of the tribunal, such as its *compétence de la compétence*,[110] the prohibition of *non liquet*,[111] the obligation for the tribunal to deal with all questions submitted to it if a party fails to appear or to present his case,[112] and the rules in respect of the adoption of the award, including the obligation to state the reasons, as discussed above.[113]

### 3.4.1 *The principle of* jura novit curia

The principle of *jura novit curia*, namely, that the court of the arbitral tribunal knows the law and that it must apply the law *ex officio*, a principle related to the maxim *da mihi factum dabo tibi jus* ('give me the facts and I shall give you the law'), is one of the basic principles of judicial procedure. It implies that the contents of the applicable law need not be proven by the parties as factual elements need to be proven, a principle since long recognized by the ICJ in respect of international judicial proceedings. In the 1974 *Fisheries Jurisdiction* case, where one of the parties failed to appear before the court, the ICJ noted:

> The Court however, as an international judicial organ, is deemed to take judicial notice of international law, and is therefore required in a case falling under Article 53 of the Statute, as in any other case, to consider on its own initiative all rules of international law which may be relevant to the settlement of the dispute. It being the duty of the Court itself to ascertain and apply the relevant law in the given circumstances of the case, the burden of establishing or proving rules of international law cannot be imposed upon any of the parties, for the law lies within the judicial knowledge of the Court.[114]

[109] See, for example, in relation to the applicable law: Article 42(1) of the ICSID Convention: 'The Tribunal shall decide a dispute *in accordance with such rules of law as may be agreed by the parties*. In the absence of such agreement, the Tribunal shall apply the law of the Contracting State party to the dispute (including its rules on the conflict of laws) and such rules of international law as may be applicable' (emphasis added). See, generally, Böckstiegel, 'The Role of the Arbitrators in Investment Treaty Arbitration', p. 369, and Wittich, 'The Limits of Party Autonomy in Investment Arbitration', p. 54.
[110] Article 41(2) of the ICSID Convention. [111] Article 42(2) of the ICSID Convention.
[112] Article 45 of the ICSID Convention. [113] Article 48 of the ICSID Convention.
[114] International Court of Justice, *Fisheries Jurisdiction (United Kingdom* v. *Iceland)*, Judgment, *ICJ Reports*, 1974, 3, para. 17. See also the Separate Opinion of Judge de Castro to the *Fisheries Jurisdiction* case (p. 79), and International Court of Justice, *Military and Paramilitary Activities in and against Nicaragua*, Judgment, *ICJ Reports*, 1986, 14, 24–25. The application generally of this principle in international criminal proceedings is, however, not generally accepted. For a discussion, see International Criminal Tribunal for the Former Yugoslavia, *Prosecutor* v. *Zoran Kupreskic, Mirjan Kupreskic, Vlatko Kupreskic, Drago Josipovic, Dragan Papic and Vladimir Santic*, Case No. IT-95-16-T, Judgment, 14 January 2000.

The only traditional exception to this principle is municipal law, which is not covered by the maxim in international judicial proceedings.[115]

In national judicial proceedings, the principle similarly applies, with the exception of foreign laws which are to be proven by the parties.[116] However, as far as arbitral procedure is concerned, the question is whether any law generally needs to be proven by the parties in the same way as the facts, or whether arbitral tribunals are free to establish the contents of the applicable law irrespective of the arguments of the parties.[117] The practice in international commercial arbitration is far from uniform, as is the practice in national arbitration.[118]

Every discussion of this principle undoubtedly ties in with the principles relating to the applicable law, and it should thus be kept in mind that the arbitrator is in any event bound by the applicable law as defined by the parties.[119] Moreover, it should be added that the principle of *jura novit curia* has in principle no bearing on the rule that tribunals are prohibited from deciding *ultra petita*.[120] That particular principle, which delineates the mandate of the tribunal, is indeed unconnected to the question of *which law applies* to the merits of the case, and whether or not the tribunal is bound by the submissions of the parties in this respect. The question, rather, is to what extent the tribunal may take into consideration legal arguments which have not been presented or pleaded by the parties to the dispute within the applicable law as defined by the parties.

Several authors have noted that the principle *iura novit curia* is inappropriate generally in international arbitration, because the very notion of 'foreign law' has no practical relevance in international arbitration since there is no *lex fori*.[121] Generally, international arbitration

[115] See, for instance, Permanent Court of International Justice, *Brazilian Loans*, Judgment, 12 July 1929, *PCIJ Reports*, Series A 20/21 (1929), p. 124. For a discussion of the application of this principle before the ICJ, see André Nollkaemper, 'The Role of Domestic Courts in the Case Law of the International Court of Justice', *Chinese Journal of International Law*, 5(2) (2006): 301.

[116] This exception, however, is again subjected to several exceptions. In respect of the status of foreign law in Italy, see Francesco Galgano, 'The New *Lex Mercatoria*', *Annual Survey of International & Comparative Law*, 2 (1995): 99.

[117] See, generally, Gabrielle Kaufmann-Kohler, 'Globalization of Arbitral Procedure', *Vanderbilt Journal of Transnational Law*, 36(4) (2003): 1313, 1331 ff.

[118] *Ibid.*, p. 1332. [119] See below Chapter 4.

[120] See, however, Teresa Giovannini, 'International Arbitration and *Jura Novit Curia*: Towards Harmonization', *Transnational Dispute Management*, 9(3) (2012): 3.

[121] See, for instance, Gabrielle Kaufmann-Kohler, 'The Governing Law: Fact or Law? A Transnational Rule on Establishing its Content', in Markus Wirth (ed.), *Best Practices in*

rules, as well as national laws on international arbitration, are silent on the power of arbitral tribunals in this respect. A notable exception are the Rules of Arbitration of the LCIA, which have taken over the provisions of the UK Arbitration Act. The LCIA Rules of Arbitration provide that it is up to the arbitral tribunal itself to decide whether it should take the initiative in identifying the contents of the applicable law.[122] Despite that exception, one can generally say that the application of the principle of *iura novit curia* in international commercial arbitration is met with certain reluctance in scholarship,[123] and is subject to divergences in national laws.[124]

## *Jura novit curia* in the practice of ICSID tribunals

The practice of arbitral tribunals in investment treaty arbitration shows a clear departure from the practice of international commercial arbitration. This has been confirmed by numerous annulment decisions rendered under the ICSID Convention in which Ad Hoc Committees have refrained from annulling awards based on arguments other than those presented by the parties.[125] In *Klöckner* v. *Cameroon*, for instance, the Ad Hoc Committee summarized the application of the principle as follows:

As for the Tribunal itself, when in the course of its deliberations it reached the provisional conclusion that the true legal basis for its decision could well be

*International Arbitration*, ASA Swiss Arbitration Association Conference, January 27, 2006, Zurich, Special Series No. 26 (Basel: Association Suisse de l'Arbitrage, 2006), p. 84; Gabrielle Kaufmann-Kohler, 'Iura novit arbiter: Est-ce bien raisonnable?' in Anne Héritier and Laurent Hirsch (eds.), *De Lege Ferenda. Réflexions sur le droit désirable en l'honneur du Professeur Alain Hirsch* (Geneva: Editions Slatkine, 2004), p. 74; and Giovannini, 'International Arbitration and *Jura Novit Curia*', p. 2.

122 Article 22.1(c) of the LCIA Arbitration Rules: 'Unless the parties at any time agree otherwise in writing, the Arbitral Tribunal shall have the power, on the application of any party or of its own motion, but in either case only after giving the parties a reasonable opportunity to state their views . . . to conduct such enquiries as may appear to the Arbitral Tribunal to be necessary or expedient, including whether and to what extent the Arbitral Tribunal should itself take the initiative in identifying the issues and ascertaining the relevant facts and the law(s) or rules of law applicable to the arbitration, the merits of the parties' dispute and the Arbitration Agreement.'

123 See, generally, International Law Association, Committee on International Commercial Arbitration, Final Report, 'Ascertaining the Contents of the Applicable Law in International Commercial Arbitration', Rio de Janeiro Conference, 2008, available at: www.ila-hq.org/en/committees/index.cfm/cid/19, accessed 20 April 2012.

124 For a discussion, see Giovannini, 'International Arbitration and *Jura Novit Curia*', pp. 4–6.

125 Christoph Schreuer, 'Three Generations of ICSID Annulment Proceedings', in Emmanuel Gaillard and Yas Banifatemi (eds.), *Annulment of ICSID Awards* (Huntington, NY: Juris, 2004), p. 30.

different from either of the parties' respective arguments, it was not, subject to what will be said below, in principle prohibited from choosing its own argument. Whether to reopen the proceeding before reaching a decision and allow the parties to put forward their views on the arbitrators' 'new' thesis is rather a question of expedience. The real question is whether, by formulating its own theory and argument, the Tribunal goes beyond the 'legal framework' established by the Claimant and Respondent. This would for example be the case if an arbitral tribunal rendered its decision on the basis of tort while the pleas of the parties were based on contract. Within the dispute's 'legal framework,' arbitrators must be free to rely on arguments which strike them as the best ones, even if those arguments were not developed by the parties (although they could have been). Even if it is generally desirable for arbitrators to avoid basing their decision on an argument that has not been discussed by the parties, it obviously does not follow that they therefore commit a 'serious departure from a fundamental rule of procedure.' Any other solution would expose arbitrators to having to do the work of the parties' counsel for them and would risk slowing down or even paralyzing the arbitral solution to disputes.[126]

The Ad Hoc Committee in *Vivendi I* also confirmed, more implicitly, the application of that principle and the discretion of the tribunal to decide on its interpretation of the law and facts:

Claimants contend the Tribunal's decision came unannounced, and that they had no opportunity to present arguments on the decision to dismiss their claim on the merits on grounds related to Article 16(4) of the Concession Contract. It may be true that the particular approach adopted by the Tribunal in attempting to reconcile the various conflicting elements of the case before it came as a surprise to the parties, or at least to some of them. But even if true, this would by no means be unprecedented in judicial decision-making, either international or domestic, and it has nothing to do with the ground for annulment contemplated by Article 52(1)(d) of the ICSID Convention.[127]

This consideration was cited and adopted by the Committee in *Helnan* v. *Egypt*.[128]

In *RSM Production Corporation* v. *Grenada*, the Committee likewise arrogated itself the power to consider arguments not raised by the parties:

[126] *Klöckner Industrie-Anlagen GmbH and others* v. *United Republic of Cameroon and Société Camerounaise des Engrais*, ICSID Case No. ARB/81/2, Decision of the Ad Hoc Committee, 3 May 1985. See also *Wena Hotels Ltd* v. *The Arab Republic of Egypt*, ICSID Case No. ARB/98/4, Decision on Annulment, 5 February 2002, para. 70.

[127] *Compañiá de Aguas del Aconquija SA and Vivendi Universal* v. *Argentina*, ICSID Case No. ARB/97/3, Decision on Annulment, para. 84.

[128] *Helnan International Hotels A/S* v. *Arab Republic of Egypt*, ICSID Case No. ARB/05/19, Decision on the Application for Annulment, 14 June 2010, para. 23.

Although not cited by the Applicant or the Respondent, there are a number of other arbitral decisions which deal with the power of international courts and tribunals to reopen a case for newly discovered evidence. On the basis of the principle of *jura novit curia*, the Committee is able to consider the relevance of those decisions.[129]

Whether or not the existence of the principle of *jura novit curia* implies an *obligation* on the tribunal to effectively exercise that power is subjected to different views. The Ad Hoc Committee in *Mitchell* v. *Congo* argued that there is no such obligation, but that this may nevertheless be expected from a tribunal:

the Arbitral Tribunal would have been welcome to address ex proprio motu the other provisions of the Treaty, which might potentially excuse taking such measures against the Claimant. A comparable approach would have been along the lines of the adage *jura novit curia* – on which the DRC leaned heavily during the Annulment Proceeding – but this could not truly be required of the Arbitral Tribunal, as it is not, strictly speaking, subject to any obligation to apply a rule of law that has not been adduced; this is but an option – and the parties should have been given the opportunity to be heard in this respect – for which reason it is not possible to draw any conclusions from the fact that the Arbitral Tribunal did not exercise it.[130]

In *Enron* v. *Argentina*, the Ad Hoc Committee also argued that:

from the material before it, the parties in their arguments before the Tribunal do not appear to have expressly identified and argued the questions set out above, which would provide an explanation for why the Tribunal did not expressly address them. A Tribunal is not required to address expressly every argument put by a party, and a Tribunal is therefore certainly not required to address arguments that have not been put by parties.[131]

Despite this general principle, the Committee in *Enron* v. *Argentina* decided to annul the original arbitral award on the basis that the tribunal had failed to apply the applicable law.[132] This, however, does not per se reverse the general principle that arbitral tribunals have no *obligation* to apply the *jura novit curia* principle. The Committee simply

[129] *RSM Production Corp.* v. *Grenada*, ICSID Case No. ARB/05/14, Decision on RSM Production Corporation's Application for a Preliminary Ruling, 29 October 2009, para. 23.

[130] *Patrick Mitchell* v. *Democratic Republic of the Congo*, ICSID Case No. ARB/99/7, Decision on the Application for Annulment of the Award, 1 November 2006, para. 57.

[131] *Enron Corporation and Ponderosa Assets LP* v. *The Argentine Republic*, ICSID Case No. ARB/01/3, Decision on the Application for Annulment of the Argentine Republic, 30 July 2010, para. 375.

[132] *Ibid.*, paras 376 ff.

posed the limits of the application of the principle: while tribunals are not under an obligation to consider legal arguments not raised by the parties, this may not result in a failure to apply the law as is defined by the parties. In other words, even though parties may not have raised fundamental legal arguments which form part of the applicable law, in this case international legal norms applicable to the interpretation of the 'only way' requirement contained in Article 25(1)(a) of the ILC Articles on State Responsibility, arbitral tribunals are not exempt from applying the relevant applicable legal rules. Based on these cases, it seems that international investment tribunals operating under the ICSID Convention are not bound by the sole legal arguments presented by the parties, in the sense that they are not under an obligation to base their award on the arguments presented by the parties. This principle, however, does not permit a deviation from the applicable law as defined by the parties to the dispute.

## *Jura novit curia* and investment treaty arbitration outside the ICSID context

Outside the formal ICSID context, the application of the maxim *jura novit curia* in investment treaty arbitration is slightly more contested. Being essentially based on the procedural rules applicable to international commercial arbitration, the application of the principle *jura novit curia* has not uniformly been accepted in non-ICSID arbitrations, essentially because of the emphasis on the principle of party autonomy in international commercial arbitration.[133] However, several tribunals in non-ICSID arbitration have also upheld the inherent power of investment tribunals to apply legal arguments that have not been advanced by the parties, which may prove that in treaty-based investment arbitration, even outside the ICSID framework, the principle should be applied. The Tribunal in *CME* v. *Czech Republic*, conducted under the UNCITRAL Arbitration Rules, argued that it was not 'bound to research, find and apply national law which has not been argued or referred to by the parties and has not been identified by the parties and the Tribunal to be essential to the Tribunal's decision'.[134] This statement, however, concerns the application of national law, and it is thus unlikely whether

133 Kaufmann-Kohler, 'Iura novit arbiter: Est-ce bien raisonnable?', p. 72 and Giuditta Cordero-Moss, 'Tribunal's Powers versus Party Autonomy', in Peter Muchlinski, Frederico Ortino and Christoph Schreuer (eds.), *The Oxford Handbook of International Investment Law* (Oxford University Press, 2009), pp. 1210–11.

134 *CME* v. *Czech Republic*, UNCITRAL, Final Award, para. 411.

the tribunal envisaged postulating a general principle applicable to international law as well. Referring to 'ICSID practice', the Tribunal in *Bogdanov* v. *Moldova* conducted under the SCC Arbitration Rules, a case in which the respondent did not participate,[135] considered that:

> In respect of international arbitration taking place in Sweden, it is sometimes suggested that the principle *iura novit curia* applies, but the parties should be notified of new legal sources introduced by the arbitrator, so that they have the possibility to comment on them ...[136]
>
> ... the Arbitral Tribunal is not limited to the arguments made by the parties. As long as the Arbitral Tribunal limits its evaluation to the facts as presented by the parties, it remains free, within the borders of the applicable law (particularly, as long as it remains within the frame of the legal sources mentioned in the proceeding), to give the legal qualifications and determine the legal consequences that it deems appropriate, even if they were not pleaded by the parties ... In the present proceedings, even though the Claimant did not invoke any specific article of the BIT, the BIT constitutes the legal basis of the arbitral proceedings, as the Claimant has initiated the present proceedings under the BIT, and has listed the BIT as one of the legal sources to be applied in the decision. Therefore, consideration of the BIT may not be deemed as a surprise to any of the parties ...[137]

The reference here to 'international arbitration taking place in Sweden', on the one hand, seems to indicate that this dictum is based on Swedish arbitral practice and rules. At the same time, it is important to note the arbitrator's reference in the second paragraph to the fact that 'the BIT constitutes the legal basis of the arbitral proceedings'.

In its 1979 award in the case *BP Exploration Co. (Libya) Ltd* v. *The Government of the Libyan Arab Republic*, the Tribunal composed of a sole arbitrator found that tribunals are not only entitled, but also 'compelled to undertake an independent examination of the legal issues deemed relevant by it, and to engage in considerable legal research going beyond the confines of the materials relied upon by the Claimant. The conclusions in the Award therefore are based on a broader consideration of the issues than that permitted by the format of the Claimant's arguments in support of its claim.'[138] This consideration was based on the absence of the respondent in the procedure before the Tribunal.

[135] *Iurii Bogdanov, Agurdino-Invest Ltd and Agurdino-Chimia JSC* v. *Republic of Moldova*, SCC Case No. 93/2004, Arbitral Award, 22 September 2005, para. 2.2.1, p. 10.

[136] *Ibid.* [137] *Ibid.*, para. 4.2.2, p. 14.

[138] *BP Exploration Co. (Libya) Ltd* v. *The Government of the Libyan Arab Republic*, Award, *International Law Reports*, 53 (1979): 297 at 313 (p. 22 of the original award).

## *Jura novit curia* and the need to invite parties to comment on arguments not presented by the parties

A related question is whether, if the tribunal has decided to base its reasoning on legal argument other than those advanced by the parties, it should invite the parties to comment on that specific legal argument. This is required in some national legal systems,[139] but is generally not considered compulsory in investment treaty arbitration conducted under the ICSID Convention.[140] Although not explicitly stated in the ICSID Arbitration Rules, this follows from the various annulment decisions that have consistently refrained from annulling decisions that were based on legal arguments not pleaded by the parties, and have thus held that the tribunal may base its award on legal reasons not pleaded by the parties, without the need to invite the parties to further comment on this. The Ad Hoc Committee in *Mitchell* v. *Congo*, however, did argue that parties should be heard when a tribunal exercises its authority to apply legal arguments other than those presented by the parties.[141] In practice, on certain occasions, tribunals have asked parties to comment upon decisions published at a later stage in the proceedings that, as a consequence, had not been addressed by the parties in their submissions.[142] Outside the formal ICSID context, practice is as divided as it is in respect of the application as such of the principle, and may depend on the applicable *lex fori*.[143]

There are obviously limits to the idea that an arbitral tribunal may apply legal arguments not presented by the parties, which are the result of the arbitral character of the dispute settlement method. If the tribunal, for instance, introduced a new sources of law, such as a treaty, which had not been included in the pleadings by the parties, or which would require the parties to introduce new evidence or facts that were

139 In France, for example. See Catherine Kessedjian, 'Principe de la contradiction et arbitrage', *Revue de l'arbitrage*, 3 (1995): 381, 399.

140 See Schreuer, 'Three Generations of ICSID Annulment Proceedings', p. 30.

141 *Mitchell* v. *Congo*, ICSID Case No. ARB/99/7, para. 57.

142 For a discussion, see Andres Rigo Sureda, 'Precedent in Investment Treaty Arbitration', in Christina Binder, Ursula Kriebaum, August Reinisch and Stephan Wittich (eds.), *International Investment Law for the 21st Century. Essays in Honour of Christoph Schreuer* (Oxford University Press, 2009), pp. 834–5, and the cases *Malaysian Historical Salvors SDN, BHD* v. *Malaysia*, ICSID Case No. ARB/05/10, Award, 17 May 2007, and *Zhinvali Development Ltd* v. *Republic of Georgia*, ICSID Case No. ARB/00/1, Award, 24 January 2003 (unpublished).

143 For a discussion of this, see Cordero-Moss, 'Tribunal's Powers versus Party Autonomy', p. 1241 and Giovannini, 'International Arbitration and *Jura Novit Curia*', p. 9.

not relevant in light of the original arguments presented by the parties, an invitation for comments seems advisable if not necessary.[144] In general, as long as the tribunal's reasoning is purely legal in character, in the sense that the tribunal uses a different legal qualification for facts that have been advanced by the parties, nothing prevents the tribunal from applying the legal reasoning it sees fit, within the boundaries, of course, of the applicable law. This should be even more the case when the tribunal is asked to apply the rules and principles of public international law.[145]

### *Jura novit curia* and the public international law foundation of investment treaty arbitration

The reasons behind the general acceptance of the application of the *jura novit curia* principle in investment treaty arbitration, at least as far as ICSID arbitration is concerned, evidently lies in the public international law character of investment disputes, and the application of public international law to the dispute as a matter of applicable law. There are generally no provisions in the ICSID Arbitration Rules, nor in BITs, on which such power may be based. Clearly, such powers cannot be founded on the *ex aequo et bono* provisions contained in certain investment treaties.[146] Such power lies within the inherent powers of international investment tribunals. This, however, does not explain why international investment tribunals specifically have such an inherent power, especially when compared with international commercial arbitration.[147] The only reasonable and logical explanation, which warrants the application of the principle of *jura novit curia* in investment treaty arbitration, is the application of public international law as part of the applicable law.[148] Referring to the ICJ's opinion in the *Fisheries Jurisdiction* case cited above, Paulsson argues that the public international law character of international investment disputes justifies an

[144] Cordero-Moss, 'Tribunal's Powers versus Party Autonomy', p. 1241. See also ILA, Committee on International Commercial Arbitration, Final Report, 'Ascertaining the Contents of the Applicable Law in International Commercial Arbitration'.

[145] See also Schill, 'Crafting the International Economic Order', p. 422.

[146] See, however, David M. Bigge, '*Iura Novit Curia* in Investment Treaty Arbitration: May? Must?', Kluwer Arbitration Blog, 29 December 2001, available at: http://kluwerarbitrationblog.com/blog/2011/12/29/iura-novit-curia-in-investment-treaty-arbitration-may-must, accessed 24 April 2012.

[147] This has however been argued by certain authors. See, for instance, Bigge, '*Iura Novit Curia* in Investment Treaty Arbitration'.

[148] See also Schill, 'Crafting the International Economic Order', p. 425.

application of the *jura novit curia* principle to international investment tribunals. After having posed the question 'whenever they are created by treaties which refer to the applicability of international law, are international tribunals in investment disputes organs of the international legal system and therefore bound to apply international law whether or not it is pleaded by the parties?', Paulsson argues that 'a tribunal in an investment dispute cannot content itself with inept pleadings, and simply uphold the least implausible of the two'.[149] This consideration is premised on the application of public international law to the dispute and the involvement of a state acting in its sovereign capacity. The legal reasoning of international investment tribunals cannot depend solely on the arguments brought by the parties. Accepting the opposite would run counter to the public dimension of international investment disputes. It cannot reasonably be accepted that the award, which undoubtedly has broader implications than the mere parties to the dispute, such as the nationals of the state the sovereign powers of which are being scrutinized by an arbitral tribunal, could rely on under-researched and incomplete legal arguments.[150] The legal reasoning of an arbitral award in international investment law cannot depend on the choice and quality of counsel, who are responsible for the legal argumentation brought before the arbitral tribunal.[151] This in addition again emphasizes the need for the appointment of arbitrators who have a specific knowledge of the principles of public international law.

More fundamentally, the question may be raised whether the principle of party autonomy in international commercial arbitration, which serves as a model for investment treaty arbitration, should also be applied rigidly in the latter form of arbitration. Indeed, the whole discussion on the application of the principle of *jura novit curia* in public international law and investment treaty arbitration, and the difference with the principles applicable to international commercial arbitration relate more generally to the distinction between inquisitorial and adversarial proceedings.

### 3.4.2 *Inquisitorial versus adversarial proceedings*

The specific powers of arbitrators in international arbitral proceedings in respect of fact-finding differ substantially according to the inquisitorial

[149] Paulsson, 'International Arbitration and the Generation of Legal Norms', p. 14.
[150] See also Schill, 'Crafting the International Economic Order', p. 422. [151] *Ibid.*

or adversarial character of the proceedings. It is traditionally considered that this dichotomy is the result of the opposition between the more adversarial role of judges and arbitrators in common law legal systems and the relatively more inquisitorial role of judges and arbitrators in civil law legal systems. Whether or not this distinction is justified, in particular, in view of the question of whether both types of systems may exist in a 'pure' form, is subject to debate.[152] It is not our purpose here to engage in this discussion. However, whether or not the international arbitrator in arbitral proceedings has an adversarial or an inquisitorial role is relatively more controversial, *a fortiori* when the dispute is an international investment dispute.

## The sources of the power of arbitral tribunals

In general, the powers of arbitral tribunals can be inferred from several sources: the agreement of the parties and the law applicable to the arbitral procedure, which includes the national arbitration law of the seat of the arbitration.[153] In international commercial arbitration, neither the adversarial nor the inquisitorial approaches apply in a pure form. Arbitral tribunals have, even in common law systems, considerable powers to act on their own initiative, including the possibility of applying legal arguments not presented by the parties, as was shown in the previous section. The relevance of either the common law or civil law system in depicting generally the powers and duties of arbitrators is thus limited, and there is a relative convergence in all applicable arbitration rules in respect of the powers of arbitrators, occasionally through the drafting of documents such as the 2010 IBA 'Rules on the Taking of Evidence in International Arbitration',[154] which have now gathered wide support and recognition as the applicable standards in

[152] See Cordero-Moss, 'Tribunal's Powers versus Party Autonomy', p. 1211.

[153] See, generally, Blackaby *et al.*, *Redfern & Hunter on International Arbitration*, para. 6.107. In relation to investment tribunals, see Chester Brown, 'The Inherent Powers of International Courts and Tribunals', *British Yearbook of International Law*, 76 (2005): 195; Chester Brown, *A Common Law of International Adjudication* (Oxford University Press, 2007), pp. 36 ff; and Martins Paparinskis, 'Inherent Powers of ICSID Tribunals: Broad and Rightly So', in Todd Weiler and Ian Laird (eds.), *Investment Treaty Arbitration and International Law* (Huntington, NY: JurisNet, 2012), pp. 11–76.

[154] International Bar Association, 'IBA Rules on the Taking of Evidence in International Arbitration', adopted by a resolution of the IBA Council 29 May 2010, available at: www.ibanet.org/Publications/publications_IBA_guides_and_free_materials.aspx, accessed 8 January 2014.

international commercial arbitration.[155] Also, under the majority of the arbitration rules, the tribunal generally has broad powers to determine the procedure, provided that the parties have not decided otherwise and subjected, of course, to such limitations as respect for the principle *audi alteram partem*.[156] Article 17 of the UNICTRAL Arbitration Rules, for instance, provides that:

> the arbitral tribunal may conduct the arbitration in such manner as it considers appropriate, provided that the parties are treated with equality and that at an appropriate stage of the proceedings each party is given a reasonable opportunity of presenting its case. The arbitral tribunal, in exercising its discretion, shall conduct the proceedings so as to avoid unnecessary delay and expense and to provide a fair and efficient process for resolving the parties' dispute.[157]

The remaining divergences will often be decided as a function of the legal culture and training of the specific arbitrator.[158] Because arbitration is based on the consent of the parties, the arbitrators generally have no specific inquisitorial powers *as such* besides those powers provided for under the relevant procedural rules, and those conferred to the tribunal by the parties. Therefore, it is difficult to categorize the powers of arbitrators in international commercial arbitration as adversarial or inquisitorial.

In investment treaty arbitration under the ICSID Convention, the powers of the arbitral tribunal are derived from the legal instrument granting jurisdiction to the tribunal, mainly BITs or multilateral treaties such as the NAFTA or the ECT, and the procedural rules contained in the ICSID Convention and the ICSID Rules of Arbitration. The power of investment tribunals in non-ICSID arbitration similarly is regulated by the international legal instrument in which the consent to arbitration is expressed, and the procedural rules of the arbitration institution that has been identified by the parties (LCIA, SCC or ICA, for instance), or the UNCITRAL Arbitration Rules in the case of ad hoc arbitration. ICSID

155 Blackaby *et al.*, *Redfern & Hunter on International Arbitration*, paras 5.08 ff.

156 *Ibid.*, paras 5.14 ff. See also, generally, Margaret L. Moses, *The Principles and Practice of International Commercial Arbitration* (Cambridge University Press, 2008), pp. 165 ff.

157 See also Article 15 of the ICC Rules of Arbitration: '1. The proceedings before the Arbitral Tribunal shall be governed by these Rules and, where these Rules are silent, by any rules which the parties or, failing them, the Arbitral Tribunal may settle on, whether or not reference is thereby made to the rules of procedure of a national law to be applied to the arbitration. 2. In all cases, the Arbitral Tribunal shall act fairly and impartially and ensure that each party has a reasonable opportunity to present its case.'

158 Kaufmann-Kohler, 'Globalization of Arbitral Procedure', p. 1331.

arbitration being completely a-national, the national laws of the seat of the arbitration have no influence on the conduct of the proceedings, which, obviously, is not the case in non-ICSID administered proceedings.

## General principles on the power of arbitral tribunals

Although there are several notable differences between the arbitration rules of the ICSID Convention and the procedural rules applicable under other rules of arbitration, some of which I have highlighted above, the general principles regulating the specific powers generally of ICSID arbitrators do not differ substantially from international commercial arbitration, with the exception of independent or *proprio motu* enquiries by arbitral tribunals.

As is the case in international commercial arbitration, ICSID tribunals, for instance, have considerable discretion in regulating procedural questions:

> Any arbitration proceeding shall be conducted in accordance with the provisions of this Section and, except as the parties otherwise agree, in accordance with the Arbitration Rules in effect on the date on which the parties consented to arbitration. If any question of procedure arises which is not covered by this Section or the Arbitration Rules or any rules agreed by the parties, the Tribunal shall decide the question.[159]

One of the examples that is illustrative of the relative convergence of procedural rules in international commercial arbitration and investment treaty arbitration is the regulation of the tribunal's powers in respect of questions of fact and document production. In national and international litigation the procedure relating to the production of documents is clearly established in the procedural rules of the court or tribunal. Similarly, in national arbitrations, the question of document production and the role that the arbitrators may take in this respect does not pose significant problems in view of the applicable procedural law and customs.[160] In international commercial arbitration and investment treaty arbitration, however, the question is more complicated in view of the complexity in the applicable legal rules. First, as far as the burden of proof is concerned, it is generally admitted that in international commercial arbitration, as it is the case in international judicial proceedings, the parties are required to present the facts in

[159] Article 44 of the ICSID Convention.
[160] Blackaby *et al.*, *Redfern & Hunter on International Arbitration*, para. 6.104.

support of their case.[161] This is required for instance by Article 24 of the UNCITRAL Arbitration Rules, as well as by the Rules of Procedure of the ICJ.[162] Secondly, in general, arbitration rules provide for the possibility that the arbitral tribunal can request additional information and documents from the parties, and can appoint experts, as is the case in international litigation.[163] Article 43 of the ICSID Convention, for instance, provides that 'except as the parties otherwise agree, the Tribunal may, if it deems it necessary at any stage of the proceedings, (a) call upon the parties to produce documents or other evidence, and (b) visit the scene connected with the dispute, and conduct such inquiries there as it may deem appropriate'. Article 27(3) of the UNCITRAL Arbitration Rules similarly provides that: 'at any time during the arbitral proceedings the arbitral tribunal may require the parties to produce documents, exhibits or other evidence within such a period of time as the arbitral Tribunal shall determine'. The rules of arbitration of the LCIA have a similar provision, since the tribunal has the authority 'to order any party to produce to the Arbitral Tribunal, and to the other parties for inspection, and to supply copies of, any documents or classes

161 *Ibid.*, para. 6.92.

162 See, for instance, Articles 38 and 49 of the Rules of the Court. See also, for example, the judgment of the court in the *Pulp Mills* case, in which the court reiterated that: 'To begin with, the Court considers that, in accordance with the well-established principle of *onus probandi incumbit actori*, it is the duty of the party which asserts certain facts to establish the existence of such facts. . . . It is of course to be expected that the Applicant should, in the first instance, submit the relevant evidence to substantiate its claims . . .' (International Court of Justice, *Pulp Mills on the River Uruguay (Argentina* v. *Uruguay)*, Judgment, 20 April 2010, *ICJ Reports*, 2010, 14, paras 162–163).

163 See, for instance, Article 48 of the Statute of the ICJ: 'The Court shall make orders for the conduct of the case, shall decide the form and time in which each party must conclude its arguments, and make all arrangements connected with the taking of evidence.' See also Articles 49 ('The Court may, even before the hearing begins, call upon the agents to produce any document or to supply any explanations. Formal note shall be taken of any refusal') and 50 ('The Court may, at any time, entrust any individual, body, bureau, commission, or other organization that it may select, with the task of carrying out an enquiry or giving an expert opinion'). This has, moreover, been considered to be an inherent power of international courts and tribunals 'derived from the need for international courts to carry out their functions in the settlement of the dispute' (Brown, 'The Inherent Powers of International Courts and Tribunals', p. 90).

of documents in their possession, custody or power which the Arbitral Tribunal determines to be relevant'.[164]

## *Independent* or *proprio motu* enquiries by arbitral tribunals in investment treaty arbitration

In respect of *independent* or *proprio motu* enquiries by arbitral tribunals, differences between international commercial arbitration and investment treaty arbitration appear more clearly.

First, in respect of the failure of one of the parties to appear, the ICSID Convention provides that in such situation 'the other party may request the Tribunal to deal with the questions submitted to it and to render an award', but at the same time adds that the failure to appear 'shall not be deemed an admission of the other party's assertions'.[165] The UNCITRAL Arbitration Rules similarly provide that 'if a party, duly notified under these Rules, fails to appear at a hearing, without showing sufficient cause for such failure, the arbitral tribunal may proceed with the arbitration'.[166] Thus, in the event of a failure of one of the parties to participate in the proceedings, and the failure to produce the necessary factual information that may counter the claim presented by the claimant, the tribunal may proceed with the dispute. However, in particular, in international investment disputes, taking into consideration the public international law character of the dispute and the involvement of a state, the tribunal should investigate the relevance and legal value of the claimant's factual information. This principle is clearly included in the ICSID Convention, but is common in many other international proceedings. Thus, the Statute of the ICJ similarly, but more explicitly, provides that: 'Whenever one of the parties does not appear before the Court, or fails to defend its case, the other party may call upon the Court to decide in favour of its claim. The Court must, before doing so, satisfy itself, not only that it has jurisdiction ... but also that the claim is well founded in fact and law.'[167] Contrary to international commercial arbitration and arbitration under the main common and civil law jurisdictions where the arbitrators generally do not have, or have only limited, independent

[164] Article 22.1(e) of the LCIA Rules of Arbitration. See also Article 20 of the ICC Rules of Arbitration, and Article 26 of the SCC Rules of Arbitration.

[165] Article 45 of the ICSID Convention.

[166] Article 30(2) of the UNCITRAL Arbitration Rules.

[167] Article 53 of the ICJ Statute.

fact-finding powers,[168] international investment tribunals should effectively engage in fact-finding, in particular, when interests of third parties are involved.[169] This can, of course, be done by using the powers granted to international investment tribunals under the ICSID Convention, which I have discussed above. At the same time, giving international arbitrators too broad an inquisitorial role would run counter to the very nature of arbitration.

Secondly, differences may exist in respect of the power of arbitral tribunals to order the production of certain documents, and the sanctions which may apply in case of a failure of one of the parties to produce documents requested by the tribunal. The ICSID Rules of Arbitration authorize the tribunal: 'if it deems it necessary at any stage of the proceeding ... [to] (a) call upon the parties to produce documents, witnesses and experts; and (b) visit any place connected with the dispute or conduct inquiries there'.[170] If a party fails to produce the requested documents, the Rules do not provide for a presumption that the document is adverse to the interests of that party, but simply note that 'the Tribunal shall take formal note of the failure of a party to comply with its obligations under this paragraph and of any reasons given for such failure'.[171] The 2010 IBA Rules on the Taking of Evidence in International Arbitration, however, on the contrary, provide for the possibility that the Arbitral Tribunal can in the event of failure to produce a document the production of which has been ordered by the tribunal, conclude that the document is adverse to the interests of that party.[172]

[168] For a discussion, see ILA, Committee on International Commercial Arbitration, Final Report, 'Ascertaining the Contents of the Applicable Law in International Commercial Arbitration', p. 5 (fn. 10).

[169] See also Schill, 'Crafting the International Economic Order', pp. 423–4.

[170] Rule 34(2)(a) of the ICSID Arbitration Rules. It is also interesting to note that the same Article of the ICSID Arbitration Rules explicitly authorizes the tribunal, 'if it deems it necessary at any stage of the proceeding', to 'visit any place connected with the dispute or conduct inquiries there'. Such power is very similar to the power of the ICJ to conduct *in situ* visits: 'The Court may at any time decide, either *proprio motu* or at the request of a party, to exercise its functions with regard to the obtaining of evidence at a place or locality to which the case relates, subject to such conditions as the Court may decide upon after ascertaining the views of the parties' (Article 66 of the Rules of the Court). Although not often used in practice, and despite the absence of any explicit provision to this effect in arbitration rules generally, it is also generally admitted that tribunals in international commercial arbitration have the power to conduct *in situ* visits. See Blackaby *et al.*, *Redfern & Hunter on International Arbitration*, para. 6.175. See also Article 7 of the IBA Rules on the Taking of Evidence in International Arbitration.

[171] Rule 34(3) of the ICSID Arbitration Rules.

[172] Article 9.5 of the IBA Rules on the Taking of Evidence in International Arbitration.

A similar rule is contained in the, non-binding, UNCITRAL Notes on Organizing Arbitral Proceedings, which provide that the tribunal, in case of failure to produce the requested documentary evidence, 'is free to draw its conclusions from the failure and may make the award on the evidence before it'.[173] The UNCITRAL Rules, however, provide only that 'if a party, duly invited by the arbitral tribunal to produce documents, exhibits or other evidence, fails to do so within the established period of time, without showing sufficient cause for such failure, the arbitral tribunal may make the award on the evidence before it'.[174] Based on their discretion in the application of procedural rules, in the absence of such regulations in the applicable arbitration rules and the agreement between the parties, several tribunals have turned to or adopted the IBA Rules on the Taking of Evidence in International Arbitration as the relevant applicable rules in respect of the production of documents.[175] Likewise, several ICSID tribunals operating under the ICSID Additional Facility have explicitly referred to the fact that the tribunal may draw adverse inferences in the event of the refusal to produce the requested documents.[176]

Because of the involvement of a state in investment treaty arbitration, and the assessment by the tribunal of the exercise by a state of its sovereign powers, limitations exist in respect in the production of documents. First of all, investment treaties may limit the production of certain documents. Thus, Article 2102 of the NAFTA provides that 'nothing in this Agreement shall be construed to require any Party to furnish or allow access to any information the disclosure of which it determines to be contrary to its essential security interests'. Similar wording is contained in certain BITs, in addition to the protection given to certain documents by the so-called 'deliberative and pre-decisional privileges' or

173 UNCITRAL Notes on Organizing Arbitral Proceedings, para. 51.

174 Article 30(3) of the UNCITRAL Arbitration Rules.

175 See, for example, *CME Czech Republic BV* v. *Czech Republic*, UNCITRAL, Partial Award, 13 September 2001, para. 46, in which the Tribunal noted that 'In accordance with Art. 15.1 of the UNCITRAL Arbitration Rules, the Tribunal decided to conduct the arbitration in the manner it considers appropriate. For this purpose, the Tribunal decided, to the extent appropriate, to apply the IBA Rules.' See also *International Thunderbird Gaming Corp.* v. *The United Mexican States*, UNCITRAL, Procedural Order No. 2, 31 July 2003.

176 See, for example, *Waste Management, Inc.* v. *The United Mexican States*, ICSID Case No. ARB (AF)00/3, Procedural Order Concerning Disclosure of Documents, 1 October 2002, para. 6; and *Feldman* v. *The United Mexican States*, ICSID Case No. ARB(AF)/99/11, Procedural Order No. 2, 3 May 2000, para. 8

'Crown privileges'. BITs may thus limit the possibility of arbitral tribunals ordering the production of documents that are protected by certain privileges. Article 38(7) of the Canadian Model FIPA, for example, provides that 'the Tribunal shall not require a Party to furnish or allow access to information the disclosure of which would impede law enforcement or would be contrary to the Party's law protecting Cabinet confidences, personal privacy or the financial affairs and accounts of individual customers of financial institutions, or which it determines to be contrary to its essential security'. This principle has usually been upheld by international tribunals, and was also included in Article 9(2)(f) of the IBA Rules on the Taking of Evidence in International Arbitration. Tribunals have, however, at the same time imposed on states the burden of proving the application of certain privileges to the documents requested. As noted by the Tribunal in *ADF Group* v. *United States*, for instance:

> the Tribunal noted the general objection entered by the Respondent to the extent the documents are 'protected from disclosure by applicable law, including without limitation, documents protected by the attorney–client and government deliberative and pre-decisional privileges'. The Tribunal ruled that for it to be able to determine the applicability of the privileges adverted to, the Respondent will have to specify the documents in respect of which one or more privilege is claimed and the nature and scope of the particular privilege claimed, and show the applicability of the latter to the former. This was a matter for future determination, should the Respondent decide actually to withhold, under claim of privilege, particular documents it should otherwise make available to the Claimant.[177]

The Tribunal in *Biwater Gauff* v. *Tanzania* indicated that the doctrine of 'public interest immunity', which is included in the Tanzanian Constitution and had been invoked by that state in the course of the proceedings, 'is not a general principle of law as understood for the purposes of article 38 (1)(c) of the ICJ Statute. Neither is it provided for in the ICSID Convention or the ICSID Arbitration Rules (which endow ICSID Tribunals with broad powers to order the production of documents)', and that 'accepting Respondent's theory would create an imbalance between the parties, which the Tribunal considers unacceptable. It is indeed one of the most fundamental principles of international

[177] *ADF Group Inc.* v. *United States of America*, ICSID Case No. ARB(AF)/00/1, Award, 9 January 2003, para. 38.

arbitration that the parties should be treated with equality.'[178] At the same time, the Tribunal held that 'the only ground which might justify a refusal by the Republic to produce documents to this Tribunal is the protection of privileged or politically sensitive information, including State secrets'.[179] The Tribunal then, as the Tribunal in *ADF Group* v. *United States*, imposed on the respondent the obligation to:

> identify the relevant document(s) and indicate the reasons why in conformity with the above mentioned principles the document concerned should be withheld, or disclosed subject to specific restrictions in order to preserve confidentiality ... The Tribunal emphasizes in this respect that the fact that a document could be adverse to the position of the Respondent in this arbitration is not sufficient to qualify the document as politically sensitive.[180]

## Tribunal-appointed experts

Finally, reference should be made to the power of arbitral tribunals to appoint experts to assist the tribunal. In general, the main arbitration rules grant the tribunal the power to appoint its own expert, often explicitly, such as in the ICC, LCIA and UNCITRAL Rules of Arbitration,[181] provided that the equality of the parties is respected, and that parties are given the opportunity to present fully their case.[182]

Neither the ICSID Convention nor the ICSID Arbitration Rules explicitly provide for this possibility, contrary to the rules mentioned above. However, in a limited number of cases, tribunals have resorted to the appointment of experts in order to assist the tribunal in the valuation of the damage.[183] This power has been founded on Article 43 of the ICSID

[178] *Biwater Gauff (Tanzania) Ltd* v. *United Republic of Tanzania*, ICSID Case No. ARB/05/22, Procedural Order No. 2, 23 May 2006, paras 8–9.

[179] *Ibid.* [180] *Ibid.*

[181] See, for instance, Article 25(4) ICC Rules of Arbitration; Article 21(1)(a) of the LCIA Rules of Arbitration; and Article 29(1) of the UNCITRAL Arbitration Rules.

[182] Claus von Wobeser, 'The Arbitral Tribunal-appointed Expert', *Transnational Dispute Management*, 4(3) (2007): 2.

[183] See, for instance, *CMS Gas Transmission Co.* v. *The Argentine Republic*, ICSID Case No. ARB/01/8, Award, 12 May 2005; *LG&E Energy Corp., LG&E Capital Corp. and LG&E International Inc.* v. *The Argentine Republic*, ICSID Case No. ARB/02/1, Award on Damages, 25 July 2007; *Sempra* v. *The Argentine Republic*, ICSID Case No. ARB/02/16, Award, 28 September 2007; *Enron Corporation and Ponderosa Assets LP* v. *The Argentine Republic*, ICSID Case No. ARB/01/3, Award, 22 May 2007; and *National Grid plc* v. *The Argentine Republic*, UNCITRAL, Award, 3 November 2008. For a complete list, see Schreuer *et al.*, *The ICSID Convention*, in their discussion of Article 43 (at paras 11 and 97). For a discussion of this practice, see Joshua B. Simmons, 'Valuation in Investor–State Arbitration: Toward a More Exact Science', *Berkeley Journal of International Law*, 30(1) (2012): 196.

Convention, which allows the tribunal to: 'except as the parties otherwise agree ... if it deems it necessary at any stage of the proceedings, (a) call upon the parties to produce documents or other evidence, and (b) visit the scene connected with the dispute, and conduct such inquiries there as it may deem appropriate'. Article 44 of the ICSID Convention contains the more general power of tribunals to decide any procedural question not covered by the ICSID Convention or the ICSID Arbitration Rules.[184] There is no substantial difference between the practice and the regulation of tribunal-appointed experts in international commercial arbitration or investment treaty arbitration. It is, however, important to point out that neither the ICSID Convention nor the ICSID Arbitration Rules contain a specific provision granting tribunals an explicit power to appoint experts, which tends to confirm a more adversarial than inquisitorial role of arbitration.

In the practice of investment treaty arbitration, the question of tribunal-appointed experts has not attracted much attention because of the limited use of this possibility and because the appointment has in the majority of the cases – with a couple of exceptions, one of which I will discuss below – been approved by the parties either explicitly or implicitly, or by the party participating in the proceedings.[185] This practice, it has been noted, may be valuable in providing the tribunal with the necessary technical and financial information necessary to proceed to the valuation of the damage and the compensation owed by the respondent state, and may, because of that, strengthen the legitimacy of the award.[186]

In the recent *Abaclat* case, however, the Tribunal decided to appoint an expert, not to assist the tribunal in the valuation of the damage, but essentially to examine and verify the information contained in a

[184] Article 44: 'Any arbitration proceeding shall be conducted in accordance with the provisions of this Section and, except as the parties otherwise agree, in accordance with the Arbitration Rules in effect on the date on which the parties consented to arbitration. If any question of procedure arises which is not covered by this Section or the Arbitration Rules or any rules agreed by the parties, the Tribunal shall decide the question.'

[185] For a discussion, see *Abaclat and others (case formerly known as Giovanna a Beccara and others)* v. *The Argentine Republic*, ICSID Case No. ARB/07/5, Procedural Order No. 15, 20 November 2012, Dissenting Opinion of Dr Torres Bernárdez, paras 41 ff.

[186] Simmons, 'Valuation in Investor–State Arbitration', p. 242. See also the Separate Opinion of Domingo Belo Janeiro in *Siemens* v. *Argentina*, ICSID Case No. ARB/02/8, Award and Separate Opinion, paras 4–5. See, however, David Caron, Matti Pellonpää and Lee M. Caplan, *The UNCITRAL Arbitration Rules. A Commentary* (Oxford University Press, 2006), p. 668.

database which contained the details of the claimants in this 'mass claims' procedure.[187] The decision of the Tribunal to appoint an expert with this mandate, and the appointment of the specific expert without the express agreement of both parties to the dispute, has been criticized severely by Arbitrator Santiago Torres Bernardez.[188] Torres Bernardez has not only opposed the terms and conditions of the expertise,[189] but, more importantly, the legal ground for such appointment.[190] The dissenting arbitrator pointed to the lack of agreement of the respondent state to conclude that it was a breach of Articles 43 and 44 of the ICSID Convention, and of Article 34 of the ICSID Arbitration Rules.[191] Considering the exceptional character of this case and the absence of consent of both parties, it is difficult to draw any firm conclusions from it, despite the fact that, absent consent of the parties, the capacity of tribunals to appoint experts is controversial.

[187] *Abaclat* v. *Argentina*, ICSID Case No. ARB/07/5, Procedural Order No. 15, 20 November 2012, para. 19.
[188] *Ibid.*, Dissenting Opinion of Dr Torres Bernárdez. [189] *Ibid.*, paras 46 ff.
[190] *Ibid.*, paras 6 ff. [191] *Ibid.*, para. 44.

# 4 The applicable law and non-investment considerations in investment treaty arbitration

The ICSID Convention as such does not contain any rules on the substantive obligations of states towards foreign investors. The Convention merely establishes the procedure to be applied to the settlement of investment disputes between states and foreign investors under the jurisdictional conditions set out in Article 25 of the Convention.

That investment treaty arbitration is now a dispute settlement method aimed primarily at establishing whether the host state has violated its international obligations under an international investment agreement implies that the applicable law essentially consists of public international law. This is not to say that municipal law has no role to play, but its application to the dispute as such will be limited compared with public international law.

The purpose of this chapter is not to provide a general overview of the applicable law in investment treaty arbitration.[1] Instead, I will establish the main principles applicable in investment treaty arbitration, and in doing so clearly establish the pre-eminent influence of public international law. A summary of the general rules on the applicable law is warranted, in particular, the question of whether and to what extent public international law applies to investment treaty arbitration generally. I will then focus especially on the question of whether investment tribunals may consider international human rights instruments and rules, as well as international investment agreements and rules of customary law.

[1] On this, see Yas Banifatemi, 'The Law Applicable in Investment Treaty Arbitration', in Katia Yannaca-Small (ed.), *Arbitration under International Investment Agreements. A Guide to the Key Issues* (Oxford University Press, 2010), pp. 191–210.

I will thus first briefly address the relevant rules on the applicable law in investment treaty arbitration, before moving to the question of whether international investment tribunals can contemplate non-investment considerations and, in particular, how conflicts between investment obligations and human rights obligations may be, and have been, addressed.

## 4.1 The applicable law in investment treaty arbitration: basic principles

Because of the modelling of investment treaty arbitration on international commercial arbitration,[2] and as a consequence of the fact that investment arbitration is an arbitral procedure, the principle of party autonomy, including in defining the law applicable to the merits of the dispute, is of primary importance.[3] As an application of this, the ICSID Convention contains, in relation to the applicable law, a *renvoi* to the choice of the parties, and in the absence thereof, to the law of the contracting state party to the dispute and the relevant rules of international law.

### *4.1.1 Choice of the parties and Article 42(1) of the ICSID Convention*

In principle, the legal instrument providing for the competence of an arbitral tribunal to settle the dispute determines the legal rules to be applied for the settlement of the dispute. If the instrument contains no specific provision in relation to the applicable law, the procedural rules chosen by the parties will often contain a clause which will enable the

[2] See Aron Broches, 'The Convention on the Settlement of Investment Disputes Between States and Nationals of Other States', *Recueil des Cours*, 136 (1972): 388 ff.

[3] The applicable law provision in the ICSID Convention is irrelevant for the purposes of establishing the jurisdiction of the Centre. As has been confirmed on various occasions by arbitral tribunals and ad hoc committees, the choice of law provisions in a treaty, and Article 42 of the ICSID Convention, apply only to the substance of the dispute. As the Ad Hoc Committee in *CMS Gas* v. *Argentina*, for instance, noted: 'The Committee first recalls that the jurisdiction of the Centre is determined not by Article 42(1) of the ICSID Convention but by Article 25. The competence of the Tribunal is governed by the terms of the instruments expressing the parties' consent to ICSID arbitration, i.e. in the present case the Argentina–United States BIT. In consequence, as the Tribunal correctly decided, "the applicable jurisdictional provisions are only those of the Convention and the BIT, not those which might arise from national legislation. Argentine law is irrelevant in this respect, as recognized in the Award and in many other ICSID decisions' (*CMS Gas Transmission Co.* v. *The Argentine Republic*, ICSID Case No. ARB/01/8, Decision on Annulment, para. 68 (internal footnotes omitted)).

tribunal to determine the law it should apply. Thus, in accordance with Article 42(1) of the ICSID Convention, an investment tribunal is required to 'decide a dispute in accordance with such rules of law as may be agreed by the parties'. At the same time, Article 42(1) of the ICSID Convention provides that 'in the absence of such agreement, the Tribunal shall apply the law of the Contracting State party to the dispute (including its rules on the conflict of laws) and such rules of international law as may be applicable'. A similar rule is provided for under the UNCITRAL Arbitration Rules, although tribunals operating under those rules of procedure have a wider discretion in determining the applicable law, failing a specific choice of law made by the parties: 'The arbitral tribunal shall apply the rules of law designated by the parties as applicable to the substance of the dispute. Failing such designation by the parties, the arbitral tribunal shall apply the law which it determines to be appropriate.'[4]

Article 42 of the ICSID Convention thus establishes that the law chosen by the parties constitutes the applicable law and, in the absence thereof, that the tribunal should apply the law of the host state and the relevant rules of international law. This system, it has been noted, offers both flexibility (the reference to the choice made by the parties) and certainty (the second limb of Article 42(1) of the ICSID Convention).[5] It should, moreover, be added that a tribunal established under the ICSID Convention is prohibited from making a finding of *non liquet* on the ground of silence or obscurity of the law,[6] and that a failure to apply the law may under the ICSID system be a ground for annulment because of 'manifest excess of power'.[7]

The majority of BITs today include applicable provisions very similar to the second limb of Article 42(1) of the ICSID Convention.[8] Still, a certain number of BITs do not contain any specific applicable law clause, which implies that the applicable law will be determined in accordance with the second limb of Article 42(1) of the ICSID Convention.[9]

It should be added that the fact that the arbitral proceedings are between a state and a non-state actor does not invalidate the applicable law clause contained in investment treaties and the ICSID Convention,

4 Article 35(1) of the UNICTRAL Arbitration Rules.
5 Schreuer *et al.*, *The ICSID Convention*, p. 550, para. 2.
6 Article 42(2) of the ICSID Convention.
7 Article 52(1)(lit b) of the ICSID Convention. See, generally, Lalive, 'On the Reasoning of International Arbitral Awards'.
8 See Kulick, *Global Public Interest in International Investment Law*, pp. 11 ff.
9 See, for instance, the Model BITs of France and Germany.

since it is generally accepted that the consent expressed by the states in their investment treaty is stipulated for the benefit of their respective nationals,[10] and that the law applicable to the dispute has thus been chosen by the mutual consent of the parties.[11] By filing a request for arbitration, the foreign investor not only expresses consent to the arbitration, but also to the applicable law clause.

### *4.1.2 Public international law as the applicable law*

Since the main objective of an international investment tribunal is to rule upon the international legal responsibility of the host states, the reliance on public international law rules to this effect is completely justified and suitable. The application of international law is in essence the logical consequence of the fact that investment tribunals are nowadays mandated to consider whether there has been a violation of an international treaty, despite the fact that the majority of the earlier cases concerned so-called 'contract claims'.[12] The preponderant view before the rise of treaty-based investment arbitration was that municipal law was to be applied first by an ICSID arbitral tribunal.[13] International law was applied only when municipal law was not in conformity with international law, often termed as the 'corrective function of international law', or when no rules of municipal law applied, the so-called 'complementary' or 'supplementary' function of international law.[14]

These principles, of course, hold true today when the tribunal is required to apply municipal law principally,[15] although this doctrine recently has been subjected to criticism.[16] The 'corrective' and 'complementary' or 'supplementary' functions of international law were the main reason why, in early arbitral decisions under the ICSID Convention, international law was considered to be of limited

[10] See also, above, Chapter 2.

[11] Banifatemi, 'The Law Applicable in Investment Treaty Arbitration', pp. 194–5. See, however, *AAPL* v. *Sri Lanka*, ICSID Case No. ARB/87/3, paras 19–20.

[12] See, generally, Antonio Parra, 'Applicable Law in Investor–State Arbitration', in Arthur Rovine (ed.), *Contemporary Issues in International Arbitration and Mediation* (Leiden: Martinus Nijhoff, 2008), p. 3.

[13] See Broches, 'The Convention on the Settlement of Investment Disputes Between States and Nationals of Other States', p. 392.

[14] See *Klöckner* v. *Cameroon*, ICSID Case No. ARB/81/2, para. 69, and *Amco Asia Corp. and others* v. *Republic of Indonesia*, ICSID Case No. ARB/81/1, Decision on Annulment, 16 May 1986, para. 22. See, generally, Schreuer *et al.*, *The ICSID Convention*, p. 583, paras 104–15.

[15] For a recent example, see *Autopista Concesionada de Venezuela CA* v. *Bolivarian Republic of Venezuela*, ICSID Case ARB/00/5, Award, 23 September 2003, para. 207.

[16] For a discussion, see Kulick, *Global Public Interest in International Investment Law*, pp. 27 ff.

applicability. It is also for this reason that the drafting history of Article 42 of the ICSID Convention is of only limited relevance in contemporary investment arbitration, which is principally treaty-based. When an international investment treaty applies, and therefore when a tribunal is requested to determine whether the state has breached its obligations under the applicable investment treaty and incurs international responsibility for such breaches, international law undoubtedly forms the principal applicable law.[17] International law then applies because the subject matter of the dispute before the international investment tribunal is regulated by international law rather than municipal law. In *LG&E* v. *Argentina*, the Tribunal thus held that 'the fact that there is no contract between the Argentine Republic and LG&E favours in the first place the application of international law, inasmuch as we are dealing with a genuine dispute in matters of investment which is especially subject to the provisions of the Bilateral Treaty complemented by the domestic law'.[18]

### *4.1.3 The relevance of municipal law*

Some authors have noted that international investment tribunals are concerned, at the same time, with a variety of other issues which would be alien to the international responsibility of the state, and thus alien to public international law, such as the 'existence, nature and scope of the private rights comprising the investment'.[19] International law is not then considered to be a 'self-sufficient legal order in the sphere of foreign investment'.[20] Clearly, in those cases, the applicable law may be a combination of both international law and municipal law, but the fact remains that investment tribunals confronted with a treaty claim are primarily concerned with establishing the international responsibility of a state according to the relevant principles of public international law. This traditional view is reflected in Article 3 of the ILC Articles on the Responsibility of States for Internationally Wrongful Acts, which enounces that 'the characterization of an act of a State as internationally wrongful is governed by international law. Such

[17] See *AAPL* v. *Sri Lanka*, ICSID Case No. ARB/87/3, paras 19 ff. The Tribunal in that case, however, argued that the choice of law derived not only from the fact that a BIT was at the basis of its jurisdiction, but also, and perhaps primarily, because international law was relied upon by the parties to the dispute.

[18] *LG&E Energy Corp., LG&E Capital Corp. and LG&E International Inc.* v. *The Argentine Republic*, ICSID Case No. ARB/02/1, Decision on Liability, 3 October 2006, para. 98.

[19] Douglas, *The International Law of Investment Treaty Claims*, p. 8. [20] *Ibid.*

characterization is not affected by the characterization of the same act as lawful by internal law.'

Of course, municipal laws may play an important role for two main reasons. First, every investment, in order to qualify as such, must exist within a domestic legal system.[21] This is not to say that municipal law has a determinant role to play in the qualification of protected investments, since, as is widely acknowledged, it is the applicable international investment treaty that regulates which types of investment are protected under the treaty.[22] However, whether there *is* an investment is a matter regulated by domestic law, as is the scope of the rights granted and the nature of the rights granted, and, for example, the existence and scope of governmental commitments towards the investment.[23] On the other hand, whether the investment is an investment *protected* under the applicable investment treaty, and thus qualifies as such under that treaty, is regulated by international law. Some investment treaties, as an application of these principles, explicitly provide for an obligation for investments to be made in accordance with the domestic laws of the host state.[24]

Secondly, municipal law is the applicable legal system in order to assess whether there has been a breach of a contractual obligation. This assessment might be necessary, either because the contract itself has provided that the arbitral tribunal has jurisdiction in this respect, or because the analysis of whether a treaty obligation has been breached first requires an analysis of the existence of a contract breach, for example, in the event of an umbrella clause.[25] Such an enquiry may lead the tribunal to investigate whether or not contractual obligations have been met, but this is not to say that international law and municipal law operate at the same level. As the ILC noted in its commentary to Article 3, referring to international investment law:

[21] Newcombe and Paradell, *Law and Practice of Investment Treaties*, para. 2.11. [22] *Ibid.*

[23] *Ibid.*, para. 2.12.

[24] In *Inceysa*, for instance, the Tribunal's jurisdiction was predetermined by the requirement of an investment made in accordance with Salvadoran law, which, according to the Tribunal, included a requirement of 'good faith'. By falsifying the facts, Inceysa had violated the principle of good faith from the time it made its investment and, therefore, it did not make it in accordance with Salvadoran law. Faced with this situation, the Tribunal could only declare its incompetence to hear Inceysa's complaint, since its investment cannot benefit from the protection of the BIT (*Inceysa Vallisoletana SL* v. *Republic of El Salvador*, ICSID Case No. ARB/03/26, Award, 2 August 2006, para. 230).

[25] Cf., above, Chapter 1.

It is true that in such a case, compliance with internal law is relevant to the question of international responsibility. But this is because the rule of international law makes it relevant, e.g., by incorporating the standard of compliance with internal law as the applicable international standard or as an aspect of it. Especially in the fields of injury to aliens and their property and of human rights, the content and application of internal law will often be relevant to the question of international responsibility.[26]

Tribunals and ad hoc committees have equally confirmed these principles. As noted, for instance, by the Committee in *Vivendi I*: 'whether there has been a breach of the BIT and whether there has been a breach of contract are different questions. Each of these claims will be determined by reference to its own proper or applicable law – in the case of the BIT, by international law; in the case of the Concession Contract, by the proper law of the contract.'[27] Similarly, the Tribunal in *Azurix* v. *Argentina* stated that:

Azurix's claim has been advanced under the BIT and, as stated by the Annulment Committee in *Vivendi II*, the Tribunal's inquiry is governed by the ICSID Convention, by the BIT and by applicable international law. While the Tribunal's inquiry will be guided by this statement, this does not mean that the law of Argentina should be disregarded. On the contrary, the law of Argentina should be helpful in the carrying out of the Tribunal's inquiry into the alleged breaches of the Concession Agreement to which Argentina's law applies, but it is only an element of the inquiry because of the treaty nature of the claims under consideration.[28]

This clear division of applicable law in function of the dispute submitted to the jurisdiction of the arbitral tribunal is very well reflected in the 2012 US Model BIT. The model treaty provides that in the event of a dispute in relation to a claim based on an alleged violation of 'an obligation under Articles 3 through 10' (the standards of treatment), the tribunal will 'decide the issues in dispute in accordance with this Treaty and applicable rules of international law'.[29] However, when the dispute relates to a claim based on the alleged violation of an investment authorization, or an investment agreement, the tribunal shall apply:

[26] Commentary to Article 3, ILC Articles on State Responsibility, UN Doc. A/56/10, para. 7

[27] *Compañiá de Aguas del Aconquija SA and Vivendi Universal* v. *Argentina*, ICSID Case No. ARB/97/3, Decision on Annulment, para. 96.

[28] *Azurix* v. *Argentina*, ICSID Case No. ARB/01/12, Award, para. 67.

[29] Article 30(1) of the 2012 US Model BIT.

(a) the rules of law specified in the pertinent investment authorization or investment agreement, or as the disputing parties may otherwise agree; or
(b) if the rules of law have not been specified or otherwise agreed:
    (i) the law of the respondent, including its rules on the conflict of laws; and
    (ii) such rules of international law as may be applicable.[30]

## 4.2 Non-investment norms in investment treaty arbitration: the consideration of human rights obligations by international investment tribunals

Human rights considerations in investment treaty arbitration are a relatively recent phenomenon. The main explanation for this is the silence, generally, of international investment treaties on human rights issues. The main multilateral investment treaties, NAFTA and the ECT, make no mention of human rights. Although states have recently effectively included references to human rights norms in their BITs,[31] the majority of contemporary BITs do not mention human rights.

Despite this relative absence of human rights in arbitral decisions, recent cases brought before investment tribunals have shown an increase in human rights considerations, but these remain relatively reluctant to engage in human rights arguments brought by one of the parties, despite the sometimes obvious relevance of human rights issues and the general importance of human rights compliance by host states.[32] It is interesting to note that many arbitral tribunals have, despite their reluctance to assess human rights considerations raised as a circumstance precluding wrongfulness, in fact relied on the jurisprudence of human rights courts, in particular the European Court of Human Rights (ECtHR), in determining whether the rights of the investor have been breached.[33] It is noteworthy that arbitral tribunals have thus recognized that they do not operate in an exclusive legal regime. Indeed, references to human rights courts' decisions, most often in assessing whether or not an expropriation has taken

[30] Article 30(2) of the 2012 US Model BIT (internal footnotes omitted).

[31] For a discussion, see Bruno Simma, 'Foreign Investment Arbitration: A Place for Human Rights?', *International and Comparative Law Quarterly*, 60(3) (2011): 573, 581.

[32] *Ibid.*, p. 578.

[33] For an analysis of case law in this respect, see Moshe Hirsch, 'Investment Tribunals and Human Rights: Divergent Paths', in Pierre-Marie Dupuy, Francesco Francioni and Ernst-Ulrich Petersmann (eds.), *Human Rights in International Investment Law and Arbitration* (Oxford University Press, 2009), pp. 99 ff.

place,[34] show not only the close relation between both branches of law,[35] but also the fact that arbitral tribunals can as a matter of principle consider human rights law.[36]

I will focus here on human rights considerations invoked by host states to 'justify' breaches of their investment obligations. This chapter is thus not concerned with human rights obligations of the foreign investors, nor with the human rights obligations of host states towards foreign investors.[37] Case law in respect of the latter two issues will,

[34] See, for example, *Técnicas Medioambientales Tecmed SA* v. *The United Mexican States*, ICSID Case No. ARB(AF)/00/2, Award, 29 May 2003, para. 122.

[35] The investment treaty and human rights regimes, indeed, share several common features. Besides the similarity in the weakness of the position of individuals and foreign investors in relation to the state, the grant of rights of protection to both individuals and investors has also resulted in the creation of specific dispute settlement mechanisms to address alleged violations of these rights by the state. To a certain extent, the direct access of individuals to investment treaty arbitration is analogous to the direct access of individuals to international human rights courts and bodies. The main difference between human rights litigation and investment arbitration is that in international human rights litigation, the states that have accepted the direct claims rights of individuals have also, and principally, accepted such a right for claims of their own nationals. Also, the protection afforded to foreign investors is still conditioned by the principle of reciprocity between the two states, while it is generally acknowledged that the protection of individual human rights has an objective character which is not conditioned by the principle of reciprocity (see Pierre-Marie Dupuy, 'Unification Rather than Fragmentation of International Law? The Case of International Investment Law and Human Rights Law', in Pierre-Marie Dupuy, Francesco Francioni and Ernst-Ulrich Petersmann (eds.), *Human Rights in International Investment Law and Arbitration* (Oxford University Press, 2009), p. 48).

[36] See also Francesco Francioni, 'Access to Justice, Denial of Justice, and International Investment Law', in Pierre-Marie Dupuy, Francesco Francioni and Ernst-Ulrich Petersmann (eds.), *Human Rights in International Investment Law and Arbitration* (Oxford University Press 2009), p. 63. However, some tribunals have been more cautious in recognizing the relevance of the ECtHR jurisprudence for investment law. The Ad Hoc Committee in *Azurix* v. *Argentina*, for instance, in responding to the argument raised by Argentina that the ECtHR case law in respect of access of shareholders could be applied to investment law, noted that 'as the extent of the protections afforded by an investment protection treaty depends in each case on the specific terms of the treaty in question, the Committee regards comparisons with differently-worded treaties as of limited utility, especially treaties outside the field of investment protection' (*Azurix Corp.* v. *The Argentine Republic*, ICSID Case No. ARB/01/12, Decision on the Application for Annulment of the Argentine Republic, 1 September 2009, para. 128).

[37] On these questions, see Eric De Brabandere, 'Human Rights Considerations in International Investment Arbitration', in Malgosia Fitzmaurice and Panos Merkouris (eds.), *The Interpretation and Application of the European Convention of Human Rights: Legal and Practical Implications* (Leiden: Martinus Nijhoff, 2012), pp. 183–215; Marc Jacob, 'International Investment Agreements and Human Rights', INEF Research Paper Series on Human Rights, Corporate Responsibility and Sustainable Development 03/2010 (Duisburg: Institute for Development and Peace,

however, be mentioned to the extent that they make clear the distinction between jurisdiction and applicable law.

I will first address the question of whether investment tribunals can consider non-investment arguments, in particular, human rights arguments, taking into account the limited scope of the jurisdiction of investment tribunals. As will be noted, a distinction should indeed be made between the limited jurisdiction of investment tribunals and the applicable law. I will next address the 'conflict' between human rights obligations and investment treaty obligations generally. I will discuss the applicable rules on treaty conflict, and how investment tribunals have dealt with human rights invoked as a defence for a breach of an investment treaty obligation, when the 'conflict' between both sets of norms is most apparent.

### *4.2.1 The limited jurisdiction of international investment tribunals and human rights law as part of the applicable law*

The specificity of the regime of investment treaty arbitration is important since it partly explains the relative reluctance by investment tribunals to engage in the consideration of non-investment arguments. Since the direct access of foreign investors to investment treaty arbitration is accepted only because it is part of the protection offered to the investor for claims arising out of the investment, the scope of authority of the arbitral tribunal is at the same time *limited* to these types of dispute. The consent of the states, expressed through the signature of bilateral and multilateral investment treaties, is given only for claims directly related to the investment, and cannot therefore be extended to any types of conflict between the investor and the home state. This, however, does not imply that the tribunal may not take into account other (treaty) obligations of states, if applicable.

Investment treaty arbitration is a specific type of mixed dispute settlement which is, as is every forum for international dispute settlement, limited by the compromissory clause in which states have expressed their consent to the jurisdiction of the arbitral tribunal. The scope of jurisdiction is defined and limited by the agreement of the states party to the treaty granting jurisdiction or, in the event of consent otherwise expressed, by that instrument. The tribunal thus has no

University of Duisburg-Essen, 2010), available at: www.humanrights-business.org/files/international_investment_agreements_and_human_rights.pdf; and Ursula Kriebaum, 'Foreign Investments and Human Rights: The Actors and Their Different Roles', *Transnational Dispute Management*, 10 (2013): 1.

competence in matters that fall outside the responsibility given to the tribunal by the parties, nor can the tribunal apply a legal system that has not been defined by the parties as the applicable law.[38]

## The jurisdiction of arbitral tribunals

The jurisdiction of a tribunal is limited to the specific category of dispute that the parties have accepted for submission to the court or tribunal. This principle was discussed by the Arbitral Tribunal in *Channel Tunnel* v. *France and United Kingdom*, in which the Tribunal also clearly distinguished between the jurisdiction of the tribunal, namely, the source of the parties' rights and obligations which the tribunal is asked to enforce, and the law applicable to the dispute.[39] The claimant argued that France and the United Kingdom had breached their obligations under the Concession Agreement and the bilateral treaty, but claimed that the obligations of states in this respect should be read in conjunction with other international obligations of the states, including the ECHR.[40] The Tribunal rejected this argument, and stated that the Concession Agreement does not action any

> contractual commitment by the States Parties that they will comply with their own or European Law. Whether or not they did so would be a matter for their own courts or for the European courts ... In short, national and European law claims against the States are to be the subject of proceedings before the appropriate national or European forums. By contrast it is for the Tribunal to deal with disputes involving the application of the Concession Agreement.[41]

A investment tribunal, which has jurisdiction over a certain dispute, cannot extend this jurisdiction to other categories or types of dispute between the parties. Article 25 of the ICSID Convention limits the jurisdiction of the Centre 'to any legal dispute arising directly out of an investment'. Concomitantly, investment agreements contain provisions delimiting the scope of application of the treaty, and thus the jurisdiction of tribunals established under that treaty. If the jurisdiction of the tribunals is limited to 'investment disputes', the *scope* of the tribunal's jurisdiction does not extend to other types of dispute. This

[38] Collier and Lowe, *The Settlement of Disputes in International Law*, p. 227.

[39] *Channel Tunnel Group* v. *France and United Kingdom*, Partial Arbitral Award, 30 January 2007, available at: www.pca-cpa.org/showpage.asp?pag_id=1184, paras 134 ff, accessed 17 January 2014.

[40] *Ibid.*, paras 107–110. [41] *Ibid.*, para. 148.

principle has been illustrated in the *Biloune* v. *Ghana* case,[42] which concerned the arrest and detention for thirteen days of a foreign investor, Biloune, who was eventually deported to Togo. The Tribunal noted that its jurisdiction under the agreement between the investor and the host state was limited to disputes relating to an investment.[43] The Tribunal held that it was, therefore, not competent to deal with every human rights violation of the foreign investor, but only to the extent that such a violation affects the investment and thus becomes an investment dispute.[44] More recently, the Tribunal in *Bernhard von Pezold and others* v. *Zimbabwe* refused the extension of the claim to include human rights, based on its limited jurisdiction. Although in this case the additional 'claim' was made by a non-disputing party under ICSD Arbitration Rule 37(2)(a), the principles reiterated by the tribunal are highly relevant, and also distinguish, although not very clearly, between the applicable law and the jurisdiction of an investment tribunal:

> The Petitioners, in effect, seek to make a submission on legal and factual issues that are unrelated to the matters before the Arbitral Tribunals. The Arbitral Tribunals agree in this regard with the Claimants that the reference to 'such rules of general international law as may be applicable' in the BITs does not incorporate the universe of international law into the BITs or into disputes arising under the BITs. Moreover, neither Party has put the identity and/or treatment of indigenous peoples, or the indigenous communities in particular, under international law, including international human rights law on indigenous peoples, in issue in these proceedings.
>
> ... the Petitioners propose to make a submission on the putative rights of the indigenous communities as 'indigenous peoples' under international human rights law, a matter outside of the scope of the dispute, as it is presently constituted. Indeed, as the Claimants have noted, in order for the Arbitral Tribunals to consider such a submission, they would need to consider and decide whether the indigenous communities constitute 'indigenous peoples' for the purposes of grounding any rights under international human rights law. Setting aside whether or not the Arbitral Tribunals are the appropriate arbiters of this decision, the decision itself is clearly outside of the scope of the dispute before the Tribunals.[45]

[42] *Biloune and Marine Drive Complex Ltd* v. *Ghana Investments Centre and the Government of Ghana*, UNCITRAL, Award on Jurisdiction and Liability, 27 October 1989, *International Law Reports*, 95 (1989): 184.

[43] *Ibid.*, p. 188. [44] *Ibid.*, p. 203.

[45] *Bernhard von Pezold and others* v. *Republic of Zimbabwe*, ICSID Case No. ARB/10/15, Procedural Order No. 2, 26 June 2012, paras 57–60.

Jurisdiction, however, is very different from the question of the law applicable to the dispute,[46] but they are without doubt connected, especially when one deals with specific regime-related dispute settlement mechanisms.

## Human rights as part of the applicable law

The limited scope of jurisdiction of an arbitral tribunal does not imply that the tribunal cannot as a matter of principle consider human rights issues raised by either party as applicable law. In practice, the wording of the compromissory clause is paramount not only for the limitation of the scope of the jurisdiction of the tribunal, but also for the law to be applied by the tribunal. This was highlighted by a decision by an arbitral tribunal in an arbitration established by application of a compromissory clause in the OSPAR Convention.[47] The Tribunal drew attention to Article 32(6)(a) of the OSPAR Convention, which notes that the tribunal shall decide 'according to the rules of international law and, in particular, those of the OSPAR convention'. Therefore the Tribunal accepted that the primary source of applicable law would be the OSPAR Convention, but also customary law and general principles, except if there is a *lex specialis* between the parties.[48] As far as other conventional law is concerned, the Tribunal referred to Article 2 of the OSPAR Convention, which delineates the general obligations of the parties under the convention: 'The Contracting Parties shall, *in accordance with the provisions of the Convention*, take all possible steps to prevent and eliminate pollution.'[49] The Tribunal, because of this explicit provision, concluded that other conventional law could not be applied, since its competence was not intended to extend to obligations under other instruments. Accepting the opposite would, according to the Tribunal, turn the OSPAR Arbitral Tribunal into a generalized dispute settlement forum, which clearly was not the intention of the parties when signing the OSPAR Convention.

Clearly, the wording of the compromissory clause is essential. When deciding on an investment dispute, there is no reason for the tribunal to exclude *ipso facto* human rights considerations *as a matter of applicable law*. Article 42 of the ICSID Convention provides that, in the absence of

[46] See International Law Commission, Final Report of the ILC Study Group on the issue of Fragmentation of International Law, UN Doc. A/CN.4/L.682, 13 April 2006, para. 44.

[47] *Ireland* v. *United Kingdom* ('OSPAR Arbitration'), PCA, Final Award, 2 July 2003, *International Legal Materials*, 42 (2003).

[48] *Ibid.*, paras 80 ff. [49] Emphasis added.

an agreement to the contrary, 'the Tribunal shall apply the law of the Contracting State party to the dispute (including its rules on the conflict of laws) and such rules of international law as may be applicable'. Moreover, the majority of the investment treaties provide for the application of international law to the dispute. For instance, Article 1131 of the NAFTA provides that investment tribunals set up under Chapter Eleven of the Agreement, 'shall decide the issues in dispute in accordance with this Agreement and applicable rules of international law'. Another example is Article 26(6) of the ECT, which provides that tribunals 'shall decide the issues in dispute in accordance with this Treaty and applicable rules and principles of international law'. The United States Model BIT similarly provides that 'the tribunal shall decide the issues in dispute in accordance with this Treaty and applicable rules of international law'.[50] These provisions open the door for the application of customary rules of international law to investment disputes, and, as some authors have also argued, international treaty law.[51] However, considering the specific and limited jurisdiction of investment tribunals, human rights considerations will in effect be taken into consideration only provided that the party that invokes these considerations can effectively prove and demonstrate the conflict between these two norms in the event of an *investment dispute*.[52]

A parallel can be drawn with the settlement of international trade disputes under the WTO. Article 3(2) of the WTO Dispute Settlement Understanding (WTO DSU) notes that the WTO Dispute Settlement System applies only to issues arising under the WTO Agreements, since it aims to 'preserve the rights and obligations of Members under the covered agreements, and to clarify the existing provisions of those agreements in accordance with customary rules of interpretation of public international law'. At first sight, therefore, when human rights norms are at stake, neither the WTO Panels nor the WTO Appellate Body could apply the human rights norms in question, and the WTO Dispute Settlement Institutions would generally not have jurisdiction to take into consideration human rights claims.[53] However, despite the limited jurisdiction of the WTO Dispute Settlement Institutions to WTO claims,

50 Article 30, 2012 United States Model BIT, available at: www.ustr.gov/sites/default/files/BIT%20text%20for%20ACIEP%20Meeting.pdf, accessed 28 December 2012.

51 Dupuy, 'Unification Rather than Fragmentation of International Law?', p. 56.

52 *Ibid.*, p. 59.

53 For a discussion, see Jan Klabbers, *Treaty Conflict and the European Union* (Cambridge University Press, 2009), p. 107.

it has been argued that as a matter of applicable law, the entire corpus of international law is binding on both parties to a dispute, and human rights can thus be part of the *applicable law*.[54] The Final Report of the ILC Study Group on the issue of Fragmentation of International Law similarly noted that 'there seems . . . little reason of principle to depart from the view that general international law supplements WTO law unless it has been specifically excluded and that so do other treaties which should, preferably, be read in harmony with the WTO covered treaties'.[55]

Consequently, when states invoke human rights obligations to justify a breach of their investment treaty obligations, there is no reason why the tribunal so established under the investment agreement should be barred from taking such argument into consideration as a matter of applicable law. Practice, however, shows that very few tribunals have effectively done so.

### *4.2.2 Conflicts between human rights and investment obligations*

First, it should be pointed out that the notion of 'conflict' is used here to denote a conflict in the international legal obligations of the host state *in concreto*. In other words, there is no automatic conflict between human rights norms and investment protection provisions.[56] What I address here is a particular situation in which a state is confronted with conflicting obligations under a human rights instrument and an investment protection instrument.

In essence, in the event of a conflict between a state's human rights obligations and its obligations under an international investment treaty, the wording of these treaties and the application of the general principles of international law, including the law on the responsibility of states for internationally wrongful acts, will be determinant. Generally, states can include human rights provisions in their treaties.[57] However, as mentioned, such a reference to human rights norms is usually lacking. It is, nevertheless, generally acknowledged that states need to take into account their various international legal

54 Joost Pauwelyn, 'Bridging Fragmentation and Unity: International Law as a Universe of Inter-Connected Islands', *Michigan Journal of International Law*, 25(4) (2003/4): 903, 910.

55 ILC, Final Report of the ILC Study Group on the Issue of Fragmentation of International Law, UN Doc. A/CN.4/L.682, para. 169.

56 See also Yannick Radi, 'The "Human Nature" of International Investment Law', *Transnational Dispute Management*, 10 (2013): 1, 2 ff.

57 See Simma, 'Foreign Investment Arbitration', pp. 573, 581.

obligations, including those related to human rights, when signing posterior treaties.[58] When states thus negotiate and sign an investment treaty, they are under an obligation to take into consideration their human rights obligations contained in international treaties. The same rule also needs to be applied to those human rights obligations that form part of customary international law.[59] As mentioned, however, there is no *a priori* incompatibility of human rights obligations and investment protection obligations, although a state can be confronted with a clear conflict of obligations in a particular situation. As a consequence, when signing investment treaties states do not necessarily omit to take into account their human rights obligations.

### Treaty interpretation and treaty conflicts

Although the potential conflict between human rights norms and the investment obligations of states can be described as a clash of 'values' materialized by the two different sets of norms, such a characterization is not useful in effectively solving the conflict.[60] A conflict of values cannot be solved by the application of a rule of international law, for such a solution would depend on the subjective hierarchicization by the community of states of rules in function of their representation of certain values.[61] Moreover, some authors have defended the view that many of the rights granted to foreign investors under international investment treaties and trade agreements are *in themselves* human rights,[62] or at least that they share the same underlying principle, which is to protect the individual from the power of the state.[63] This thus creates a conflict between different human rights norms that cannot be solved unless through the characterization of certain human rights as more fundamental than others, which, except for *jus cogens* norms, is absent in current international (human rights) law. Hierarchy of treaties and norms also is of no avail in solving conflicts between human rights treaties and investment treaties simply because

58 See Jan B. Mus, 'Conflicts between Treaties in International Law', *Netherlands International Law Review*, 45(3) (1998): 208, 227.

59 See Dupuy, 'Unification Rather than Fragmentation of International Law?', p. 53.

60 Klabbers, *Treaty Conflict and the European Union*, pp. 33 ff.

61 See ILC, Final Report of the ILC Study Group on the issue of Fragmentation of International Law, UN Doc. A/CN.4/L.682, Part F.

62 Ernst-Ulrich Petersmann, 'Human Rights and International Trade Law: Defining and Connecting the Two Fields', in Thomas Cottier, Joost Pauwelyn, and Elisabeth Bürgi (eds.), *Human Rights and International Trade* (Oxford University Press, 2005), pp. 29–94.

63 Simma, 'Foreign Investment Arbitration', p. 576.

international law currently contains no rules in this respect, with the exception of Article 103 of the UN Charter, which is of little relevance in the event of conflicts between human rights treaties and international investment law.[64]

The Vienna Convention on the Law of Treaties (VCLT)[65] offers some guidance for treaty interpretation and for solving treaty conflicts,[66] although one should be reminded of the fact that the rules contained in the VCLT were essentially drafted to interpret treaties, not to solve conflicts between treaties or treaty obligations. The VCLT provides in its Article 30, entitled 'Application of successive treaties relating to the same subject matter', that:

> 1. Subject to Article 103 of the Charter of the United Nations, the rights and obligations of States Parties to successive treaties relating to the same subject matter shall be determined in accordance with the following paragraphs.
> 2. When a treaty specifies that it is subject to, or that it is not to be considered as incompatible with, an earlier or later treaty, the provisions of that other treaty prevail.
> 3. When all the parties to the earlier treaty are parties also to the later treaty but the earlier treaty is not terminated or suspended in operation under Article 59, the earlier treaty applies only to the extent that its provisions are compatible with those of the later treaty.
> 4. When the parties to the later treaty do not include all the parties to the earlier one:
>    (a) as between States Parties to both treaties the same rule applies as in paragraph 3;
>    (b) as between a State party to both treaties and a State party to only one of the treaties, the treaty to which both States are parties governs their mutual rights and obligations.
> 5. Paragraph 4 is without prejudice to Article 41, or to any question of the termination or suspension of the operation of a treaty under Article 60 or to any question of responsibility which may arise for a State from the conclusion or application of a treaty the provisions of which are incompatible with its obligations towards another State under another treaty.

[64] For a discussion of this possibility in international environmental treaties, see Malgosia Fitzmaurice and Olufemi Elias, *Contemporary Issues in the Law of Treaties* (Utrecht: Eleven, 2005), pp. 341 ff.

[65] Vienna Convention on the Law of Treaties, 23 May 1969, 1155 UNTS 331.

[66] See Diane A. Desierto, 'Conflict of Treaties, Interpretation, and Decision-making on Human Rights and Investment during Economic Crises', *Transnational Dispute Management*, 10 ( 2013): 1.

One of the most important rules contained in that Article is *lex posterior derogat anteriori*, subject to certain conditions as expressed in paragraphs 3 and 4, namely, the rule that a later treaty prevails over an earlier one. However, this rule cannot solve every conflict of norms. First, it is not self-evident to assert that both human rights obligations and obligations under investment treaties can be considered as relating to the 'same subject matter', as required by Article 30 of the VCLT. In addition, the VCLT does not offer an adequate solution to treaty conflict when the parties to the treaty are not identical.[67] Indeed, an application of the *lex posterior derogat anteriori* principle to these types of treaty conflict will often be contrary to the *inter partes* effect of international treaties, since the parties to the two treaties are not the same. And even when one limits the application of the rule to the states party to both treaties, it is hard to find a general rule on the priority of either the *lex posterior* or the *lex prior*.[68]

The same can be said in respect of the application of the *lex specialis derogat generali* principle, which does not always offer a solution to conflicts between human rights and investment treaties or norms.[69] The *lex specialis* principle implies that, in the event of normative conflicts between matters regulated by a general and a specific rule, the specific rule takes precedence over the general rule.[70] Besides the fact that it is in practice not easy to determine which rule constitutes the 'general' or the 'specific' rule, the application of the *lex specialis* principle to human rights/investment conflicts is not self-evident.[71] The conflict of norms is one that applies to the conflicting obligations of the host state in a concrete situation, but both sets of rules do not necessarily cover the same subject matter. Taking into consideration that the application of

[67] Klabbers, *Treaty Conflict and the European Union*, p. 87. See also Final Report of the ILC Study Group on the Issue of Fragmentation of International Law, UN Doc. A/CN.4/L.682, para. 243.

[68] For a discussion, see Final Report of the ILC Study Group on the Issue of Fragmentation of International Law, UN Doc. A/CN.4/L.682, paras 234–250.

[69] On this principle generally and on the application of the principle to treaty conflicts (in particular, between human rights and humanitarian law), see Jean d'Aspremont, 'Articulating International Human Rights and International Humanitarian Law: Conciliatory Interpretation under the Guise of Conflict of Norms-Resolution', in Malgosia Fitzmaurice and Panos Merkouris (eds.), *The Interpretation and Application of the European Convention of Human Rights: Legal and Practical Implications* (Leiden: Martinus Nijhoff, 2012), pp. 3–31.

[70] Final Report of the ILC Study Group on the Issue of Fragmentation of International Law, UN Doc. A/CN.4/L.682, para. 56.

[71] *Ibid.*, para. 58.

the principle presupposes a conflict between two norms that deal with the same subject matter, and whose scope of application overlaps, it is to be doubted whether the *lex specialis* principle even applies in this case.[72] As also noted by the ILC in its commentary to the Articles on State Responsibility which contain a rule on *lex specialis* for the international responsibility of states,[73] for the rule to apply, 'there must be some actual inconsistency between them, or else a discernible intention that one provision is to exclude the other'.[74] Under human rights treaties or customary law, the state has obligations towards the individuals within its jurisdiction, while under investment treaties, states have taken up obligations in respect of the treatment of foreign investors. Therefore, it is not so much a question of which set of rules is more general or specific than the other, but rather that the two sets of state obligations are applicable in *different areas* and may simply amount to conflicting obligations of the state in a particular situation.

Article 31(3)(c) of the VCLT, which requires that 'any relevant rule of international law applicable in the relations between the parties' should be taken into account (the so-called 'systemic integration' of treaties) in the interpretation, is also of little avail in solving conflicts between treaties. Indeed, as with the other provisions, Article 31(3)(c) is a principle for the interpretation of treaties, not for settling treaty conflicts.[75] One should, however, not overlook that Article 31(3)(c) of the Vienna Convention may, in certain situations, provide the necessary framework for integrating human rights in the interpretation of certain BIT provisions.[76]

In practice, in the case of conflicts between a state's human rights and investment obligations, the so-called principle of 'political decision' will often be employed, although it is not as such a *method* to solve conflicts.[77] It is merely a practical and pragmatic policy solution to such conflicts. In essence, the principle holds that when treaty conflict cannot be solved through interpretation, the state 'simply' faces the choice of respecting one treaty and breaching its obligations under the other. When making such a decision, it is understood that a state having

72 See d'Aspremont, 'Articulating International Human Rights and International Humanitarian Law'.
73 Article 55, ILC Articles on State Responsibility, UN Doc. A/56/10.
74 *Ibid.*, Commentary to Article 55, para. 4.
75 Simma, 'Foreign Investment Arbitration', p. 584.
76 See extensively on this, *ibid.*, pp. 584–6.
77 Klabbers, *Treaty Conflict and the European Union*, pp. 88–9.

to decide which treaty obligations it will breach will need to make a balanced decision. As a consequence of the application of the principle of 'political decision', the state will be in breach of either one of its obligations in the event of a conflict between two treaties. When a state has breached its human rights obligations through the signature or application of an international investment treaty, or vice versa, there is no doubt that the state holds responsibility for the breach of these rights. When the responsibility of the host state towards the foreign investor is engaged because of an alleged breach of the provisions of the investment treaty, as a consequence of a conflict with the state's human rights obligations, the foreign investor can thus bring a claim before an international arbitral tribunal provided that the treaty contains a clause to this effect. The question then is whether and how investment tribunals can assess the responsibility of the state for the breach of its obligations under international investment law, while taking into account the human rights obligations of the host state. This has notably been the case when human rights obligations are invoked as a defence against international responsibility.

## Human rights obligations raised as a defence against responsibility

A recurrent type of dispute before international investment tribunals relates to one of the reasons behind the involvement of foreign corporations in states, namely, the privatization of public services, such as water supply, sewage systems and waste management.[78] Many states have in recent decades privatized public services, and have granted concessions and lease contracts to foreign investors in these areas. Conflicts may then arise, *in concreto*, between a state's obligations in respect of economic and social rights, and its obligations towards the foreign investor.

It is generally acknowledged that there is a duty on the state to ensure that private companies operating in their territory do not interfere with

[78] See, generally, Pierre Thielbörger, 'The Human Right to Water versus Investor Rights: Double-Dilemma or Pseudo-Conflict?', in Pierre-Marie Dupuy, Francesco Francioni and Ernst-Ulrich Petersmann (eds.), *Human Rights in International Investment Law and Arbitration* (Oxford University Press 2009), p. 487; Stephen C. McCaffrey, 'The Human Right to Water', in Edith Brown Weiss, Laurence Boisson de Chazournes and Nathalie Bernasconi-Osterwalder (eds.), *Fresh Water and International Economic Law* (Oxford University Press 2005), pp. 93–115; and Laurence Boisson de Chazournes, *Fresh Water in International Law* (Oxford University Press, 2013).

the enjoyment of human rights, including those contained in the International Covenant on Economic, Social and Cultural Rights.[79] Since human rights are obligations on the host state, the state is under an obligation to ensure respect for the human rights on its territory, including protection from the acts of foreign investors. Regulations and laws adopted by host states in the exercise of their public authority in order to ensure respect for these human rights can, nevertheless, enter into conflict with certain provisions of investment treaties or investment contracts that states have negotiated and signed with foreign investors. The question, then, is whether the human rights obligations of the state can be invoked as a defence to justify the breach of an international investment agreement. Essentially, human rights raised as a defence can take the form of two claims. Either the state asserts that the protection of human rights can function as a form of 'necessity' – which precludes the wrongfulness of the breach of the investment treaty as matter of treaty law ('non-precluded measures clauses'), or through the application of the general rules on circumstances precluding wrongfulness in the Articles on State Responsibility – or it can be maintained that, in the case where a breach of the 'fair and equitable treatment' standard (FET)[80] or of the prohibition on indirect or 'creeping' expropriations is invoked by the investor, these rules do not preclude action taken by the host state to protect human rights.[81] I will focus here on the first type of argument, which forms part of the applicable law and the jurisdiction of tribunals debate, considering the focus of this book is on the procedural implications of the public international law character of investment treaty arbitration.

In case of the invocation of human rights considerations by host states to justify a breach of their obligations under an international investment treaty, foreign investors have on most occasions generally argued that the human rights obligations of the host state, although as

79 See for a discussion Simma, 'Foreign Investment Arbitration', p. 576.

80 See Radi, 'The "Human Nature" of International Investment Law', pp. 9 ff.

81 On the relation between the 'fair and equitable treatment' standard and human rights, see Ionna Knoll-Tudor, 'The Fair and Equitable Treatment Standard and Human Rights Norms', in Pierre-Marie Dupuy, Francesco Francioni and Ernst-Ulrich Petersmann (eds.), *Human Rights in International Investment Law and Arbitration* (Oxford University Press, 2009), p. 339, and Annika Wythes, 'Investor–State Arbitrations: Can the "Fair and Equitable Treatment" Clause Consider International Human Rights Obligations?', *Leiden Journal of International Law*, 23(1) (2010): 241, 241–56. See also Simma, 'Foreign Investment Arbitration', p. 589, and Timothy G. Nelson, 'Human Rights and BIT Protection: Areas of Convergence, *Journal of World Investment & Trade*, 11(1) (2011): 27, 27–47.

such relevant with regard to the obligations of the host state, are irrelevant to the determination of a breach of that state's obligations under investment treaties. This dichotomy is very well reflected in *Suez* v. *Argentina*, one of the few cases in which human rights considerations were relatively extensively discussed.[82] Argentina and *amicus curiae* submissions argued that human rights laws required that Argentina adopt measures to ensure that the right water was supplied, and that, as a consequence, the Tribunal should consider this obligation in interpreting and applying the relevant provisions of the investment treaty.[83] The claimants, on the other hand, argued 'that what is at issue in these cases is whether Argentina breached its legal commitments under the BITs and that human rights law is irrelevant to that determination'.[84]

In fact, the Argentine Government has invoked human rights considerations on many occasions to defend the emergency measures it adopted during the economic crisis which started in 2001. The argument raised by Argentina was, essentially, that in the event of an economic crisis that compromises the basic human rights of its citizens, an investment treaty could not prevail over emergency measures taken by the government to remedy the effects of the crisis and thus preserve the basic human rights of its nationals.[85] In the majority of the cases the Argentine defence and the conflict faced by the Argentine Government were not upheld or taken into consideration. Arbitral practice, indeed, shows that tribunals have been relatively reluctant to engage in a discussion of the conflict between a state's investment and human rights obligations, either as a claim relating to the existence of 'necessity' or in analysing a violation of the FET standard.[86]

In *Azurix*, Argentina raised a conflict between the BIT and human rights treaties that protect consumers' rights.[87] One of the experts

[82] *Suez, Sociedad General de Aguas de Barcelona SA and Vivendi Universal SA* v. *The Argentine Republic*, ICSID Case No. ARB/03/19, Decision on Liability, 30 July 2010.

[83] *Ibid.*, para. 256. [84] *Ibid.*, para. 255.

[85] See, for example, *CMS Gas* v. *Argentina*, ICSID Case No. ARB/01/8, Decision on Annulment, para. 114.

[86] I should mention here that several of the cases analysed below have been the subject of annulment procedures under the rules provided for in the ICSID Convention. Although the annulment proceedings have not always resulted in a nullification of the decisions of the tribunals in respect of the discussed subject matter, these judgments do not necessarily reflect the final and binding outcome of the procedures. They are, however, indicative of how tribunals generally have dealt with human rights considerations brought by the host state, and are thus mentioned and discussed for this reason.

[87] *Azurix* v. *Argentina*, ICSID Case No. ARB/01/12, Award, para. 254.

intervening for Argentina, Dr Solomoni, opined that 'a conflict between a BIT and human rights treaties must be resolved in favor of human rights because the consumers' public interest must prevail over the private interest of service provider'.[88] The Tribunal avoided the conflict by noting that 'the matter has not been fully argued and the Tribunal fails to understand the incompatibility in the specifics of the instant case'.[89] Similarly, in *Siemens* v. *Argentina*, Argentina claimed that 'the human rights so incorporated in the Constitution would be disregarded by recognizing the property rights asserted by the Claimant given the social and economic conditions of Argentina'.[90] Argentina cited the *Tecmed* v. *Mexico* award, in which the tribunal had discussed and accepted the relevance of ECtHR case law in assessing whether or not an expropriation had taken place, in order to weaken the amount of compensation to be afforded to Siemens.[91] However, the *Siemens* Tribunal distinguished between the cases, and noted that the human rights issues raised in *Tecmed* concerned the determination of whether an expropriation had taken place, and not the determination of the amount of compensation. The Tribunal noted that the human rights argument in this respect had not been developed by Argentina, and that 'without the benefit of further elaboration and substantiation by the parties, it is not an argument that, *prima facie*, bears any relationship to the merits of this case', a rather cryptic statement that seems to imply that the Tribunal considered that it had no jurisdiction over the question.[92]

In *Sempra* v. *Argentina*, the tribunal was more open to human rights considerations, and recognized the potential conflict between human rights obligations and investment obligations.[93] Argentina claimed that its responsibility was excluded 'by the rules of international law governing the state of necessity, whether customary or contained in the Treaty'.[94] The argument was principally that institutional survival and the preservation of the constitutional order, including respect for the

[88] *Ibid.* [89] *Ibid.*, para. 261.
[90] *Siemens* v. *Argentina*, ICSID Case No. ARB/02/8, Award and Separate Opinion, para. 75.
[91] *Tecmed* v. *Mexico*, ICSID Case No. ARB(AF)/00/2.
[92] *Siemens* v. *Argentina*, ICSID Case No. ARB/02/8, Award and Separate Opinion, para. 79.
[93] *Sempra* v. *Argentina*, ICSID Case No. ARB/02/16, Award. That decision was, however, entirely annulled on the ground of manifest excess of powers, mainly for failing to apply Article XI of the BIT, which contained a treaty-based 'necessity' exception: *Sempra Energy International* v. *The Argentine Republic*, ICSID Case No. ARB/02/16, Decision on the Argentine Republic's Request for Annulment of the Award, 29 June 2010.
[94] *Ibid.*, para. 98.

provisions of the American Convention on Human Rights, justified the infringements of the rights of the investor.[95] The Tribunal recognized that the question 'raises the complex relationship between investment treaties, emergency and the human rights of both citizens and property owners'.[96] However, when assessing whether the constitutional order and the survival of the state were imperilled by the crisis and, therefore, whether it could constitute 'necessity' under customary international law, the Tribunal held that:

> the constitutional order was not on the verge of collapse, as evidenced by, among many examples, the orderly constitutional transition that carried the country through five different Presidencies in a few days' time, followed by elections and the reestablishment of public order. Even if emergency legislation became necessary in this context, legitimately acquired rights could still have been accommodated by means of temporary measures and renegotiation.[97]

Here again, the Tribunal analysed the human rights defences raised by Argentina by reference to the conditions under which 'necessity' can invoked in general customary international law. A similar reasoning was held by the Arbitral Tribunal in *Biwater Gauff*. Tanzania claimed that the investor 'had created a real threat to public health and welfare', and that 'water and sanitation services are vitally important, and the Republic has more than a right to protect such services in case of a crisis: it has a moral and perhaps even a legal obligation to do so'.[98] The Tribunal considered, however, that 'there was no necessity or impending public purpose to justify the Government's intervention in the way that took place'.[99]

In *LG&E* v. *Argentina*, the Tribunal concluded that the measures adopted by Argentina were 'necessary to maintain public order and protect its essential security interests'.[100] Although the Tribunal never explicitly referred to human rights, it noted that Argentina responded to the crisis by adopting measures to 'ensure the population's access to basic health care goods and services'.[101] The Tribunal, thus, essentially analysed whether the situation in Argentina could be considered to be a state of emergency, as understood under Article XI of the US–Argentina

95 *Ibid.*, para. 331. 96 *Ibid.*, para. 332. 97 *Ibid.*, para. 332.

98 *Biwater Gauff (Tanzania) Ltd* v. *United Republic of Tanzania*, ICSID Case No. ARB/05/22, Award, 24 July 2008, paras 434 and 436.

99 *Ibid.*, para. 515.

100 *LG&E* v. *Argentina*, ICSID Case No. ARB/02/1, Decision on Liability, para. 226.

101 *Ibid.*, para. 234.

BIT and the Articles on State Responsibility.[102] A similar reasoning was given by the Arbitral Tribunal in *Continental* v. *Argentina*.[103] The Tribunal noted that the measures taken by Argentina to protect constitutional guarantees and fundamental liberties were justified, and that the state had a significant margin of appreciation in deciding the type of measures to take.[104] The Tribunal there also did not explicitly refer to the human rights obligations of Argentina.

The Tribunal in *Suez* v. *Argentina* mentioned above refused to accept the necessity claim, considering that the strict conditions set by the Articles on State Responsibility were not met.[105] In respect of the claim that Argentina's human rights obligations trumped its investment treaty obligations specifically, the Tribunal argued that it cannot 'find a basis for such a conclusion either in the BITs or international law. Argentina is subject to both international obligations, that is, human rights and treaty obligations, and must respect both of them equally. Under the circumstances of these cases, Argentina's human rights obligations and its investment treaty obligations are not inconsistent, contradictory or mutually exclusive.' Thus, as discussed above, Argentina could have 'respected both types of obligations'.[106] It is interesting to point out that the Tribunal approached the issue from the perspective of a conflict of norms as part of the assessment of the 'necessity' claim. This view is very much in line with the general idea set out above that there is no automatic conflict between the two norms, and one norm does not prevail over the other.

Investment tribunals remain relatively reluctant to take human rights into consideration when dealing with investment claims. They generally take little account of the conflicting investment and human rights obligations of states, at least when it comes down to responding to the argument of whether human rights obligations may amount to a form of 'necessity' under international law. Although admittedly the *intent* of the government is of no relevance for an assessment of the alleged breach of the state's investment obligations, such decisions do not address in detail the human rights defences of the host states and their conflicting obligations, which nevertheless form part of the

102 *Ibid.*, paras 245 ff.
103 *Continental Casualty Co.* v. *The Argentine Republic*, ICSID Case No. ARB/03/9, Award, 5 September 2008.
104 *Ibid.*, paras 180 ff.
105 *Suez/Vivendi* v. *Argentina*, ICSID Case No. ARB/03/19, Decision on Liability, para. 258.
106 *Ibid.*, para. 262.

applicable law.[107] In addition to the legal principles in respect of the applicable law and the limited jurisdiction of investment tribunals explained above, the predominantly private and commercial character of investment arbitration and proceedings may also explain the lack of arbitrators' enthusiasm to address human rights considerations.[108]

[107] On the claim that human rights considerations could in any event not influence the decision of the arbitration on the merits, but arguably only on the calculation of compensation, see Knoll-Tudor, 'The Fair and Equitable Treatment Standard and Human Rights Norms', p. 342.

[108] On the absence of arbitrators' acquaintance with the specialized field of human rights as an explanatory element, see *ibid.*

# 5 Transparency and public access in investment treaty arbitration

Traditionally, international commercial arbitration is conducted in a relatively confidential and private manner, even in the absence of an explicit confidentiality provision in the arbitration agreement.[1] Neither the existence of a dispute nor the procedural details of the settlement of the dispute are made public; nor is there any access by non-disputing parties to the proceedings.[2] The main reason behind this practice is that the dispute and the agreement underlying the dispute are of a private nature,[3] and that sensitive business and commercial information should not be disclosed.[4] Some authors have, nevertheless, recently questioned the validity of such arguments.[5] In any event, the majority of the arbitration rules provide that awards may not be published without the parties' agreement,[6] and even in the absence of such explicit rules, it is accepted that proceedings are conducted in a confidential way.[7]

[1] There has, indeed, been a tendency over the past couple of years to diminish or question the confidentiality of arbitral proceedings generally. See Blackaby *et al.*, *Redfern & Hunter on International Arbitration*, para. 2.152, and for an extensive discussion, Alberto Malatesta and Rinaldo Sali (eds.), *The Rise of Transparency in International Arbitration* (Huntington, NY: Juris, 2013).

[2] Blackaby *et al.*, *Redfern & Hunter on International Arbitration*, paras 2.145 ff.

[3] Moses, *The Principles and Practice of International Commercial Arbitration*, p. 162.

[4] Schreuer *et al.*, *The ICSID Convention*, p. 834.

[5] Stefano Azzali, 'Introduction: Balancing Confidentiality and Transparency', in Alberto Malatesta and Rinaldo Sali (eds.), *The Rise of Transparency in International Arbitration* (Huntington, NY: Juris, 2013), p. xxiii.

[6] See, for instance, Articles 32(5) and 25(4) of the UNCITRAL Arbitration Rules.

[7] Paolo Comoglio and Chiara Roncarolo, 'Presenting the Guidelines for the Publication of Arbitral Awards: Aiming to the Circulation of a Solid Arbitral Case Law', in Alberto Malatesta and Rinaldo Sali (eds.), *The Rise of Transparency in International Arbitration* (Huntington, NY: Juris, 2013), p. 2.

For legitimate reasons, investment treaty arbitration has departed from the commercial arbitration principles of privacy and confidentiality. This is evidenced by the modification in 2006 of the ICSID Arbitration Rules, and the adoption in July 2013 of specific rules on 'transparency in treaty-based investor–State arbitration' by UNCITRAL.[8] It should be noted that it is precisely and only for *treaty-based* investment arbitration that the new rules have been adopted, which again shows that the public international law (treaty) foundation of investment treaty arbitration influences the conduct of arbitration. The new UNCITRAL rules on transparency, however, apply only to treaties that provide for arbitration under the UNCITRAL Arbitration Rules, which are signed after the entry into force of the new rules, although the parties can agree to the application of the rules for arbitration initiated under a treaty concluded prior to the adoption of these rules.[9]

The principles of confidentiality and privacy should clearly be distinguished.[10] The first concept revolves around the secrecy of the proceedings, by which is meant the question of whether information about the proceedings and the final outcome thereof can, or should, be made available to the public (confidentiality versus transparency).[11] The second relates to whether the proceedings are purely private, or whether parties other than the disputing parties may have access to the proceedings (privacy versus non-party access). The first question will be addressed in section 5.2, the second in section 5.3. Before examining the practice and the procedural rules in respect of these questions, it seems important to first briefly determine why the debates on confidentiality

[8] UNCITRAL Press Releases, 'UNCITRAL adopts Transparency Rules for Treaty-based Investor–State Arbitration and Amends the UNCITRAL Arbitration Rules', UN Doc. UNIS/L/186, 12 July 2013. See also United Nations General Assembly, UNCITRAL, Report of Working Group II (Arbitration and Conciliation) on the Work of its 58th Session, New York, 4–8 February 2013, UN Doc. A/CN.9/765, 13 February 2013.

[9] United Nations General Assembly, UNCITRAL, Report of Working Group II (Arbitration and Conciliation), UN Doc. A/CN.9/765, para. 20.

[10] For a discussion of definition of the two concepts, see Jack J. Coe, 'Transparency in the Resolution of Investor–State Disputes: Adoption, Adaptation and NAFTA Leadership', *University of Kansas Law Review*, 54(4) (2005/6): 1339, 1342; and Rémy Gerbay, 'Confidentiality vs Transparency in International Arbitration: The English Perspective', *Transnational Dispute Management*, 9 (2012): 3.

[11] For a discussion of the terminology in this respect, see Alessandra Asteriti and Christian Tams, 'Transparency and Representation of the Public Interest in Investment Treaty Arbitration', in Stephan W. Schill (ed.), *International Investment Law and Comparative Public Law* (Oxford University Press, 2010), pp. 787–8.

versus transparency and privacy versus non-party access are of relevance in investment treaty arbitration.

## 5.1 Why investment treaty arbitration should be transparent and public

In order to better grasp the reasons behind the move away from a relatively private and confidential procedure in investment treaty arbitration, it is important to understand the reasons behind this development. There are several practical and theoretical reasons for increasing both the transparency and non-party access to investment treaty arbitration. More generally, these arguments are related to the public international law character of investment treaty arbitration, which instils the need for transparency and public participation in investment treaty arbitration. Indeed, that investment tribunals are engaged in assessing the exercise by states of their sovereign prerogatives inevitably causes tensions between the commercial and closed character of the proceeding and the public international law character of such disputes.

First, one should point to the fact that, considering that one of the main policy reasons behind the existence of investment protection and investment treaty arbitration is to enhance the confidence of foreign investors in the investment climate of the host state, any secrecy as to the outcome of certain decisions by the host state would in effect undermine that very purpose.[12] Similar arguments can, in fact, be made in respect of the foreign investor in order to maintain its reputation generally,[13] and to satisfy internal or external corporate social responsibility requirements.[14] In general, transparency and public access to the procedure signifies that neither party has anything to hide.[15]

Generally, international commercial arbitration does not as such form part of a specific legal regime which has a similar objective. The fact that investment protection treaties have an objective that is broader than the mere settlement of investment disputes, indeed, justifies a departure from the private and closed character of international

[12] Schreuer *et al.*, *The ICSID Convention*, p. 838. [13] *Ibid.*

[14] See, generally, Peter Muchlinski, 'Human Rights, Social Responsibility and the Regulation of International Business: The Development of International Standards by Intergovernmental Organisations', *Non-State Actors and International Law*, 3(1) (2003): 123, 123–52.

[15] Coe, 'Transparency in the Resolution of Investor–State Disputes', p. 1361.

commercial arbitration, which, largely, is concerned with the settlement of the dispute between two or more private parties.

Secondly, and most importantly, the public international law character of investment treaty arbitration differentiates it from international commercial arbitration as I explained in Part I. The fact that the questions put to an investment tribunal generally concern the respect by states of their international legal obligations, and that the acts complained of relate to issues of general public interest, such as environmental legislation, labour standards or other social and economic rights, militate in favour of both transparency and non-party access to the proceedings.[16] Because of the potential effects of this decision on the nationals of the state, there is a general public interest in the outcome of the procedure.[17] Moreover, since investment tribunals may award substantial damages to foreign investors for a state's exercise of its sovereign powers, secrecy in the procedure is indeed improper.[18] This feature of investment arbitration stands in sharp contrast to dispute settlement in international commercial arbitration.[19] In other words, international commercial arbitration is usually restricted to having a private function, that is, the resolution of the dispute between the parties, while investment treaty arbitration not only has a private function, but, at the same time, has a very important public aspect, which exceeds the private bilateral relations between the parties.[20]

Thirdly, because of the involvement of a state, public reporting responsibilities may be applicable in the sense that states and state organs may be bound by principles of open government expected of public authorities, and democratically elected governments may need to report to their electorate.[21] This has even been explicitly adopted by certain national courts in respect of international commercial arbitration is which a state organ or agency is involved, although not without controversy. For instance, as noted by Mason CJ in the *Esso Australia Resources Ltd and others* v. *The Honourable Sidney James* case in Australia,

16 Christina Knahr and August Reinisch, 'Transparency versus Confidentiality in International Investment Arbitration: The Biwater Gauff Compromise', *Law and Practice of International Courts and Tribunals*, 6(1) (2007): 97, 113.

17 See Meg Kinnear, Eloïse Obadia and Michael Gagain, 'The ICSID Approach to Publication of Information in Investor–State Arbitration', in Alberto Malatesta and Rinaldo Sali (eds.), *The Rise of Transparency in International Arbitration* (Huntington, NY: Juris, 2013), p. 108.

18 *Ibid.*

19 For a discussion, see Blackaby, 'Public Interest and Investment Treaty Arbitration', p. 1.

20 *Ibid.* 21 *Ibid.*, p. 4.

'there may be circumstances, in which third parties and the public have a legitimate interest in knowing what has transpired in an arbitration, which would give rise to a "public interest" exception'.[22] Similar case law exists in the United Kingdom.[23]

Fourthly, the legitimacy of the arbitral process as such is of high importance in investment treaty arbitration, as I have discussed in Chapter 3 on the role and function of the arbitrators. Public access to the outcome and conduct of the arbitral process is, therefore, important to inspire confidence in the arbitral mechanism.

Fifthly, public availability of decisions enhances access to the reasoning of arbitral tribunals, and thus enables host states and foreign investors to better be acquainted with the strengths and weaknesses of their case, despite the fact that there is no binding precedent in international law generally and in investment treaty arbitration.[24] Transparency, moreover, leads to predictability, which in turn may serve the interests of both states and investors.[25]

It has, however, been argued that a purely commercial arbitration dispute may directly impact the public as well, and that likewise states participate in commercial arbitration disputes without this necessarily having affected the privacy and confidentiality of international commercial arbitration.[26] As a consequence, it has been argued that instead of legitimizing the arbitral procedure through transparency, the power of arbitrators to adjudicate upon investment disputes should be replaced by another form of dispute settlement.[27] This argument is based on the idea that in international commercial arbitration, in the event of the presence of a public policy which would hinder the private settlement of the dispute through arbitration, the principle of

[22] High Court of Australia, *Esso Australia Resources Ltd and others* v. *The Honourable Sidney James Plowman and others*, FC No. 95/014, [1995] HCA 19, para. 38. See also Supreme Court of New South Wales, *Commonwealth of Australia* v. *Cockatoo Dockyard Pty Ltd*, [1995] 36 NSWLR 662.

[23] See, for example, Court of Appeal of England and Wales, *Ali Shipping Corp.* v. *Shipyard Trogir* [1999] 1 WLR 314. For discussion, see Gerbay, 'Confidentiality vs Transparency in International Arbitration'.

[24] See De Brabandere, 'Arbitral Decisions as a Source of International Investment Law', pp. 245–88.

[25] For a similar claim in respect of international commercial arbitration, see Azzali, 'Introduction: Balancing Confidentiality and Transparency', p. xiv.

[26] Ruth Teitelbaum, 'A Look at the Public Interest in Investment Arbitration: Is it Unique? What Should We do About It?', *Berkeley Journal of International Law Publicist*, 5 (2010): 54, 56.

[27] *Ibid.*, p. 58.

arbitrability establishes whether or not the case should be settled in court rather than through arbitration.[28] This argument, however, mistakenly applies the principle of arbitrability in international commercial arbitration to investment treaty arbitration. Indeed, investment treaty arbitration is more akin to interstate judicial dispute settlement, as was pointed out earlier, and the principle of arbitrability does not apply as it does in international commercial arbitration. As a consequence, the states' consent to settle investment disputes through arbitration, expressed in an investment treaty, cannot be limited in application of the principle of arbitrability. In addition, because arbitrability of certain disputes is essentially regulated by the domestic laws of states, a state would not be able to rely on its own national law to withdraw its consent to arbitrate.

## 5.2 Transparency versus confidentiality in investment treaty arbitration

The need to ensure transparency and public access to investment arbitration, as will be pointed out, is paramount, but here again such an adaptation of the arbitration rules may not denature the very concept of arbitral proceedings.[29] The choice of arbitration by states as the main method to settle investment disputes needs to be respected. The question is only how one can make the necessary adaptations to the current system in order to maintain its viability. Investment treaty arbitration has appropriately departed from the secrecy of the proceedings by making available to the public information about the proceedings and the final outcome thereof, and allowing hearings to be open to the public without impinging on the arbitral character of the proceedings. The rules in this respect are still very much subject to the consent of the parties, and have not yet fully been adopted in practice.

### *5.2.1 Public access to information and documents in investment treaty arbitration*

Article 48(5) of the ICSID Convention provides that 'the Centre shall not publish the award without the consent of the parties'. Rule 48(4) of the ICSID Arbitration Rules reiterates this provision, but adds that 'the Centre shall, however, promptly include in its publications excerpts of the legal

[28] *Ibid.* [29] Coe, 'Transparency in the Resolution of Investor–State Disputes', p. 1354.

reasoning of the Tribunal'.[30] This latter section was modified in 2006 in order to enhance the transparency of investment arbitration under the ICSID Convention.[31] Previously, Rule 48(4) provided that the ICSID *may* publish excerpts of the award,[32] which in turn was a modification of the initial rule which prohibited publication.[33] If parties have agreed to publish the award of the tribunal, the Secretary-General is mandated to take the necessary steps to arrange for the publication of the award or the minutes and other records of proceedings.[34] It should be added that the ICSID Secretary-General is equally under an obligation to register and make publicly available all requests for conciliation or arbitration brought under the ICSID Convention, which includes at least the names of the parties involved in the dispute and the date of registration of the case.[35] Although this practice now seems uncontroversial, it should be noted that in the 1960s, when this regulation was introduced, the ICSID was a pioneer, and this modification of the regulation was adopted especially because of the 'public nature of the institution'.[36] At the same time, several rules in the ICSID Convention or Arbitration Rules are intended to maintain a certain form of privacy in the conduct of the proceedings, but in essence this is necessary to safeguard the fairness and efficiency of the proceedings. Rule 6(2) of the ICSID Arbitration Rules, for instance, provides that an arbitrator should sign a declaration stating that he or she will 'keep confidential all information coming to my knowledge as a result of my participation in this proceeding, as well as the contents of any award made by the Tribunal'.

In practice, the vast majority of awards rendered under the ICSID Convention have been made available to the public, by the ICSID Secretariat and the consent of the parties, or by (one of) the parties to

[30] For a general overview of rules on transparency under the ICSID Convention, see Kinnear, Obadia and Gagain, 'The ICSID Approach to Publication of Information in Investor–State Arbitration', pp. 107 ff.

[31] ICSID Secretariat, 'Suggested Changes to the ICSID Rules and Regulations', Working Paper of the ICSID Secretariat, 12 May 2005, available at: http://icsid.worldbank.org/ICSID/FrontServlet?requestType=ICSIDPublicationsRH&actionVal=ViewAnnouncePDF&AnnouncementType=archive&AnnounceNo=14_1.pdf, accessed 20 September 2011.

[32] For a discussion, see Schreuer *et al.*, *The ICSID Convention*, p. 835.

[33] Kinnear, Obadia and Gagain, 'The ICSID Approach to Publication of Information in Investor–State Arbitration', p. 114.

[34] Regulations 22 and 23, ICSID Administrative and Financial Regulations. [35] *Ibid.*

[36] Kinnear, Obadia and Gagain, 'The ICSID Approach to Publication of Information in Investor–State Arbitration', p. 112; and Antonio R. Parra, *The History of the ICSID* (Oxford University Press, 2012), p. 104.

the dispute, or by subsequent litigation in domestic courts or tribunals. Decisions other that the final award are treated by the ICSID Secretariat in the same way as awards, and similarly have very often been made public either by the ICSID Secretariat with the consent of the parties, or by one of the parties.[37]

The rules and regulations regulating the publication of the award are addressed to the ICSID only, and do not therefore prohibit any of the parties from publicizing the award, unless, of course, both parties have agreed to keep the decision confidential or unless there is a confidentiality order issued by the tribunal.[38] I should add here that the intentions of the state parties to the investment treaty, or the ICSID Convention, are important, and trump the wishes of the parties to the dispute.[39] The tribunal is bound by the rules on transparency and confidentiality incorporated in the treaty granting it jurisdiction and by the procedural rules of the ICSID Convention. This implies that in cases where no such rules are provided in the investment treaty, the tribunal is free to determine the applicable procedural rules in consultation with the parties.

The public release of documents and information other than the decisions of tribunals is not regulated by the ICSID Convention or the ICSID Arbitration Rules. The question thus is whether, and to what extent, there is a general principle of confidentiality in investment treaty arbitration. The Tribunal in *Biwater Gauff* v. *Tanzania*, which gave a highly detailed analysis of the confidential character or not of a large number of types of document and information susceptible of being available in the course of arbitral proceedings, took the position that 'in the absence of any agreement between the parties on this issue, there is no provision imposing a general duty of confidentiality in ICSID arbitration, whether in the ICSID Convention, any of the applicable Rules or otherwise. Equally, however, there is no provision imposing a general rule of transparency or non-confidentiality in any of these sources.'[40] The same is true in respect of the UNCITRAL Arbitration Rules.[41] The drafting history of the ICSID also reveals that parties were not prohibited from publishing their pleadings, but that they may agree otherwise 'if they feel that publication may exacerbate the dispute'.[42]

37 Schreuer *et al.*, *The ICSID Convention*, p. 838. 38 *Ibid.*, p. 836.

39 For a discussion, see Roberts, 'Clash of Paradigms', p. 48.

40 *Biwater Gauff (Tanzania) Ltd* v. *United Republic of Tanzania*, ICSID Case No. ARB/05/22, Procedural Order No. 3, 29 September 2006, para. 121.

41 *Ibid.*, para. 132. 42 For a discussion, see *ibid.*, para. 125.

This had already been confirmed by the Tribunal in *Amco* v. *Indonesia* in 1983.[43]

Similar conclusions have been reached by tribunals operating under the ICSID Additional Facility Rules. The Tribunal in *Metalclad* v. *Mexico*, for instance, noted that:

> there remains nonetheless a question as to whether there exists any general principle of confidentiality that would operate to prohibit public discussion of the arbitration proceedings by either party. Neither the NAFTA nor the ICSID (Additional Facility) Rules contain any express restriction on the freedom of the parties in this respect. Though it is frequently said that one of the reasons for recourse to arbitration is to avoid publicity, unless the agreement between the parties incorporates such a limitation, each of them is still free to speak publicly of the arbitration. It may be observed that no such limitation is written into such major arbitral texts as the UNCITRAL Rules or the draft Articles on Arbitration adopted by the International Law Commission.[44]

The *Biwater Gauff* Tribunal also noted that the change in the ICSID Arbitration Rules in 2006, 'clearly reflect an overall trend in this field towards transparency',[45] and concluded that:

> subject to the restrictions on disclosure of specific documents ... neither party should be prevented from engaging in general discussion about the case in public, provided that any such public discussion is restricted to what is necessary (for example, pursuant to the Republic's duty to provide the public with information concerning governmental and public affairs), and is not used as an instrument to further antagonise the parties, exacerbate their differences, unduly pressure one of them, or render the resolution of the dispute potentially more difficult.[46]

This statement is in line with the Tribunal's finding in *Metalclad*, in which it argued that 'it would be of advantage to the orderly unfolding

[43] *Amco Asia Corporation and others* v. *Republic of Indonesia*, ICSID Case No. ARB/81/1, Decision on Request for Provisional Measures, 9 December 1983, *ICSID Reports*, 1993, para. 4. In that case, the respondent had requested the Tribunal to order the claimant not to unilaterally release information about the case, which was rejected by the Tribunal. See also, more recently, *Abaclat and others (case formerly known as Giovanna a Beccara and others)* v. *The Argentine Republic*, ICSID Case No. ARB/07/5, Procedural Order No. 3 (Confidentiality Order), 27 January 2010.

[44] *Metalclad Corp.* v. *The United Mexican States*, ICSID Case No. ARB(AF)/97/1, Decision on a Request by the Respondent for an Order Prohibiting the Claimant from Revealing Information, 27 October 1997, paras 9–10.

[45] *Biwater Gauff* v. *Tanzania*, ICSID Case No. ARB/05/22, Procedural Order No. 3, para. 122.

[46] *Ibid.*, para. 149.

of the arbitral process and conducive to the maintenance of working relations between the Parties if during the proceedings they were both to limit public discussion of the case to a minimum, subject only to any externally imposed obligation of disclosure by which either of them may be legally bound'.[47]

In respect of minutes and records of hearings, pleadings and memorials, and the correspondence in respect of the proceedings, tribunals seem to operate more carefully, and show a clear tendency to prohibit the publication of these in the absence of the consent of the parties. This is essentiality the result of Regulation 22 of the ICSID Administrative and Financial Regulations, which provides that the ICSID Secretary-General may only publish the minutes and other records of proceedings if both parties so consent, contrary to the question of publicly discussing the case, which is not regulated by the ICSID Convention. In *Biwater Gauff*, the Tribunal, while being open to discussions about the case in public, prohibited the parties from disclosing the minutes or record of the hearings, the documents produced in the arbitral proceedings by the opposing party, the pleadings or memorials, and the correspondence between the parties and/or the Arbitral Tribunal.[48] In a recent case, *Telefónica* v. *Mexico*, an ICSID Additional Facility Tribunal, while noting that there is neither a principle of confidentiality nor a principle of transparency, adopted the same principles.[49] This decision was severely criticized by one of the arbitrators in a Dissenting Opinion, since the Tribunal, in view of the competing claims of the claimant and the respondent, unjustifiably upheld a 'presumption of confidentiality'.[50]

Outside the formal context of the ICSID, awards and decisions of investment tribunals have not normally been published.[51] The UNCITRAL

[47] *Metalclad* v. *Mexico*, ICSID Case No. ARB(AF)/97/1, Decision on a Request by the Respondent, paras 9–10.

[48] *Biwater Gauff* v. *Tanzania*, Procedural Order No. 3, para. 42. See also *Abaclat* v. *Argentina*, ICSID Case No. ARB/07/5, Procedural Order No. 3 (Confidentiality Order), 27 January 2010, paras 100 ff.

[49] *Telefónica SA* v. *The United Mexican States*, ICSID Case No. ARB(AF)/12/4, Procedural Order No. 1, 8 July 2013.

[50] *Telefónica SA* v. *The United Mexican States*, ICSID Case No. ARB(AF)/12/4, Dissent to Procedural Order No. 1, 8 July 2013.

[51] One way in which awards have, however, been made public is through subsequent litigation in domestic courts or tribunals, which, as will be pointed out later, is more probable than in the event of ICSID arbitration because of the presence of automatic enforcement mechanisms in the ICSID Convention, and the absence of review by domestic courts and tribunals. See, for example, *Adria Beteiligungs GmbH* v. *The Republic of Croatia*, UNCITRAL, Award, 21 June 2010, the contents of which were partly made

Arbitration Rules generally provide that hearings are to be held *in camera* and that awards are to be made public only with the consent of both parties. The 2013 UNCITRAL Rules on Transparency, however, show a clear departure from the principle of confidentiality as far as investment treaty arbitration is concerned. Article 2, for instance, provides that the parties to the dispute should communicate to the 'repository' the notice of arbitration, which will then make public the identities of the parties, the economic sector in which the dispute has arisen and the treaty on which the claim is based.[52] The main official documents of the arbitral proceedings are also to be made available to the public.[53]

Before the adoption of these rules, which have not yet been used in practice, several tribunals operating under the UNICTRAL Arbitration Rules in proceedings in respect of the NAFTA have also accepted that investment treaty arbitration is subject to different rules, compared with international commercial arbitration:

> The Tribunal considers that, whatever may be the position in private consensual arbitrations between commercial parties, it has not been established that any general principle of confidentiality exists in an arbitration such as that currently before this tribunal. The main argument in favour of confidentiality is founded on a supposed implied term in the arbitration agreement. The present arbitration is taking place pursuant to a provision in an international treaty, not pursuant to an arbitration agreement between disputing parties.[54]

It is true that the NAFTA was one of the first treaties to take on the need for increased transparency. As is the case with other investment treaties, the NAFTA contains no general provision providing for confidentiality of arbitration under its Chapter Eleven. On the other hand, certain provisions of the NAFTA are explicitly aimed at ensuring

public through excerpts quoted in the Ruling on the Application to Set-Aside the Award by the Hague Court, 15 August 2012, available at: www.italaw.com/sites/default/files/case-documents/italaw1221.pdf.

52 United Nations General Assembly, United Nations Commission on International Trade Law, Settlement of Commercial Disputes: Preparation of a Legal Standard on Transparency in Treaty-based Investor–State Arbitration, Note by the Secretariat, UN Doc. A/CN.9/WG.II/WP.17, 30 November 2012, para. 22, and UN General Assembly, UNCITRAL, Report of Working Group II UN Doc. A/CN.9/765, para. 90.

53 UNCITRAL, UN Doc. A/CN.9/WG.II/WP.17, para. 25, and UNCITRAL, UN Doc. A/CN.9/765, para. 91.

54 *S.D. Myers, Inc.* v. *Government of Canada*, UNCITRAL, Procedural Order No. 16 (concerning confidentiality in materials produced in the arbitration), 13 May 2000, para. 8. The Tribunal, however, subsequently limited the possibility of the parties making public certain documents to the pleadings, procedural orders and the award (para. 16).

transparency, in particular, through the access of other NAFTA state parties to the proceedings, which I will discuss in the next section, and on the publication of awards.[55] Moreover, in its 'Notes of Interpretation of Certain Chapter Eleven Provisions',[56] the NAFTA Free Trade Commission considered that:

> Nothing in the NAFTA imposes a general duty of confidentiality on the disputing parties to a Chapter Eleven arbitration, and, subject to the application of Article 1137(4), nothing in the NAFTA precludes the Parties from providing public access to documents submitted to, or issued by, a Chapter Eleven tribunal.
>
> ... In accordance with Article 1120(2), the NAFTA Parties agree that nothing in the relevant arbitral rules imposes a general duty of confidentiality or precludes the Parties from providing public access to documents submitted to, or issued by, Chapter Eleven tribunals, apart from the limited specific exceptions set forth expressly in those rules.
>
> ... Each Party agrees to make available to the public in a timely manner all documents submitted to, or issued by, a Chapter Eleven tribunal, subject to redaction of:
>
> 1. confidential business information;
> 2. information which is privileged or otherwise protected from disclosure under the Party's domestic law; and
> 3. information which the Party must withhold pursuant to the relevant arbitral rules, as applied.[57]

Following the NAFTA example, which also paved the way for the 2006 remodelling of certain ICSID Arbitration Rules, the quest for more transparency in investment treaty arbitration has also been reflected in certain recent BITs. The 2012 US Model BIT, for instance, provides that the respondent shall, after receiving the notice of intent, the notice of arbitration, pleadings, memorials and briefs submitted to the tribunal by a disputing party, and any written non-disputing party submissions, minutes or transcripts of hearings of the tribunal, and orders, awards, and decisions of the tribunal, 'promptly transmit them to the non-disputing Party and make them available to the public'.[58] Of course, this obligation is subject to several exceptions, such as in

[55] Article 1137(4) of the NAFTA, in which the United States and Canada agreed in advance to publicize awards of arbitral tribunals operating under Chapter Eleven, Mexico referring instead to the applicable arbitration rules.

[56] NAFTA Free Trade Commission, Notes of Interpretation of Certain Chapter 11 Provisions, 31 July 2001, available at: www.international.gc.ca/trade-agreements-accords-commerciaux/disp-diff/NAFTA-Interpr.aspx?lang=en&view=d, accessed 6 February 2013.

[57] Section A. [58] Article 29(1), 2012 US Model BIT.

relation to 'protected information'.[59] Similarly, the Canadian Model FIPA provides that 'all documents submitted to, or issued by, the Tribunal shall be publicly available, unless the disputing parties otherwise agree, subject to the deletion of confidential information' and that 'any Tribunal award under this Section shall be publicly available, subject to the deletion of confidential information'.[60]

## 5.3 Non-disputing party access to investment treaty arbitration

The question of non-disputing party access to investment treaty arbitration is very much linked to the question of transparency generally of those proceedings, but in actual fact relates more to the question of privacy of proceedings than transparency. In addition, because of the specific rules that have been designed, in the ICSID Arbitration Rules and in several investment agreements, in respect of submissions by non-disputing parties, the topic deserves special consideration. Because of the increasing use by non-disputing parties of the possibilities provided for under these instruments to gain access to investment treaty arbitration proceedings, it is likely that this particular mechanism in effect constitutes one of the most adequate tools to ensure public access to the proceedings generally and, for that reason, may generate positive outcomes.[61] In general, the increased acceptance in international dispute settlement of non-governmental organization (NGO) participation as *amici curiae* has been hailed as 'permitt[ing] the emergence in international law of the idea of civil society as an important participant in the resolution of investment disputes',[62] and as an enhancement of transparency in international dispute settlement.[63]

[59] Article 29(2) and (4), 2012 US Model BIT.

[60] Article 39(3) and (4), Canadian Model FIPA.

[61] However, others have pointed out that this form of participation alone cannot improve the transparency of investment arbitration, since this does not imply the right to receive pleadings or to attend hearings, nor would such participation enhance the democratic legitimacy of investment arbitration since NGOs are *of themselves* non-democratic in the sense that they are not accountable to their members or to the general public (Charles H. Brower II, 'Structure, Legitimacy, and NAFTA's Investment Chapter', *Vanderbilt Journal of Transnational Law*, 36(1) (2003): 37, 72–3).

[62] Francisco Francioni, 'Access to Justice, Denial of Justice and International Investment Law', *European Journal of International Law*, 20(3) (2009): 729, 742.

[63] Laurence Boisson de Chazournes, 'Transparency and *Amicus Curiae* Briefs', *Journal of World Investment and Trade*, 5(2) (2004): 333.

I will first discuss public access to the hearings, before analysing the concept and practice of non-disputing party submissions in international law.

### 5.3.1 *Public access to the hearings*

Next to the increase in transparency in respect of access to documents and information on the proceedings, recent years have seen an increase in public hearings of investment treaty arbitration, at least in respect of those proceedings conducted under the ICSID Convention. Public access to hearings is very close to the notion of transparency, since by allowing third parties to attend the hearings, public information about the dispute, as well as the arguments of the parties, are made public. Public access does not mean, however, that access is granted to all hearings – restrictions may operate to safeguard confidential and other protected information.

As was the case in respect of the transparency of the proceedings, NAFTA has proved to be a precursor in relation to public access to hearings. Already in 2002, in the *UPS* v. *Canada* case, the Tribunal had authorized public hearings based on the consent of the parties.[64] Public hearings were also authorized in the merits phase, 'except for those parts of the hearing which involve confidential information'.[65] Public hearings also took place in the subsequent *Methanex* v. *United States* and *Canfor* v. *United States* cases in 2004.[66]

ICSID Arbitration Rule 32(2), modified in 2006, provides that:

> unless either party objects, the Tribunal, after consultation with the Secretary-General, may allow other persons, besides the parties, their agents, counsel and

[64] ICSID News Release, *United Parcel Service of America, Inc.* v. *Government of Canada*, NAFTA/UNCITRAL Arbitration Rules Proceeding, 28 May 2001, available at: https://icsid.worldbank.org/ICSID/FrontServlet?requestType=CasesRH&actionVal=OpenPage&PageType=AnnouncementsFrame&FromPage=NewsReleases&pageName=Archive_%20Announcement6, accessed 11 February 2013.

[65] ICSID News Release, *United Parcel Service of America, Inc.* v. *Government of Canada*, NAFTA/UNCITRAL Arbitration Rules Proceeding, 7 December 2005, available at: https://icsid.worldbank.org/ICSID/FrontServlet?requestType=CasesRH&actionVal=OpenPage&PageType=AnnouncementsFrame&FromPage=NewsReleases&pageName=Archive_%20Announcement23, accessed 11 February 2013.

[66] *Methanex Corp.* v. *United States of America*, UNCITRAL, Final Award of the Tribunal on Jurisdiction and Merits, 3 August 2005, para. 8. The transcripts of the hearings in *Canfor* v. *United States of America*, which was consolidated with two other cases in 2005 (*Tembec, Inc. and others* v. *United States of America* and *Terminal Forest Products Ltd* v. *United States of America*) are also available on the website of the US Department of State at: www.state.gov/s/l/c7424.htm, accessed 11 February 2013.

advocates, witnesses and experts during their testimony, and officers of the Tribunal, to attend or observe all or part of the hearings, subject to appropriate logistical arrangements. The Tribunal shall for such cases establish procedures for the protection of proprietary or privileged information.[67]

In effect, this provision reversed the private character of the proceedings by requiring one of the parties to object to the opening of the oral hearings to the public.[68] In other words, compared with, for instance, the publication of the awards, which is prohibited unless the parties agree to publication, the principle here is that an ICSID tribunal may allow the public to attend the hearings, after consultation with the ICSID Secretary-General, unless one of the parties objects. The revised version, while reversing the logic of the private character of hearings, does nevertheless authorize any of the parties to veto public access to the hearings. The result is thus essentially the same, but the rationale is fundamentally different.

Article 28(3) of the UNCITRAL Arbitration Rules contains the principle of *in camera* hearings, unless the parties otherwise agree, as is the case in general commercial arbitration. The 2013 UNCITRAL Rules on Transparency in Treaty-based Investment Arbitration, however, now provide that hearings are open to the public unless there is a need to protect confidential information or the integrity of the process.[69]

Before the introduction of this rule in the general revision of the ICSID Arbitration Rules in 2006, discussed above, tribunals generally refused requests for attendance at the hearings by non-disputing parties in the absence of the consent of both parties, which was one of the explicit requirements in the old version of Article 32(2) of the ICSID Arbitration Rules.[70] In practice, hearings still are most often held *in camera*, and are not open to the public, despite the modification of

[67] The Rule was formerly drafted as follows: 'The tribunal shall decide, with the consent of the parties, which other persons besides the parties, their agents, counsel and advocates, witnesses and experts during their testimony, and officers of the Tribunal may attend the hearings.'

[68] See, however, Schreuer *et al.*, *The ICSID Convention*, p. 699, para. 102. The authors claim that despite this new provision, the rule of 'privacy' essentially remains.

[69] UNCITRAL, UN Doc. A/CN.9/WG.II/WP.17, para. 44, and UNCITRAL, UN Doc. A/CN.9/765, para. 52.

[70] See, for instance, *Suez, Sociedad General de Aguas de Barcelona SA and Vivendi Universal SA* v. *The Argentine Republic*, ICSID Case No. ARB/03/19, Order in Response to a Petition for Participation as *Amicus Curiae*, 19 May 2005, para. 6, arguing that 'Although the Tribunal, as the Petition asserts, does have certain inherent powers with respect to arbitral procedure, it has no authority to exercise such power in opposition to a clear directive in the Arbitration Rules, which both Claimants and Respondent have agreed

Rule 32(2) in 2006, because one of the parties objects to the presence of third parties at the hearings, even when the dispute presents a clear public interest.[71] Only on a few occasions have the parties not opposed public access to the hearings, very often in conjunction with the acceptance of non-disputing party submissions.[72] I should point out that investment treaties may provide for open hearings, in which case the parties to the dispute are not in a position to refuse public participation in the hearings since the procedure to be applied by the tribunal is determined not only by the applicable rules of the arbitration institute, but also those defined by the state when expressing consent to arbitration in an investment treaty. The 2012 US Model BIT referred to above has also adopted the principle of 'open hearings', provided that the tribunal makes appropriate arrangements to safeguard protected information from disclosure,[73] as does the Canadian Model FIPA.[74]

### *5.3.2 Non-disputing party submissions in investment treaty arbitration*

Non-disputing party submissions in international proceedings imply that non-disputing parties are granted the right to submit a written statement during the proceedings, but not the right of becoming a party to the dispute.[75] The role played by non-disputing parties, in particular NGOs, in international dispute settlement generally has been visible particularly in the areas of international economic law and investment law since their right to formally submit *amicus curiae* briefs has been explicitly accepted under the ICSID Arbitration Rules, and recently in the UNCITRAL Rules on Transparency in Treaty-based Investor–State Arbitration. However, one should not overlook that this practice is also widespread in other international proceedings,[76] such as

will govern the procedure in this case.' See also *Aguas del Tunari SA* v. *Bolivia*, ICSID Case No. ARB/02/3, para. 17.

[71] See, for instance, *Biwater Gauff (Tanzania) Ltd* v. *United Republic of Tanzania*, ICSID Case No. ARB/05/22, Procedural Order No. 5, 2 February 2007, para. 71 and *Philip Morris Asia Ltd* v. *The Commonwealth of Australia*, UNCITRAL, PCA Case No. 2012-12, Procedural Order No. 5, Regarding Confidentiality, 30 November 2012.

[72] This has, for instance, been the case in *Commerce Group Corp. and San Sebastian Gold Mines, Inc.* v. *The Republic of El Salvador*, ICSID Case No. ARB/09/17, Award, 14 March 2011, and *Pac Rim Cayman LLC* v. *Republic of El Salvador*, ICSID Case No. ARB/09/12, 18 May 2011.

[73] Article 29(2), US Model BIT. [74] Article 38(1), 2007 Canada Model BIT.

[75] For a discussion of the concept, see Philippe Sands and Ruth Mackenzie, 'International Courts and Tribunals, *Amicus Curiae*', in Rüdiger Wolfrüm (ed.), *Max Planck Encyclopedia of Public International Law* (Oxford University Press, 2012), vol. II, pp. 519–26.

[76] For an overview, see Eric De Brabandere, 'NGOs and the "Public Interest": The Legality and Rationale of *Amicus Curiae* Interventions in International Economic and Investment Disputes', *Chicago Journal of International Law*, 12(1) (2011): 85.

the ECtHR,[77] the Inter-American Court of Human Rights[78] and international criminal tribunals and courts.[79]

## *Amicus curiae* in general international dispute settlement

Statutes and regulations often contain explicit rules on the procedure of third party intervention which enable a third party to participate directly in the proceedings – thus in a different capacity than as *amicus curiae* – if the third party has a legal interest that may be affected by the decision in the case as is the case at the ICJ.[80] Such an authorization is usually also accepted when the parties consent to voluntary intervention, which is included in several arbitration rules in international commercial arbitration.[81]

In investment treaty arbitration, certain rules exist in relation to the capacity of state parties to the investment agreement that are not party to the dispute to make submissions to the tribunal. In the NAFTA, for instance, parties to the NAFTA have the right 'on written notice to the disputing parties, [to] make submissions to a Tribunal on a question of interpretation of this Agreement'.[82] The 2012 US Model BIT similarly provides that 'the non-disputing Party may make oral and written submissions to the tribunal regarding the interpretation of this Treaty'.[83]

[77] Article 36(2) of the ECHR: 'The President of the Court may, in the interest of the proper administration of justice, invite any High Contracting Party which is not a party to the proceedings or any person concerned who is not the applicant to submit written comments or take part in hearings', Convention for the Protection of Human Rights and Fundamental Freedoms, 4 November 1950, 213 UNTS 222 (hereafter 'European Convention on Human Rights'.

[78] See Jo M. Pasqualucci, *The Practice and Procedure of the Inter-American Court of Human Rights* (Cambridge University Press, 2003), p. 214.

[79] See Sarah J. Williams and Hannah Woolaver, 'The Role of the *Amicus Curiae* before International Criminal Tribunals', *International Criminal Law Review*, 6(2) (2006): 151, 151–89.

[80] See, for example, Article 62 of the ICJ Statute.

[81] See, for instance, Article 22(1)(h) of the LCIA Arbitration Rules: 'Unless otherwise agreed by the parties in writing, the Arbitral Tribunal shall have the power . . . to allow, only upon the application of a party, one or more third persons to be joined in the arbitration as a party provided any such third person and the applicant party have consented thereto in writing, and thereafter to make a single final award, or separate awards, in respect of all parties so implicated in the arbitration.' Such power is, however, not foreseen in other arbitration rules, such as the ICC Arbitration Rules. For a discussion, see Thomas Bevilacqua, 'Voluntary Intervention and other Participation of Third Parties in Ongoing International Arbitrations: A Survey of the Current State of Play', *World Arbitration & Mediation Review*, 1(4) (2007): 507.

[82] Article 1128 of the NAFTA.

[83] Article 28(2), US Model BIT. See also Article 39, Canada Model FIPA.

This practice has now been taken over in the 2013 UNCITRAL Rules on Transparency.[84] These procedures, however, do not apply to the participation of non-disputing parties, outside the parties to the investment agreement, which is fundamentally different.

Voluntary submissions by non-disputing parties that are not parties to the investment treaty were, before the revision of the ICSID Arbitration Rules in 2006, not regulated. When investment tribunals were first confronted with voluntary submissions by NGOs of *amicus curiae* briefs, the tribunals that had to assess the legality and acceptability of such interventions were faced with the absence of any specific regulation or rule in that respect both in international law generally and in their own statute or rules of procedure. They have thus quite logically turned to the practice developed in other fields of international law. The question of *amicus curiae* briefs has first and foremost been discussed in the context of international trade law. This development is particularly remarkable since it gives NGOs access to international dispute settlement to represent a non-state interest, although the essence of the dispute relates purely to international legal obligations of states. The first WTO dispute in which there was NGO participation in proceedings through the submission of briefs is the *Shrimp–Turtles* dispute. The case concerned the attempt by the United States to prevent the importation of shrimp caught with the use of nets that do not have turtle-excluder devices. The case was first brought before a WTO Special Panel. Three groups of NGOs submitted briefs to the Panel in order to influence its decision.[85] The Panel rejected the unsolicited information provided by the three NGOs on legal grounds, *as a matter of principle*, because the WTO DSU allows only certain parties to intervene in WTO proceedings.[86] The Panel Report was appealed to the WTO Appellate Body, who rejected the *a contrario* interpretation given by the Panel.[87] The Appellate Body confirmed that every state has the right to attach *amicus curiae* briefs to its own submissions, and distinguished, as the Panel did, between these and others that are not part of the official submission of a state.[88] In the first case, the panel is

[84] See UNCITRAL, UN Doc. A/CN.9/765.

[85] *United States – Import Prohibition of Certain Shrimp and Shrimp Products*, Report of the Panel, Doc. No. WT/DS58/R, 15 May 1998.

[86] *Ibid.*, para. 3.129. [87] *Ibid.*, paras 102–110.

[88] *Ibid.*, para. 89: 'We consider that the attaching of a brief or other material to the submission of either appellant or appellee, no matter how or where such material may have originated, renders that material at least prima facie an integral part of that participant's submission.' See also para. 110.

obliged to take into consideration the submission since it is part of the official submission of the state. As far as voluntary submissions by NGOs are concerned, the Appellate Body argued that there is no rule in the WTO DSU that prohibits panels from accepting information voluntarily submitted to it, since 'authority to seek information is not properly equated with a prohibition on accepting information which has been submitted without having been requested'.[89]

The practice set in motion by the WTO Appellate Body has influenced similar developments in other related fields of international law. In particular, international investment tribunals have, invoking these decisions, accepted *amicus curiae* submissions by NGOs, although international arbitration traditionally is closed to participation by non-disputing parties.

## Non-disputing party submissions in investment treaty arbitration

The participation of NGOs in investment treaty arbitration has developed along the lines of their involvement in the WTO system. The ICSID Arbitration Rules did not originally contain any reference to non-disputing party submissions. The UNCITRAL Arbitration Rules likewise do not explicitly authorize or prohibit an arbitral tribunal from accepting an *amicus curiae* brief, but convey to the tribunal a wide discretion in terms of procedural rules and principles, limited only by contrary party agreement and the principle of equality.[90] The Iran–US Claims Tribunal, which functions under an amended version of the UNCITRAL Arbitration Rules, had adopted an interpretative note to Article 15 of the Rules in which it authorized the submission of *amicus curiae* briefs by parties other than Iran or the United States only 'under special

[89] *Ibid.*, para. 108. As far as the submission of *amicus curiae* briefs to the Appellate Body itself is concerned, the Appellate Body decided in a subsequent case that it had, relatively similarly to the panels, the authority to accept and consider *amicus curiae* briefs if it finds it 'pertinent and useful to do so' (*United States – Imposition of Countervailing Duties on Certain Hot-Rolled Lead and Bismuth Carbon Steel Products Originating in the United Kingdom*, Report of the Appellate Body, Doc. No. WT/DS138/AB/R, 10 May 2000, para. 42). See also *European Communities – Measures Affecting Asbestos and Asbestos-Containing Products*, Report of the Appellate Body, Doc. No. WT/DS135/AB/R, 12 March 2001, para. 52.

[90] Article 15.1: 'Subject to these Rules, the arbitral tribunal may conduct the arbitration in such manner as it considers appropriate, provided that the parties are treated with equality and that at any stage of the proceedings each party is given a full opportunity of presenting his case.'

circumstances'.[91] Although non-party submissions in proceedings before the Iran–US Claims Tribunal have been relatively limited,[92] the principled acceptance by the Tribunal of the authority to receive and consider *amicus curiae* submissions in accordance with the UNCITRAL Arbitration Rules has been used in subsequent investment arbitrations which similarly had to decide on the acceptability of *amicus curiae* briefs.

Interestingly, the acceptance of *amicus curiae* briefs was first accepted in investment treaty arbitration conducted under the UNCITRAL Rules. This development unambiguously shows, as I have highlighted in the Introduction, that it is the public international law character of investment treaty arbitration that has influenced the procedure, a development which clearly is not limited to ICSID arbitration only.

In 2001, in the ground-breaking *Methanex* v. *United States* decision,[93] a NAFTA Chapter Eleven Arbitral Tribunal, operating under the UNCITRAL Arbitration Rules, concluded that it had the power to accept *amicus curiae* briefs, by referring to the case law of the Iran–US Claims Tribunal and the cases before the WTO mentioned above. The Tribunal considered that neither the UNCITRAL Arbitration Rules nor Chapter Eleven of the NAFTA Agreement contained any explicit provision in respect of *amicus curiae* briefs.[94] The Tribunal noted that Article 15 of the UNCITRAL Arbitration Rules gives the Tribunal wide discretion in terms of procedural rules.[95] The *Methanex* Tribunal also rightly pointed out that accepting *amicus curiae* briefs from a party other than a disputing party is not the equivalent of adding that entity as a party to the arbitration.[96] It is important to point out that the Tribunal in *Methanex* invoked the need for greater transparency and called for the involvement in the case of

91 Iran-United States Claims Tribunal, Tribunal Rules of Procedure, Notes to Article 15, para. 5, 3 May 1983, available at: www.iusct.org/tribunal-rules.pdf, accessed 14 April 2010.

92 Jack J. Coe, 'The Tribunal's Transparency Features: Some Observations', in Christopher R. Drahozal and Christopher S. Gibson (eds.), *The Iran–U.S. Claims Tribunal at 25: The Cases Everyone Needs to Know for Investor–State and International Arbitration* (Oxford University Press 2007), p. 132.

93 *Methanex Corp.* v. *United States of America*, UNCITRAL, Decision of the Tribunal on Petitions from Third Persons to Intervene as *Amici Curiae*, 15 January 2001, para. 32.

94 *Ibid.*, para. 47. See, generally, Patrick Dumberry, 'The Admissibility of *Amicus Curiae* Briefs by NGOs in Investor-States Arbitration: The Precedent Set by the Methanex Case in the Context of NAFTA Chapter 11 Proceedings', *Non-State Actors and International Law*, 1(3) (2001): 201.

95 *Methanex* v. *United States*, UNCITRAL, Decision of the Tribunal on Petitions from Third Persons to Intervene as *Amici Curiae*, paras 29–32.

96 *Ibid.*, para. 30.

issues relating to the 'public interest' in support of the authority for the tribunals to receive NGO submissions.[97] The Tribunal in that case also clearly distinguished between the general capacity of a tribunal to accept *amicus curiae* briefs by NGOs, which is founded on the legal arguments mentioned above, and the appropriateness of the effective acceptance of such briefs in *a particular* case, which I will address in the next section.

Since *Methanex*, the NAFTA Free Trade Commission has issued a statement confirming that no provision in NAFTA limits the discretionary authority or arbitral tribunals to accept submissions of non-disputing parties.[98] The Statement also recommended that Chapter Eleven Tribunals adopt the outlined procedure that, *inter alia*, establishes certain requirements which will be discussed in the next section. The principled decision in *Methanex* was followed by the acceptance of *amicus curiae* briefs in several subsequent NAFTA Chapter Eleven arbitrations, including *UPS* v. *Canada*[99] and *Glamis* v. *United States*.[100] The Tribunal in *Glamis* explicitly grounded the authority to receive and consider briefs in the aforementioned 'Statement of the Free Trade Commission on non-disputing party participation',[101] without assessing the conformity of such submission with the UNCITRAL Arbitration Rules.[102]

As far as ICSID arbitration is concerned, although an early tribunal decision refused such submissions based on a rather restrictive interpretation of the consensual nature of investment arbitration,[103] several ICSID tribunals in subsequent cases have confirmed the authority to receive *amicus curiae* briefs. In *Suez/Vivendi* v. *Argentina*, an ICSID Tribunal for the first time accepted the authority to receive *amicus curiae* briefs.[104] The authority of the Panel to receive and consider *amicus curiae* briefs was founded on Article 44 of the ICSID Convention, which grants the arbitral tribunal the power to decide on procedural questions that are

[97] *Ibid.*

[98] Statement of the Free Trade Commission on Non-Disputing Party Participation, para. A.1, available at: www.international.gc.ca/trade-agreements-accords-commerciaux/assets/pdfs/Nondisputing-en.pdf, accessed 7 April 2010.

[99] *United Parcel Service of America Inc. (UPS)* v. *Canada*, UNCITRAL, Decision of the Tribunal on Petitions for Intervention and Participation as *Amici Curiae*, 17 October 2001.

[100] *Glamis Gold Ltd* v. *United States of America*, UNCITRAL, Decision on Application and Submission by Quechan Indian Nation, 16 September 2005.

[101] *Ibid.*, para. 10. [102] *Ibid.*, para. 8.

[103] *Aguas del Tunari SA* v. *Bolivia*, ICSID Case No. ARB/02/3, Appendix III, text of 29 January 2003, letter from the Tribunal to Earthjustice, counsel for petitioners.

[104] *Suez/Vivendi* v. *Argentina*, ICSID Case No. ARB/03/19, Order in Response to a Petition for Participation as *Amicus Curiae*.

not regulated by the rules of the ICSID Convention,[105] and explicitly referred to the *Methanex* Tribunal's interpretation of Article 15 of the UNCITRAL Rules. The *Suez/Vivendi* Tribunal also re-emphasized that participation as *amicus curiae* is not the equivalent of participation as a party to the arbitration, and reiterated that the function of *amicus curiae* is to provide assistance to a court or tribunal by offering expertise and arguments that the parties might not provide.[106]

The decision of the Tribunal in *Suez/Vivendi* has been followed by a formal acceptance of the authority of investment tribunals to receive *amicus curiae* briefs in both the ICSID Rules of Arbitration and several BITs. As a result of this case, the ICSID Rules of Arbitration were amended in 2006 to explicitly include, under certain conditions, the capacity of a tribunal to allow a non-disputing party which has a significant interest in the case to file a written submission:

> (2) After consulting both parties, the Tribunal may allow a person or entity that is not a party to the dispute (in this Rule called the 'non-disputing party') to file a written submission with the Tribunal regarding a matter within the scope of the dispute. In determining whether to allow such a filing, the Tribunal shall consider, among other things, the extent to which:
> 1. the non-disputing party submission would assist the Tribunal in the determination of a factual or legal issue related to the proceeding by bringing a perspective, particular knowledge or insight that is different from that of the disputing parties;
> 2. the non-disputing party submission would address a matter within the scope of the dispute;
> 3. the non-disputing party has a significant interest in the proceeding.
>
> The Tribunal shall ensure that the non-disputing party submission does not disrupt the proceeding or unduly burden or unfairly prejudice either party, and that both parties are given an opportunity to present their observations on the non-disputing party submission.[107]

The amended rules have had an immediate impact on NGO participation in investment arbitration. In *Biwater Gauff* v. *Tanzania*, for example, the parties accepted the application of this new rule to the dispute, although the dispute had been initiated before the new ICSID Rules entered into force.[108]

The 2013 UNCITRAL rules on transparency in treaty-based investment arbitration also now provide that 'third persons' may make submissions

[105] *Ibid.*, para. 16. [106] *Ibid.*, para. 13.
[107] Article 37(2) of the ICSID Arbitration Rules.
[108] *Biwater Gauff* v. *Tanzania*, Procedural Order No. 5, para. 16.

in investment treaty arbitration, provided that they have a 'significant interest in the proceedings' and that the submission would 'assist the arbitral tribunal in the determination of a factual or legal issue related to the arbitral proceedings by bringing a perspective, particular knowledge or insight that is different from that of the disputing parties'.[109]

These developments have prompted certain states to also include the possibility for NGOs to submit *amicus curiae* briefs, and the limitations thereto, in their bilateral investment treaties.[110] In the United States–Uruguay BIT, for example, the parties have agreed that the arbitral tribunal has the authority to accept and consider *amicus curiae* submissions from 'a person or entity that is not a disputing party'.[111]

## Non-disputing party submissions and the 'public interest'

Although principally used to give a voice to NGOs, the practice of *amicus curiae* briefs has also been beneficial to private or public organizations, including subnational governments.[112] Thus, in the *Electrabel* v. *Hungary* case, the European Commission used the procedure provided for under Article 37(2) of the ICSID Arbitration Rules to submit a statement relating, *inter alia*, to the jurisdiction of the Tribunal and the relation between European Community law and the Energy Charter Treaty, which provided the jurisdictional basis of the arbitration.[113] Then, however, the intervention as a non-disputing party may not necessarily be a question of transparency, but rather one of having an expert legal opinion on a specific question.[114]

109 UN General Assembly, UNCITRAL, UN Doc. A/CN.9/765, para. 35.

110 For an overview, see Kyla Tienhaara, 'Third Party Participation in Investment–Environment Disputes: Recent Developments', *Review of European Community & International Environmental Law*, 16(2) (2007): 230, 232–3.

111 Treaty Between the United States of America and the Oriental Republic of Uruguay Concerning the Encouragement and Reciprocal Protection of Investment, 4 November 2005, Article 28(3), available at: http://tcc.export.gov/static/Uruguay-11.4.05.pdf, accessed 2 April 2010.

112 On the latter, see Andrea K. Bjorklund, 'The Participation of Sub-national Government Units as *Amici Curiae* in International Investment Disputes', in Chester Brown and Kate Miles (eds.), *Evolution in Investment Treaty Law and Arbitration* (Cambridge University Press, 2011), pp. 298–315.

113 *Electrabel* v. *Hungary*, ICSID Case No. ARB/07/19, paras 4.89 ff.

114 In the *Electrabel* case, for instance, the Tribunal noted that 'while the European Commission is an expert commentator on European Community law and could accordingly assist the Tribunal by addressing several legal issues, the scope of its legal opinion should in principle be directed to addressing the following issues:
(a) European Community law and its connection with the Energy Charter Treaty;
(b) Community Law and the State Aid investigation concerning the Power Purchase

Certain international investment tribunals operating both under NAFTA Chapter Eleven and the ICSID Convention have from the start distinguished between establishing the legality of NGO participation as *amicus curiae*, discussed in the previous paragraph, and the *appropriateness* of submissions in that case, linked to the particular non-state or non-corporate interest of that case. They have very often advanced the 'public character' of the dispute as part of their reasoning on the legality of NGO submissions in those cases. The participation of NGOs in international dispute settlement has been noticeable principally in cases involving matters of public interest, namely, in cases relating to the environment and water and their connection with foreign investment. In that sense, NGO participation is thus not necessarily to the benefit of the tribunal or court, but rather to the benefit of a greater 'public interest', since the participation increases the legitimacy, transparency and openness of investment treaty arbitration.[115]

However, the possibility of *amicus curiae* submissions is not unrestricted. In practice, tribunals have pointed out that such submissions need to conform to certain conditions. These conditions boil down to the rationale behind such participation: first, the 'public' interest character of the dispute and the role of the NGO as representative of that interest; and, secondly, the consequent utility of the brief in assisting the tribunal in the sense that it presents arguments different from those of the disputing parties. Both conditions relate to the same requirement of the existence of a 'public interest' that is different from the interests of states and corporations. Indeed, the requirement of the utility of the brief in assisting the tribunal by presenting arguments *different from those of the disputing parties* implies that the NGO should, in fact, represent a 'public', that is, a non-state and non-corporate interest. The state and corporate interests are already represented by the parties. Since investment treaty arbitration is traditionally open only to states and corporations or individual investors, only state and investor interests are represented at such proceedings. NGO participation is then often perceived as a method to remedy taking into consideration the state's and the investor's interests only. The 'broader' interests represented by NGOs can either be general and related to human rights or environmental issues, or relatively specific or sectoral, such as the

Agreements signed by Hungary; and (c) the Effect of Community Decisions on the European Union's Members States, particularly Hungary' (*ibid.*, para. 24).

115 See also Sands and Mackenzie, 'International Courts and Tribunals, *Amicus Curiae*', pp. 29–31.

representation of the rights of a particular social group affected by the tribunal's or court's decision and otherwise having no access to the proceedings. The rationale of NGO participation as *amicus curiae* therefore also, relatively paradoxically, acts as inherent limitation to this participation.

Many tribunals in investment treaty arbitration have explicitly invoked the need for greater transparency in 'public interest' cases to support the idea of NGO participation as *amici curiae*. The *Methanex* Tribunal noted that the proceedings presented an issue of public interest since it involved the provision of public services and matters relating to health, which thus 'extends far beyond those raised by the usual transnational arbitration between commercial parties'.[116] The Tribunal further noted that NAFTA Chapter Eleven Arbitration could benefit from being 'more open or transparent'.[117] Similarly, the Arbitral Tribunal in *UPS* recalled the recent focus on ensuring greater transparency in investment treaty arbitration, which cannot be 'equated to the standard run of international commercial arbitration between private parties'.[118] In that case, the Tribunal thus accepted the representation of the labour rights of Canadian postal workers via *amicus curiae* submissions. In *Glamis*, NGO participation enabled indigenous peoples to participate in proceedings.[119] The *Glamis* Tribunal has indeed accepted submissions by, *inter alia*, the Quechan Indian Nation who could be affected by the outcome of its decision and would have, but for the participation through *amicus curiae* submissions, no access to the arbitral tribunal. The Statement of the Free Trade Commission that followed the *Methanex* decision also confirmed both the rationale and the limitations of *amicus curiae* briefs. The Statement requires tribunals to assess, *inter alia*, whether the non-disputing party has 'a significant interest in the arbitration; and whether there is 'a public interest in the subject-matter of the arbitration'.[120] The latter will, however, often be the case in investment treaty arbitration.

116 *Methanex* v. *United States*, UNCITRAL, Decision of the Tribunal on Petitions from Third Persons to Intervene as *Amici Curiae*, para. 49.

117 *Ibid.*

118 *UPS* v. *Canada*, UNCITRAL, Decision of the Tribunal on Petitions for Intervention and Participation as *Amici Curiae*, para. 70.

119 See, generally, Megan Davis, 'New Developments in International Advocacy: *Amicus Curiae* and the World Trade Organization', *Indigenous Law Bulletin*, 5 (2003), available at: www.austlii.edu.au/au/journals/ILB/2003/28.html, accessed 11 February 2011.

120 Statement of the Free Trade Commission on Non-disputing Party Participation, para. B.6.

As far as ICSID arbitration more generally is concerned, the *Suez/Vivendi* Tribunal explained the appropriateness of accepting *amicus curiae* by noting that the case not only involved matters of public interest which are present in all ICSID cases, but that:

> the factor that gives this case particular public interest is that the investment dispute centers around the water distribution and sewage systems of a large metropolitan area, the city of Buenos Aires and surrounding municipalities. Those systems provide basic public services to millions of people and as a result may raise a variety of complex public and international law questions, including human rights considerations. Any decision rendered in this case, whether in favor of the Claimants or the Respondent, has the potential to affect the operation of those systems and thereby the public they serve.[121]

The ICSID Rules on Arbitration amended in 2006 require the tribunal, in determining whether or not to allow the submission of a brief, to consider, *inter alia*, the extent to which the *amicus* 'has a significant interest in the proceeding'.[122] In *Biwater Gauff*, the Tribunal quoted the order in both the *Methanex* and the *Suez/Vivendi* cases in respect of the public interest character of these disputes.[123] The Tribunal equally noted, again quoting the *Methanex* decision, that even if it were admitted that there was no special or wider interest at stake, the arbitral process could generally benefit from increased transparency.[124] Thus, the Tribunal accepted the submission of a single brief by five NGOs, but denied their request for access to the documents filed by the parties and their request for presence or participation at the hearing.[125]

Because participation via this procedure is only *indirect* and cannot be equated with participation as a party to the disputes, the arguments presented by the NGOs are both limited to the subject matter of the dispute and need to represent an interest different from that of the parties. In that sense, *amicus curiae* briefs are essentially seen as beneficial to the court or tribunal since it would provide the court or tribunal with useful information and argumentation other than that presented by the parties. It has generally been accepted by various tribunals, but also under the revised ICSID Rules, that the main function of *amicus curiae* submissions is to assist the tribunal in its work, and so the briefs

[121] *Ibid.*, para. 19.
[122] ICSID Rules of Procedure for Arbitration Proceedings (Arbitration Rules) Art. 37(2)(c), available at: http://icsid.worldbank.org/ICSID/StaticFiles/basicdoc/CRR_English-final.pdf, accessed 14 April 2010.
[123] *Biwater Gauff* v. *Tanzania*, Procedural Order No. 5, paras 51–52. [124] *Ibid.*, para. 54.
[125] *Ibid.*, paras 62–72.

need to relate to questions under discussion in the dispute. Only those submissions that provide assistance to a court or tribunal by offering expertise and arguments different from those of the disputing parties will eventually be accepted by the court or tribunal.[126] Thus, the Tribunal in *Bernhard von Pezold and others* v. *Zimbabwe* refused the extension of the claim to a human rights one, a 'claim' made by a non-disputing party.[127]

The revised ICSID Arbitration Rules also limit the possibility of *amicus curiae* intervention to those submissions that 'would assist the Tribunal in the determination of a factual or legal issue related to the proceeding by bringing a perspective, particular knowledge or insight that is different from that of the disputing parties'.[128] Before the revision of the ICSID Rules, the Tribunal in *Suez/Vivendi* v. *Argentina* had already noted that NGOs that wished to submit *amicus curiae* briefs needed to satisfy it that they had the necessary expertise, experience and independence to be of assistance in the case.[129] In *Biwater Gauff* v. *Tanzania*, the final award of the Arbitral Tribunal, after having already granted leave to a group of NGOs to submit a single brief, noted that the interests, expertise and perspectives given by the NGOs 'have been demonstrated to materially differ from those of the two contending parties, and as such have provided a useful contribution to these proceedings'.[130] Likewise, the Statement of the NAFTA Free Trade Commission requires tribunals to assess, *inter alia*, the extent to which the submission would 'assist the Tribunal in the determination of a factual or legal issue related to the arbitration by bringing a perspective, particular knowledge or insight that is different from that of the disputing parties'.[131]

[126] See *Suez/Vivendi* v. *Argentina*, ICSID Case No. ARB/03/19, Order in Response to a Petition for Participation as *Amicus Curiae*, para. 13.
[127] *Bernhard von Pezold and others* v. *Zimbabwe*, ICSID Case No. ARB/10/15, Procedural Order No. 2, para. 60, and the citation accompanying n. 45, Ch. 4, above.
[128] Article 37(2) of the ICSID Arbitration Rules.
[129] *Suez/Vivendi*, ICSID Case No. ARB/03/19, Order in Response to a Petition for Participation as *Amicus Curiae*, para. 24.
[130] *Biwater Gauff* v. *Tanzania*, Procedural Order No. 3.
[131] Statement of the Free Trade Commission on non-disputing party participation, para. B.6.

# 6 Public international law remedies in investment treaty arbitration

The question of compensation in investment treaty arbitration has been a contentious area of international investment law for many years.[1] This has been the case, in particular, in relation to the calculation of compensation in cases of expropriation, but also in respect of the forms of reparation and the amounts of monetary compensation.

In relation to international investment law specifically, a differentiation must be made between two types of claims susceptible to being brought before an investment tribunal. First, in the event of a direct or lawful expropriation, the most appropriate remedy is pecuniary compensation, and although the question of which standard should be applied to the valuation of this compensation still is subject to much debate, there is little disagreement on the principle of pecuniary compensation as the only form of compensation.[2] This in effect forms part of the primary international legal norms governing expropriation, and is as such very different from the question of reparation in cases of breaches of international legal obligations. The second type of claim concerns the reparation for violations by a state of its international investment obligations in relation to claims, including reparation in cases of unlawful takings or indirect expropriations.[3] Reparation in relation to the second type of claim remains the subject of some controversy. One specific question, for instance, is whether pecuniary compensation is the most adequate form of reparation, compared with, for instance, restitution or satisfaction. Related to this question,

[1] See, for instance, the contribution from 1982 of Oscar Schachter, 'Editorial Comment. Compensation for Expropriation', *American Journal of International Law*, 78(1) (1984): 121.
[2] See McLachlan *et al.*, *International Investment Arbitration*, pp. 315 ff.
[3] In this case, pecuniary compensation has come to be the accepted method of reparation (*ibid.*, p. 331).

whether or not moral damages may or should be awarded by investment tribunals has attracted much attention in recent years, not least in view of certain cases in which tribunals have controversially awarded monetary compensation for moral damages suffered by foreign investors.[4]

At the outset, it should be noted that the right to claim reparation for an internationally wrongful act by a foreign investor is by necessary implication the result of the grant to foreign investors – individuals and corporations – of rights under the applicable investment treaties.[5] This is so irrespective of the 'direct' or 'derivative' character of these rights.

This chapter will focus on the question of compensation for non-expropriatory breaches of international law, that is, the secondary rules on reparation for internationally wrongful acts, considering the procedural focus of this book and the relative unequivocal acceptance of pecuniary compensation in the case of expropriation, with the exception of the valuation standard. This is also the area that, from the perspective of the public international law character of international investment law, is one of the most contentious aspects of the debate on reparation.

I will use here the notion of 'compensation' as used in international law, denoting a pecuniary amount awarded to cover any financially assessable damage, including loss of profits, as a consequence of an unlawful act.[6] Reparation, on the other hand, is used as the generic term covering the various ways in which damage may be repaired.

I will first address the general legal regime governing reparation in international investment law, before turning to the specific issue of non-pecuniary remedies and moral damages in investment treaty arbitration.

[4] See Patrick Dumberry, 'Compensation for Moral Damages in Investor–State Arbitration Disputes', *Journal of International Arbitration*, 27(3) (2010): 247, and Patrick Dumberry, 'Satisfaction as a Form of Reparation for Moral Damages Suffered by Investors and Respondent States in Investor–State Arbitration Disputes', *Journal of International Dispute Settlement*, 3(1) (2012): 205.

[5] Pierre d'Argent, 'Le droit de la responsabilité internationale complété? Examen des Principes fondamentaux et directives concernant le droit à un recours et à réparation des victimes de violations flagrantes du droit international des droits de l'homme et de violations graves du droit international humanitaire', *Annuaire français de droit international*, 51 (2005): 27, 44.

[6] See, however, Charles N. Brower and Michael N. Ottolenghi, 'Damages in Investor–State Arbitration', *Transnational Dispute Management*, 4 (2007): 6, noting that compensation applies only to lawful state action, while the notion of 'damages' is a remedy for unlawful state action.

## 6.1 Compensation in investment treaty arbitration

The starting point of any debate on compensation in investment treaty arbitration is the general public international law regime governing reparations for internationally wrongful acts, since investment treaty arbitration is concerned with the international responsibility of states for violation of their international obligations under international investment treaties. Despite the fact that the liability of the state resulting from the breach of the international treaty governing the protection of foreign investment has been considered to be 'civil' or 'commercial', the responsibility of a state for a breach of its investment treaty obligations is no different than its responsibility for any other breaches of its international legal obligations.[7] The appropriate rules on the reparation for damages suffered because of these violations are thus the general rules on the international responsibility of states for internationally wrongful acts, which are well established in international law, and recently codified in the ILC Articles on State Responsibility.

### 6.1.1 *The principle of 'full reparation'*

Reparation in international law is governed by two fundamental principles, enunciated by the PCIJ in its decisions in the *Chorzów Factory* case.[8] The first principle is that 'the breach of an engagement involves an obligation to make reparation in an adequate form'.[9] The second principle is the principle of 'full reparation', which implies that reparation must be made so as to re-establish the situation as it was before the breach and has since long been recognized in international law:

> The essential principle contained in the actual notion of an illegal act - a principle which seems to be established by international practice and in particular by the decisions of arbitral tribunals - is that reparation must, as far as possible, wipe out all the consequences of the illegal act and reestablish the situation which would, in all probability, have existed if that act had not been committed.[10]

These principles are reflected in Article 31 of the ILC Articles on the Responsibility of States, which state that 'the responsible State is under an obligation to make full reparation for the injury caused by the

[7] See Douglas, *The International Law of Investment Treaty Claims*, p. 7.
[8] Permanent Court of International Justice, *Factory at Chorzów*, Jurisdiction, Judgment, 26 July 1927, *PCIJ Reports*, Series A, No. 9 (1928), and Merits, Judgment No. 13, 13 September 1928, *PCIJ Reports*, Series A, No. 17 (1928).
[9] *Ibid.*, Jurisdiction, p. 21. [10] *Ibid.*, Merits, p. 47.

internationally wrongful act'. Such injury includes 'any damage, whether material or moral, caused by the internationally wrongful act of a State'.[11] The general principles in respect of reparation contained in the ILC Articles have been held to represent the customary law principles in relation to reparation, and, as will be shown, they both reflect and are reflected in a relatively consistent jurisprudence of international courts and tribunals.[12] Numerous investment tribunals have similarly recognized the principle that an internationally wrongful act results in an obligation to compensate for the economic harm suffered,[13] and that reparation should in principle be 'full reparation' for the damages suffered.[14]

However, one should keep in mind that because of the subsidiary character of the ILC Articles on the Responsibility of States, investment treaties may provide for more specific rules, which should then, as a *lex specialis*, be applied instead of the general provisions contained in the ILC Articles.[15] Investment treaties, however, only rarely provide specific rules applicable to reparation, with a few exceptions discussed in the

[11] Article 31(2) of the ILC Articles on the Responsibility of States, UN Doc. A/56/10.

[12] See James Crawford, 'State Responsibility', in Rüdiger Wolfrüm (ed.), *Max Planck Encyclopedia of Public International Law* (Oxford University Press, 2012), vol. IX, p. 31. See also *ADC Affiliates Ltd and ADC & ADMC Management Ltd* v. *The Republic of Hungary*, ICSID Case No. ARB/03/16, Award of the Tribunal, 2 October 2006, para. 495 and *Nykomb Synergetics Technology Holding AB* v. *The Republic of Latvia*, SCC Case 118/2001, Final Award, 16 December 2003, p. 38. The ILC Articles provide that the rules are 'without prejudice to any right, arising from the international responsibility of a State, which may accrue directly to any person or entity other than a State' (Article 33(2) of the ILC Articles on the Responsibility of States, UN Doc. A/56/10). This paragraph is, *inter alia*, intended to cover those situations where a non-state entity can invoke the responsibility on its own account, through a special procedure, as in investment treaty arbitration. The invocation of the responsibility of a state by entities other than states is possible only to the extent that a specific primary rule to this effect exists (see Commentary to Article 33(2), ILC Articles on the Responsibility of States, UN Doc. A/56/10, para. 4). The rules and principles relating to the forms of reparation are, however, similar when it is a non-state entity that is entitled to invoke the responsibility of a state.

[13] See, for instance, *S.D. Myers, Inc.* v. *Government of Canada*, UNCITRAL, Partial Award, 13 November 2000, paras 312–315; *CME* v. *Czech Republic*, UNCITRAL, Partial Award, paras 583 ff; *LG&E* v. *Argentina*, ICSID Case No. ARB/02/1, Award on Damages, para. 31; and *Biwater Gauff* v. *Tanzania*, Procedural Order No. 3. para. 773.

[14] See, for instance, *Metalclad Corporation* v. *Mexico*, ICSID Case No. ARB(AF)/97/1, Award, 30 August 2000, para. 122; and *Petrobart Ltd* v. *The Kyrgyz Republic*, SCC Case No. 126/2003, Arbitral Award, 29 March 2005, pp. 77 and 78.

[15] For a discussion, see David D. Caron, 'The ILC Articles on State Responsibility: The Paradoxical Relationship between Form and Authority', *American Journal of International Law*, 96(4) (2002): 857, 857–73. See also *ADC* v. *Hungary*, ICSID Case No. ARB/03/16, paras 480 ff.

next section. Investment treaties do often contain provisions in respect of compensation in cases of lawful expropriation, which are then to be applied by the tribunal, but this is not a form of reparation for an internationally wrongful act.[16]

That a breach of an investment treaty results in the obligation for the State to provide reparation for the damage caused by the breach is relatively unequivocal, as is the principle that reparation should re-establish the situation as it was before the breach. The question remains however, which *form* of reparation is most adequate in case of breach of investment protection treaties. Indeed, because of the notoriously large amounts of pecuniary compensation awarded by tribunals, one may legitimately raise the question as to whether other forms of compensation may, can or should be applied by tribunals in investment treaty arbitration.[17]

### 6.1.2 *Forms of reparation*

Article 34 of the ILC Articles provides that full reparation for the injury caused by an internationally wrongful act can take the form of 'restitution, compensation and satisfaction, either singly or in combination'. This principle has also been confirmed by various courts and tribunals, including investment tribunals.[18]

Restitution is generally considered to be the primary method of reparation, compensation being awarded only in cases where restitution is not possible. As noted by the PCIJ in the aforementioned *Chorzów Factory* case:

> Restitution in kind, or, if this is not possible, payment of a sum corresponding to the value which a restitution in kind would bear; the award, if need be, of damages for loss sustained which would not be covered by restitution in kind or payment in place of it – such are the principles which should serve to determine the amount of compensation due for an act contrary to international law.[19]

[16] See, for instance, *ADC* v. *Hungary*, ICSID Case No. ARB/03/16, para. 481.

[17] McLachlan *et al.*, *International Investment Arbitration*, p. 341. See also recently, the award of a total amount of US$936,940,000 against Libya, the second largest amount ever awarded in investment treaty arbitration: *Mohamed Abdulmohsen Al-Kharafi & Sons Co.* v. *Libya and others*, Cairo Regional Center for International Commercial Arbitration (CRCICA), Final Award, 22 March 2013.

[18] In *CMS Gas* v. *Argentina*, for instance, the Tribunal observed that: 'it is broadly accepted in international law that there are three main standards of reparation for injury: restitution, compensation and satisfaction' (*CMS Gas* v. *Argentina*, ICSID Case No. ARB/01/8, Decision on Annulment, para. 399).

[19] PCIJ, *Factory at Chorzów*, Judgment No. 13, p. 47.

This principle is reflected also in the *Wall* Advisory Opinion of the ICJ.[20]

Restitution may take two forms: 'material' or 'juridical'. In the first case, which is relatively self-explanatory, restitution may include 'return of territory, persons or property, or the reversal of some juridical act, or some combination of them'.[21] Juridical restitution, on the other hand, involves 'the modification of a legal situation either within the legal system of the responsible State or in its legal relations with the injured State', and may include the 'revocation, annulment or amendment of a constitutional or legislative provision enacted in violation of a rule of international law, the rescinding or reconsideration of an administrative or judicial measure unlawfully adopted in respect of the person or property of a foreigner or a requirement that steps be taken (to the extent allowed by international law) for the termination of a treaty'.[22] Although restitution is, in accordance with the principles established above, the primary form of reparation in order to re-establish the situation that existed before the wrongful act,[23] it is often considered by investment tribunals to be materially impossible.[24] It is, on the other hand, accepted that investment tribunals may, as a matter of principle, order non-pecuniary relief, such as an injunction or an order of certain performance as a form of restitution.[25] This form of reparation, however, is almost absent in investment treaty arbitration, with a couple of exceptions, and is discussed in the next section.

Compensation, very often termed 'damages', is subsidiary to restitution in the sense that the obligation to provide compensation for the damage caused by an internationally wrongful act exists only to the

20 'Israel is accordingly under an obligation to return the land, orchards, olive groves and other immovable property seized from any natural or legal person for purposes of construction of the wall in the Occupied Palestinian Territory. In the event that such restitution should prove to be materially impossible, Israel has an obligation to compensate the persons in question for the damage suffered. The Court considers that Israel also has an obligation to compensate, in accordance with the applicable rules of international law, all natural or legal persons having suffered any form of material damage as a result of the wall's construction' (International Court of Justice, *Legal Consequences of the Construction of a Wall in the Occupied Palestinian Territory*, Advisory Opinion, *ICJ Reports*, 2004, para. 153).

21 Commentary to Article 35, ILC Articles on the Responsibility of States, UN Doc. A/56/10, para. 5.

22 *Ibid.*, para. 5.

23 See, for instance, *CMS Gas* v. *Argentina*, Decision on Annulment, para. 400, and *Nykomb* v. *Latvia*, SCC Case 118/2001, Final Award, paras 38–39.

24 See, for instance, *ADC* v. *Hungary*, ICSID Case No. ARB/03/16, para. 495.

25 See, for instance, *Enron* v. *Argentina*, ICSID Case No. ARB/01/3, Award, para. 81.

extent that the damage is not made good by restitution.[26] Compensation then should cover 'any financially assessable damage including loss of profits insofar as it is established'.[27] As noted in the ILC Commentary to this Article, 'any financially assessable damage' means 'any damage which is capable of being evaluated in financial terms', and 'encompasses both damage suffered by the State itself (to its property or personnel or in respect of expenditures reasonably incurred to remedy or mitigate damage flowing from an internationally wrongful act) as well as damage suffered by nationals, whether persons or companies, on whose behalf the State is claiming within the framework of diplomatic protection'.[28] Compensation according to the ILC Articles does not, however, cover compensation for 'moral damage' suffered by a state, namely, 'the affront or injury caused by a violation of rights not associated with actual damage to property or persons'.[29] The reparation for moral damages suffered by the state usually takes the form of satisfaction, which is dealt with in Article 37 of the ILC Articles.[30] Compensation does, however, include 'moral damage' suffered by nationals on whose behalf the state is claiming.[31] This principle is an application of the often quoted *Lusitania* decision, in which the Umpire held that:

> That one injured is under the rules of international law, entitled to be compensated for an injury inflicted resulting in mental suffering, injury to his feelings, humiliation, shame, degradation, loss of social position or injury to his credit or to his reputation, there can be no doubt, and such compensation should be commensurate to the injury. Such damages are very real, and the mere fact that they are difficult to measure or estimate by money standards makes them none the less real and affords no reason why the injured person should not be compensated therefor as compensatory damages, but not as a penalty.[32]

Compensation, because of the frequent inappropriateness or impossibility of restitution, is the most widely used form of reparation in investment treaty arbitration.[33] Tribunals have at the same time confirmed the subsidiary character of this form of reparation, namely, that

[26] Article 36(1) of the ILC Articles on the Responsibility of States, UN Doc. A/56/10.
[27] Article 36(2) of the ILC Articles on the Responsibility of States, UN Doc. A/56/10.
[28] Commentary to Article 36, of the ILC Articles on the Responsibility of States, UN Doc. A/56/10, para. 2.
[29] *Ibid.*, para. 1. [30] *Ibid.* [31] *Ibid.*
[32] *Mixed Claims Commission (United States and Germany)*, 1 November 1923–30 October 1939, Opinion in the Lusitania Cases, UNRIAA, vol. VII, 1 November 1923, p. 40.
[33] McLachlan *et al.*, *International Investment Arbitration*, p. 341.

'quite naturally compensation is only called for when the damage is not made good by restitution'.[34] The standard used in Article 36 of the ILC Articles, namely, that compensation 'shall cover any financially assessable damage including loss of profits' has also been endorsed by several tribunals.[35]

Finally, satisfaction, the third form of reparation, is according to the ILC Articles relevant only insofar as the injury caused by a wrongful act cannot be made good by restitution or compensation.[36] Satisfaction 'may consist in an acknowledgement of the breach, an expression of regret, a formal apology or another appropriate modality'.[37] Satisfaction is very often used as the appropriate method of reparation for injuries that are not financially assessable, and, in particular, for wrongful acts that have caused moral or legal damage to the state.[38] Satisfaction usually takes the form of an acknowledgement, or finding of the breach, or a formal apology for the breach. Satisfaction is very often used as a method of reparation in interstate disputes.[39] These principles have been confirmed in various decisions of investment tribunals. Satisfaction is generally considered to be 'irrelevant' as an adequate form of reparation in investment treaty arbitration.[40] As noted, satisfaction is possible only if the injury caused cannot be made good by restitution or compensation. In *CMS Gas* v. *Argentina*, the Tribunal noted that 'as this is not a case of reparation due to an injured State, satisfaction can be ruled out at the outset'.[41] Discarding satisfaction only because the reparation is not owed to another state is, however, inappropriate, since satisfaction may in effect be an appropriate remedy in cases where both restitution and compensation are not possible. This was acknowledged by the majority in *Biwater Gauff* v. *Tanzania*: 'given that none of the Republic's violations of the BIT caused the loss and damage for which BGT now claims compensation, it follows that each of BGT's claims for damages must be

[34] *CMS Gas* v. *Argentina*, ICSID Case No. ARB/01/8, Decision on Annulment, para. 401.

[35] For example, *CME* v. *Czech Republic*, UNCITRAL, Final Award, para. 501; *CMS Gas* v. *Argentina*, Decision on Annulment, para. 401; and *LG&E* v. *Argentina*, ICSID Case No. ARB/02/1, Award on Damages, para. 41.

[36] Article 37(1) of the ILC Articles on the Responsibility of States, UN Doc. A/56/10.

[37] Article 37(2) of the ILC Articles on the Responsibility of States, UN Doc. A/56/10.

[38] Commentary to Article 37, ILC Articles on the Responsibility of States, UN Doc. A/56/10, para. 3.

[39] See, for instance, International Court of Justice, *Arrest Warrant of 11 April 2000 (Democratic Republic of the Congo* v. *Belgium)*, *ICJ Reports*, 2002, 31

[40] *LG&E* v. *Argentina*, ICSID Case No. ARB/02/1, Award on Damages, para. 32, n. 6.

[41] *CMS* v. *Argentina*, Decision on Annulment, para. 399.

dismissed, and that the only appropriate remedies for the Republic's conduct can be declaratory in nature'.[42]

## 6.2 Non-pecuniary remedies in investment treaty arbitration

Generally, international investment tribunals award monetary compensation for losses incurred as a consequence of breaches of the host state's obligations towards the foreign investor, in spite of the various possibilities of reparation available under international law. However, monetary compensation in public international law is, as mentioned, only one of several forms of reparation, which may be contrasted to the exclusive focus on pecuniary compensation in international commercial law and arbitration.[43] There is no reason to exclude *a priori* the possibility of investment tribunals awarding non-pecuniary compensation.

### *6.2.1 Can and should investment tribunals award non-pecuniary remedies in investment treaty arbitration?*

The general lack of awards of non-pecuniary compensation is the result of several considerations, which at the same time explain the importance of pecuniary compensation as a form of reparation in investment treaty disputes.

First, restitution will be legally impossible in a certain number of cases in view of the powers of the tribunal. This will, for instance, be the case when the damage was 'inflicted indirectly through loss-creating actions towards a subsidiary in the country of a Contracting State', while the arbitration was instituted by the shareholding company.[44] Then, because the entity that has suffered direct damage is not a party to the proceedings, the tribunal will not be in a position to order restitution because the reparation is aimed at remedying the damage caused to the party in the proceedings, and not the subsidiary of the disputing party. Another example is when the investment has in the mean time been transferred to a third party.[45]

[42] *Biwater Gauff* v. *Tanzania*, Procedural Order No. 3, para. 807.

[43] See Thomas W. Wälde and Borzu Sabahi, 'Compensation, Damages and Valuation in International Investment Law', in Peter Muchlinski, Frederico Ortino and Christoph Schreuer (eds.), *The Oxford Handbook of International Investment Law* (Oxford University Press, 2008), p. 1056.

[44] *Nykomb* v. *Latvia*, SCC Case 118/2001, Final Award, p. 39.

[45] *Waguih Elie George Siag and Clorinda Vecchi* v. *The Arab Republic of Egypt*, ICSID Case No. ARB/05/15, Award, 1 June 2009, para. 534, where the Tribunal stated that it 'further accepts

Secondly, in certain cases restitution has been deemed inappropriate because of the complexity or practical difficulties in reversing legal regulations which were at the origin of the breach of the state's investment obligations. In the context of the Argentinian crisis, for example, a tribunal considered that 'it would be utterly unrealistic for the Tribunal to order the Respondent to turn back to the existing regulatory framework existing before the emergency measures were adopted'.[46] Parties were, however, according to the Tribunal, free to reach an agreement which would constitute 'restitution by means of negotiation'.[47]

Thirdly, tribunals have on occasion argued that restitution is primarily to be agreed upon by the parties to the dispute, and thus, that 'absent an agreed form of restitution by means of renegotiation of contracts or otherwise, the appropriate standard of reparation under international law is compensation'.[48] This consideration, because of its formulation in absolute and principled terms, is inaccurate and does not conform to the general principles governing reparation explained above. But despite the inaccurate formulation of this principle by the Tribunal, the underlying reason is legitimate: in the absence of confidence between the foreign investor and the host state, restitution may not be practically possible.

Fourthly, tribunals have refused to order restitution based on the consideration that this would constitute an infringement on the sovereignty of states. The Tribunal in *LG&E* v. *Argentina*, for instance, argued that 'the judicial restitution required in this case would imply modification of the current legal situation by annulling or enacting legislative and administrative measures that make over the effect of the legislation in breach. The Tribunal cannot compel Argentina to do so without a sentiment of undue interference with its sovereignty.'[49] From a strict

that restitution of the Claimants' investment is not possible. The Property was conveyed to a third party in 2003. In those circumstances, the only relief that is practically available is an award of damages.'

[46] *CMS Gas* v. *Argentina*, Decision on Annulment, para. 406. [47] *Ibid.*, para. 406.

[48] *Enron* v. *Argentina*, ICSID Case No. ARB/01/3, Award, para. 359. Note, however, that this part of the decision was annulled, not because of the principles applied by the Tribunal, but essentially because the Tribunal's findings on liability were annulled, which, according to the Ad Hoc Committee inevitably leads to the annulment of the Tribunal's original decision with respect to damages (*Enron* v. *Argentina*, ICSID Case No. ARB/01/3, Decision on the Application for Annulment, para. 414). See also *Sempra* v. *Argentina*, ICSID Case No. ARB/02/16, Award, para. 401. This decision, however, was also annulled in its entirety, although the main reason was not related to the Tribunal's findings in respect of compensation.

[49] *LG&E* v. *Argentina*, ICSID Case No. ARB/02/1, Award on Damages, para. 87.

legal perspective, the imposition by a tribunal of a certain obligation as a form of restitution does not impede the sovereignty of states, not only because such power is inherent in the arbitral and judicial functions, but also because restitution in international law is generally considered to be the primary mode of reparation.[50] However, some authors have argued that the imposition of the payment of large amounts of compensation on a state has an even stronger impact on a state's sovereignty than ordering the performance of certain conduct.[51]

Fifthly, a practical consideration has been that Article 54(1) of the ICSID Convention limits the obligations on contracting states to recognize and enforce decisions of ICSID tribunals of 'the pecuniary obligations imposed by that award'.[52] As a consequence, the award of pecuniary compensation would be more effective in comparison with restitution.[53] This, however, does not imply that non-pecuniary remedies may not be awarded.

Finally, because tribunals are bound by the obligation not to rule *ultra petita*, awarding a non-pecuniary remedy may exceed the mandate of the tribunal, and thus result in an annulment of the decision in cases where the parties to the dispute have specifically requested pecuniary compensation.[54] It should be added, however, that tribunals are authorized to so rule, that is, a decision would not be *ultra petita*, if the parties to the dispute have not specified any specific form of reparation, when one of the parties has argued that restitution would be an appropriate

50 See also Christoph Schreuer, 'Non-pecuniary Remedies in ICSID', *Arbitration International*, 20(4) (2004): 325, 331.

51 See Wälde and Sabahi, 'Compensation, Damages and Valuation in International Investment Law', p. 1060. See also the Separate Opinion of Ian Brownlie in *CME* v. *Czech Republic*, UNCITRAL, Final Award, in which he noted that 'It would be strange indeed, if the outcome of acceptance of a bilateral investment treaty took the form of liabilities likely to entail catastrophic repercussions for the livelihood and economic well-being of the population of the Czech Republic' (para. 78).

52 It has, however, been argued that this principle does not limit the capacity of arbitral tribunals to order non-pecuniary relief. See Schreuer, 'Non-pecuniary Remedies in ICSID', pp. 325–6.

53 Anne van Aaken, 'Primary and Secondary Remedies in International Investment Law and National State Liability: A Functional and Comparative View', in Stephan W. Schill (ed.), *International Investment Law and Comparative Public Law* (Oxford University Press, 2010), p. 734.

54 See Wälde and Sabahi, 'Compensation, Damages and Valuation in International Investment Law', p. 1059, van Aaken, 'Primary and Secondary Remedies in International Investment Law and National State Liability', p. 734 and Brown, 'The Inherent Powers of International Courts and Tribunals', p. 191.

remedy, or when the possibility of the tribunal ordering restitution is implicit in the *petitum* of the parties.[55]

More generally, one can ask the question of whether non-pecuniary forms of reparation are more adequate forms of reparation than monetary compensation. Despite the 'primacy' of restitution as a form of reparation, it will not always be feasible, notably in view of the considerations just mentioned. This, however, does not invalidate the principle that a tribunal should first enquire whether restitution is possible, in particular, when one of the parties to the dispute has suggested this particular form of reparation. Although I do not endorse generally the analogy made between investment treaty arbitration and public law, the latter regime does offer some interesting avenues and guidance for the question of compensation. The main criticism of reparation in investment treaty arbitration from a public law perspective is that the use of compensation as a public law remedy is inappropriate to 'sanction general regulation'.[56] The analogy, in terms of remedies, between investment treaty arbitration and public law was skilfully explored by Anne van Aaken. Van Aaken notes that the traditional way to remedy governmental wrongs consists in a challenge to the particular act which allegedly infringes the rights of the national.[57] This is usually done through a procedure before the administrative courts of the state responsible for the act in question, a procedure in which, generally, the annulment of the act in question is sought. Such proceedings are essentially preventive.[58] A claim for compensation for the damage caused by that act is a relatively different type of proceedings, and is traditionally only possible as a last form of remedy and forms part of a claim in state liability.[59] Pecuniary compensation in domestic legal systems exists and is the most appropriate remedy for direct or lawful expropriation. But, of course, this is part of the primary norm as such, and in the event that a state measure results in a special loss to the holder of the right, pecuniary compensation is similarly usually awarded.[60] In those circumstances, claims in state liability are often used. However, when the claim relates to another type of state measure, the majority of national legal systems provide for access to administrative remedies, rather than claims in

[55] Wälde and Sabahi, 'Compensation, Damages and Valuation in International Investment Law', p. 1059 (and accompanying footnotes).

[56] See, for example, Van Harten, *Investment Treaty Arbitration and Public Law*, p. 145.

[57] Van Aaken, 'Primary and Secondary Remedies in International Investment Law and National State Liability', p. 726.

[58] *Ibid.*, p. 724. [59] *Ibid.*, p. 726. [60] *Ibid.*, p. 724.

pecuniary compensation through the mechanism of state liability.[61] Then restitution rather than monetary compensation is the appropriate remedy.

These considerations are, of course, very stimulating, but the question remains whether one can easily transpose the thus established principles to investment treaty arbitration. Van Aaken concludes that the most efficient way would be to arrive at a combination of pecuniary and non-pecuniary remedies, coupled with a combination of national and international levels of jurisdiction.[62] Then, the national courts and tribunals should principally consider restitution as a method of reparation, while the international legal level - investment treaty arbitration - would come into play only when access to the national level of remedy is impossible or unsatisfactory by awarding pecuniary compensation.[63] This idea, based on the principle of complementarity, is interesting, but would, however, require a revision of the entire institution of investment arbitration, including the ICSID Convention and the vast majority of international investment treaties, since it would imply a need to first exhaust the administrative court remedies before having recourse to investment treaty arbitration.

Rather than attempting to change the current system, it seems more feasible to ask the question as to whether the award of pecuniary compensation by investment tribunals is indeed the most adequate form of reparation, in particular, because the other forms of reparation may equally provide full reparation and are in line with the general principles of public international law. Without doubt, restitution may *in practice* often not be possible. However, this does not imply that, where possible, tribunals should consider whether non-pecuniary remedies may provide for an equal level of remedy.

### *6.2.2 Non-pecuniary remedies in the practice of investment tribunals*

Despite the reluctance to award non-pecuniary remedies in the practice of investment tribunals, it is generally accepted that investment tribunals have the capacity and the legal authority to award non-pecuniary remedies in addition to, or in lieu of, the pecuniary compensation.[64]

[61] *Ibid.* [62] *Ibid.*, pp. 749 ff. [63] *Ibid.*

[64] See Schreuer, 'Non-pecuniary Remedies in ICSID'. See, however, Montt, *State Liability in Investment Treaty Arbitration*, pp. 137–8. See also for a criticism, Zachary Douglas, 'Other Specific Regimes of Responsibility: Investment Treaty Arbitration and ICSID', in James Crawford, Alain Pellet and Simon Olleson (eds.), *The Law of International Responsibility* (Oxford University Press, 2010), pp. 829–32.

Several tribunals have confirmed this principle. In *Micula* v. *Romania*,[65] for instance, the Tribunal, referring to Article 35 of the ILC Articles on the Responsibility of States, noted that:

> under the ICSID Convention, a tribunal has the power to order pecuniary or non-pecuniary remedies, including restitution, i.e., re-establishing the situation which existed before a wrongful act was committed ... In addition, the Tribunal finds no limitation to its powers to order restitution in the BIT, the instrument on which the consent of the parties is based ... The Tribunal therefore does have the powers to order restitution, both under the ICSID Convention and the BIT.[66]

It should be added also that states are free to exclude the possibility of tribunals ordering non-pecuniary remedies, or to restrict or expand in any other way the tribunal's powers in this respect.[67] The ILC Articles are supplementary provisions and apply only to the extent that there is no *lex specialis*.

In at least two cases tribunals have effectively ordered restitution as the primary remedy for violation of investment treaties. Before discussing these cases, I should point out that reference to *Antoine Goetz and others* v. *Burundi*[68] as an example where restitution was ordered by a tribunal is misleading, since in that case the Tribunal did not, explicitly, find that the respondent was in breach of its obligations under the investment treaty. The Tribunal considered that the respondent could be found in breach of its obligations only in the event that it did not pay compensation in accordance with the applicable BIT.[69] The Tribunal therefore gave the respondent the choice, either to pay the required

65 *Ioan Micula and others* v. *Romania*, ICSID Case No. ARB/05/20, Decision on Jurisdiction and Admissibility, 24 September 2008.

66 *Ibid.*, paras 166–168. See also, although not as explicit as the cited passage in *Micula* v. *Romania*, *Enron* v. *Argentina*, ICSID Case No. ARB/01/3, Decision on Jurisdiction, paras 78–81.

67 See, for example, Article 34 of the 2012 US Model BIT: '1. Where a tribunal makes a final award against a respondent, the tribunal may award, separately or in combination, only: (a) monetary damages and any applicable interest; and (b) restitution of property, in which case the award shall provide that the respondent may pay monetary damages and any applicable interest in lieu of restitution.' See also Article 26(8) of the ECT, which provides that 'An award of arbitration concerning a measure of a sub-national government or authority of the disputing Contracting Party shall provide that the Contracting Party may pay monetary damages in lieu of any other remedy granted.'

68 *Antoine Goetz and others* v. *Republic of Burundi*, ICSID Case No. ARB/95/3, Award, 29 January 1999.

69 The Tribunal, indeed, noted that: 'la question de la licéité internationale de la décision du 29 mai 1995 reste en suspens' (*ibid.*, para. 131).

compensation or to provide restitution to the claimants in the form of the free zone certificate they had previously enjoyed.[70]

The first case is *ATA Construction* v. *Jordan*.[71] The Tribunal decided to order restitution of the claimant's right to arbitration which had been 'extinguished' by the application of a Jordanian law, and which had accordingly been considered by the Tribunal to be a breach of Jordan's obligations under the applicable BIT.[72] The facts of this case are peculiar in the sense that the award of pecuniary compensation would have been difficult in any case considering the relative impossibility of calculating the pecuniary damage caused by the extinction of the claimant's 'right to arbitrate'. The case, decided in 2010, is one of the first instances in which restitution was ordered by an investment tribunal.

In a second case, *Franck Charles Arif* v. *Moldova*,[73] decided in 2013, the Tribunal offered the respondent state the possibility of restitution of the investment of Mr Arif, within a limited time period, after which pecuniary compensation had to be paid by the state.[74] This case is remarkable for two reasons. First, the Tribunal unequivocally established the principles that restitution as a remedy is 'more consistent with the objectives of bilateral investment treaties'[75] and that restitution is 'the preferable remedy'.[76] Secondly, the Tribunal, in deciding on the form of reparation, adopted a pragmatic approach. The Tribunal took into account the absence of confirmation by the state of the effective possibility of restitution despite the state's suggestion that restitution would be the most appropriate form of reparation, and the absence of any supervisory powers of the Tribunal as to the implementation of the restitution. As a consequence, the Tribunal decided to award compensation as an alternative remedy in case the proposed restitution did not satisfy the claimant, or in the absence of any restitution proposal by the host state.[77] The Tribunal considered that this solution 'provides a final opportunity to preserve the investment, while also preserving Claimant's right to damages if a satisfactory restitutionary solution cannot be found'.[78] The claimant was finally given the right to opt for compensation at any time within a period of ninety days from the date

[70] *Ibid.*, para. 132.
[71] *ATA Construction, Industrial and Trading Co.* v. *The Hashemite Kingdom of Jordan*, ICSID Case No. ARB/08/2, Award, 18 May 2010.
[72] *Ibid.*, paras 131–132.
[73] *Franck Charles Arif* v. *Republic of Moldova*, ICSID Case No. ARB/11/23, Award, 8 April 2013.
[74] *Ibid.*, para. 572. [75] *Ibid.* [76] *Ibid.*, para. 571. [77] *Ibid.* [78] *Ibid.*

of the award.[79] This solution, besides being in conformity with the relevant principles on reparation in international law in that it has ordered restitution as the primary form of reparation, should also be welcomed for its pragmatism in ordering compensation as an alternative remedy in view of the fact that, as I have mentioned, foreign investment relies very much on a relationship of good faith with the host state.

## 6.3 Moral damages in investment treaty arbitration

Within the compensation debate, the question of moral damages takes a special place, not the least because claims for moral damages are increasingly being made in investment treaty arbitration. This section will focus generally on compensation for moral damages claimed by investors, and not by respondent states. Although the latter issue will be touched upon when discussing whether satisfaction may function as an adequate form of reparation for moral damages, international investment treaties do not, in general, provide legal protection to host states against acts of foreign investors, even when these submit manifestly unmeritorious claims.[80]

### *6.3.1 Moral damages in the ILC Articles on the Responsibility of States*

Again, the most logical departing point is the general regime of reparation in public international law. As noted, the ILC Articles explicitly

[79] *Ibid.*, para. 572.

[80] In *Amto* v. *Ukraine*, the Tribunal refused to accept a claim in compensation for moral damages made by the respondent state based on the following consideration: 'The jurisdiction of an Arbitral Tribunal over a State party counterclaim under an investment treaty depends upon the terms of the dispute resolution provisions of the treaty, the nature of the counterclaim, and the relationship of the counterclaims with the claims in the arbitration. Article 26(6) ECT provides that the applicable law to an ECT dispute is the Treaty itself and "the applicable rules and principles of international law". The Respondent has not presented any basis in this applicable law for a claim of non-material injury to reputation based on the allegations made before an Arbitral Tribunal. Accordingly, the Arbitral Tribunal finds that there is no basis for a counterclaim of this nature and it is accordingly dismissed' (*Amto* v. *Ukraine*, SCC Case No. 080/2005, Final Award, para. 118). For a discussion and possible exceptions to this principle, see Dumberry, 'Satisfaction as a Form of Reparation for Moral Damages', pp. 235 ff. Such claims may, however, be brought by the state against a foreign investor as a matter of private law (Ingeborg Schwenzer and Pascal Hachem, 'Moral Damages in International Investment Arbitration', in Stefan Kröll, Loukas Mistelis, Pilar Perales Viscasillas and Vikki Rogers (eds.), *International Arbitration and International Commercial Law: Synergy, Convergence and Evolution, Liber Amicorum Eric Bergsten* (Alphen aan den Rijn: Kluwer Law International, 2011), p. 427).

provide that injury includes 'any damage, whether material or moral, caused by the internationally wrongful act of a State', therefore, the obligation to compensate moral damages thus forms part of the principle of 'full reparation'.[81] The rule does not cover compensation for moral damage *to a state*, which is remedied through satisfaction, dealt with in Article 37 of the ILC Articles.[82] The moral damage referred to in the second paragraph of Article 31 thus refers to moral damages suffered by nationals (either individuals or legal persons) on whose behalf the state is claiming.[83] This is further explained in the ILC Commentary to Article 36, which relates to compensation. 'Any financially assessable damage' is there defined as 'any damage which is capable of being evaluated in financial terms', and 'encompasses both damage suffered by the State itself (to its property or personnel or in respect of expenditures reasonably incurred to remedy or mitigate damage flowing from an internationally wrongful act) as well as damage suffered by nationals, whether persons or companies, on whose behalf the State is claiming within the framework of diplomatic protection'.[84] Moral damage suffered by an individual or a company on whose behalf a state is claiming in the framework of diplomatic protection may form part of a claim in pecuniary compensation to the extent that it is financially assessable.[85] Moral damage, according to the ILC, encompasses 'loss of loved ones, pain and suffering as well as the affront to sensibilities associated with an intrusion on the person, home or private life'.[86] It is generally understood that moral damage covers all non-material damage.[87] Although in international investment arbitration the foreign

[81] Article 31(2) ILC of the Articles on the Responsibility of States, UN Doc. A/56/10.
[82] Commentary to Article 36, ILC Articles on the Responsibility of States, UN Doc. A/56/10, para. 1.
[83] *Ibid.*, para. 1. See also Sergey Ripinksy and Kevin Williams, *Damages in International Investment Law* (London: British Institute of International and Comparative Law, 2008), p. 308.
[84] Commentary to Article 36, ILC Articles on State Responsibility, UN Doc. A/56/10, para. 2.
[85] The ILC, however, considered that 'material and moral damage resulting from an internationally wrongful act will normally be financially assessible and hence covered by the remedy of compensation (Commentary to Article 37, ILC Articles on the Responsibility of States, UN Doc. A/56/10, para. 3).
[86] Commentary to Article 31, ILC Articles on the Responsibility of States, UN Doc. A/56/10, para. 5.
[87] The International Court of Justice defined 'moral damages', although not explicitly endorsing this terminology, as 'cover[ing] harm other than material injury which is suffered by an injured entity or individual' (International Court of Justice, *Ahmadou Sadio Diallo (Republic of Guinea* v. *Democratic Republic of the Congo)*, Compensation owed by

investor is initiating a claim directly against the state, the same principles apply to the direct claims right of foreign investors.

The principle that moral damages caused by an internationally wrongful act are capable of being compensated is relatively old and well established in international law, and had already been accepted in the *Lusitania* decision in 1923, quoted above,[88] in which the Umpire considered that:

> That one injured is under the rules of international law, entitled to be compensated for an injury inflicted resulting in mental suffering, injury to his feelings, humiliation, shame, degradation, loss of social position or injury to his credit or to his reputation, there can be no doubt, and such compensation should be commensurate to the injury. Such damages are very real, and the mere fact that they are difficult to measure or estimate by money standards makes them none the less real and affords no reason why the injured person should not be compensated therefor as compensatory damages, but not as a penalty.[89]

The principle that moral damages caused by an internationally wrongful act are capable of being compensated has recently been confirmed by the ICJ in the *Diallo* case, in which the court awarded an amount of US$85,000 for 'non-material injury',[90] based, *inter alia*, on the fact that Mr Diallo had been

> arrested without being informed of the reasons for his arrest and without being given the possibility to seek a remedy; that he was detained for an unjustifiably long period pending expulsion; that he was made the object of accusations that were not substantiated; and that he was wrongfully expelled from the country where he had resided for 32 years and where he had engaged in significant business activities. Thus, it is reasonable to conclude that the DRC's wrongful conduct caused Mr. Diallo significant psychological suffering and loss of reputation.[91]

Moral damages have also been awarded by the International Tribunal for the Law of the Sea in the M/V *Saiga* case, both for the detention of the

the Democratic Republic of Congo to the Republic of Guinea, Judgment, 19 June 2012, para. 18).

[88] Contrary to what is often suggested in literature, the Umpire did not in the end award compensation for moral damages, because the mandate of the Commission explicitly ruled out the award of compensation for such damages (see, for instance, Matthew T. Parish, Annalise K. Newlson and Charles B. Rosenberg, 'Awarding Moral Damages to Respondent States in Investment Arbitration', *Berkeley Journal of International Law*, 29(1) (2011): 225 and 227).

[89] *Lusitania decision*, UNRIAA, vol. VII, p. 40.

[90] ICJ, *Diallo*, Compensation owed by the DRC to the Republic of Guinea, Judgment, 19 June 2012, para. 25.

[91] *Ibid.*, para. 21.

captain and members of the crew (pecuniary compensation), and for the violations of the rights of the flag state, St Vincent and the Grenadines (satisfaction in the form of a declaration of violation).[92]

### 6.3.2 *Moral damages in investment treaty arbitration*

The question of moral damages in investment treaty arbitration has been the subject of several recent decisions. However, it should be pointed out that the question had already been addressed as early as1980 in *Benvenuti et Bonfant* v. *Congo*.[93] The claimant claimed an amount of 250,000,000 CFA to compensate, *inter alia*, for 'lost opportunities for work and investment', 'loss of credits with supplier and banks', and because the claimant saw 'its own organization at the managerial level and its own technical personnel dispersed'.[94] Although the Tribunal noted that the evidence presented by the claimant was inconclusive, and doubted the assertions made by the claimant,[95] the Tribunal, based on equitable considerations, did award compensation of 5,000,000 CFA 'in view of the measures to which B[envenuti] and B[onfant] has been subject and the suit that was the consequence thereof, which have certainly disturbed the activities of B[envenuti] and B[onfant]'.[96]

In the majority of the decisions, tribunals have dismissed claims for compensation for moral damage based on the lack of sufficient evidence to this effect. In these cases, tribunals did not engage in a discussion, generally, of the overall possibility, or lack thereof, for parties in international investment disputes to claim compensation for moral damages, nor the conditions under which such compensation might be awarded.[97]

92 International Tribunal for the Law of the Sea, *The M/V Saiga (No. 2) case (St Vincent and the Grenadines* v. *Guinea)*, Judgment, 1 July 1999, paras 175–176.

93 *Benvenuti et Bonfant* v. *Congo*, Award, 15 August 1980, *International Legal Materials*, 21(4) (1980): 740.

94 *Ibid.*, para. 4.95. 95 *Ibid.*, para. 4.96. 96 *Ibid.*

97 In *Tecmed* v. *Mexico*, the Tribunal refused to compensate for moral damages because of the absence of evidence that the acts which the Tribunal found to constitute an internationally wrongful act 'affected the Claimant's reputation and therefore caused the loss of business opportunities for the Claimant' (*Tecmed* v. *Mexico*, ICSID Case No. ARB(AF)/00/2, para. 198). In *Bogdanov* v. *Moldova*, the Tribunal likewise dismissed the claim for compensation of moral damages because the claimant 'failed to provide any factual evidence for moral damages' (*Bogdanov* v. *Moldova*, SCC Case No. 93/2004, Arbitral Award, p. 19), as did the Tribunal in *Victor Pey Casado and President Allende Foundation* v. *Republic of Chile*, ICSID Case No. ARB/98/2, Award, 8 May 2008, para. 689. In *Funnekotter and others* v. *Zimbabwe*, the Tribunal was similarly confronted with a claim in compensation for moral damages, but because the claimants had made their claim for the first time at the hearing, the Tribunal considered that they were inadmissible. The Tribunal did note in passing that the claims had already been partially

One of the first recent cases in which substantial pecuniary compensation for moral damages was given to a foreign investor is *Desert Line* v. *Yemen*[98]. In that case, the Tribunal awarded the substantial amount of US$1,000,000 to the claimant as compensation for moral damages. The claimant, engaged in the construction of asphalt roads in Yemen, initiated a claim against Yemen based, *inter alia*, on the refusal by Yemeni authorities to pay certain amounts due under contract, the pressure exerted on Desert Line to sign a settlement agreement, and the harassment and mistreatment of Desert Line's personnel by armed tribes and the Yemeni army. The Tribunal noted that 'even if investment treaties primarily aim at protecting property and economic values, they do not exclude, as such, that a party may, in exceptional circumstances, ask for compensation for moral damages. It is generally accepted in most legal systems that moral damages may also be recovered besides pure economic damages', and further argued that 'it is also generally recognized that a legal person (as opposed to a natural one) may be awarded moral damages, including loss of reputation, in specific circumstances only'.[99] The 'physical duress exerted on the executives of the Claimant', was considered by the Tribunal to be 'malicious' and 'constitutive of a fault-based liability'.[100] Compensation for the damage caused to 'the physical health of the Claimant's executives and the Claimant's credit and reputation' was thus, according to the Tribunal, justified. The amount of US$10,000,000 requested by the claimant was, however, reduced to US$1,000,000.

The Tribunal in *Lemire* v. *Ukraine* discussed the possibility of investment tribunals awarding compensation for moral damages extensively, but finally refused to award compensation for moral damages.[101] The claimant, active in the radio broadcasting industry, claimed that Ukrainian broadcasting regulators unfairly rejected more than 200 applications for new radio frequencies and engaged in an unwarranted series of inspections, and requested the award of a compensation in the sum of

compensated by the allocation of a disturbances indemnity (*Bernardus Henricus Funnekotter and others* v. *Republic of Zimbabwe*, ICSID Case No. ARB/05/6, Award, 22 April 2009, para. 140). See also recently, *AHS Niger and Menzies Middle East and Africa SA* v. *Republic of Niger*, ICSID Case No. ARB/11/11, Award, 15 July 2013, paras 146–155, where the Tribunal dismissed the claims for moral damages based on the lack of sufficient evidence.

98 *Desert Line Projects LLC* v. *The Republic of Yemen*, ICSID Case No. ARB/05/17, Award, 6 February 2008.

99 *Ibid.*, para. 289. 100 *Ibid.*, para. 290.

101 *Joseph Charles Lemire* v. *Ukraine*, ICSID Case No. ARB/06/18, Decision on Jurisdiction and Liability, 14 January 2010.

US$3,000,000 based on injury suffered 'as a consequence of harassment by the National Council . . . includ[ing] anxiety, pain and suffering'.[102] In its decision on 'jurisdiction and liability', the Tribunal sided with the Tribunal in *Desert Line*, in that it considered that compensation for moral damages may, in exceptional circumstances, be awarded by investment tribunals. The Tribunal noted that the facts in *Desert Line*, which included physical duress and a siege by the armed forces of the respondent state, were indeed 'exceptional'.[103] In *Lemire*, however, the claimant had not been subjected to physical duress, but essentially based its claim for compensation for moral damages on the fact that the respondent was involved 'in systemic bias against Gala Radio', 'jeopardiz[ed] Gala's plans to expand its activities', and 'maliciously subjected Gala to a series of inspections'.[104] The Tribunal reasoned that because certain acts of the respondent were considered to be a breach of the FET standard contained in the BIT, 'an economic indemnification' would be awarded to the claimant.[105] It referred the assessment of the existence of 'exceptional circumstances', which would merit the award of moral compensation, to the next stage of the proceedings after further briefing on the context and causation of the moral damages. In its final award, the Tribunal discussed extensively the conditions under which moral damages may be awarded in investment treaty arbitration.[106] It first established that only 'exceptional circumstances' may lead to the award of damages, thus endorsing the opinion of the Tribunal in *Desert Line*[107]. Exceptional circumstances, are present, according to the Tribunal if:

- the State's actions imply physical threat, illegal detention or other analogous situations in which the ill-treatment contravenes the norms according to which civilized nations are expected to act;
- the State's actions cause a deterioration of health, stress, anxiety, other mental suffering such as humiliation, shame and degradation, or loss of reputation, credit and social position; and
- both cause and effect are grave or substantial.[108]

Applied to the facts of the case, the Tribunal found that, although Mr Lemire had without doubt been 'mistreated', and felt 'stress and anxiety', moral damages had already been compensated through the award of economic compensation, and the facts of the case were not as 'extraordinary' as to award additional compensation for moral damages.[109]

[102] *Ibid.*, para. 475. [103] *Ibid.*, para. 476. [104] *Ibid.*, para. 479. [105] *Ibid.*, para. 486.
[106] *Joseph Charles Lemire* v. *Ukraine*, ICSID Case No. ARB/06/18, Award, 28 March 2011.
[107] *Ibid.*, paras 326 ff. [108] *Ibid.*, para. 333. [109] *Ibid.*, paras 337–344.

More recently, in *Mohamed Abdulmohsen Al-Kharafi & Sons Co.* v. *Libya and others*, an ad hoc arbitration conducted before the Cairo Regional Center for International Commercial Arbitration,[110] a Tribunal awarded the colossal sum of US$30,000,000 as compensation for 'moral damages' caused to the claimant's 'reputation in the stock market, as well as in the business and construction markets in Kuwait and around the world'.[111] This amount came in addition to the award of US$900,000,000 as compensation for 'lost profits', 'as a result of the damage to [Claimant's] worldwide professional reputation'.[112] It is important to stress, however, that the Tribunal, the jurisdiction of which was based on an investment treaty (the Unified Agreement for the Investment of Arab Capital in the Arab States), the contract between the parties and Libyan law, essentially justified the grant of compensation for moral damages on the basis of the applicable Article 225 of the Libyan Civil Code, which allows the compensation of moral damages.[113] There was no justification sought in the applicable principles of general international law. Be that as it may, the question remains whether, first, the award of a compensation for moral damages *in se* was justified, in particular, in view of the fact that compensation was also given for lost profits; and, secondly, whether the amount awarded was reasonable.

Indeed, these decisions, in particular, *Desert Line* and *Al-Kharafi* because of the effective award of financial compensation for moral damages, call for certain observations, which are not necessarily related to the question generally of the capacity of investment tribunals to award compensation for moral damages. This is indisputable under the general principles of international law. Rather, the conditions under which such compensation has been granted seem to move away both from general principles of international law and the jurisdiction of international investment tribunals.

First, the reliance in *Desert Line* on the fault criterion to establish the state's responsibility for moral damages is clearly contrary to the widespread and accepted notion that the international legal regime governing the responsibility of states for internationally wrongful acts is 'objective'. It is not fault-based, which is a criterion that might be included in a primary norm, but it does not form part of the rules on

[110] *Al-Kharafi* v. *Libya*, CRCICA, Final Award. [111] *Ibid.*, para. 369. [112] *Ibid.*, para. 382.
[113] *Ibid.*, para. 365.

state responsibility.[114] Fault or malicious intent may be taken into consideration for the determination of the *amount* of compensation, but not for the establishment of responsibility.[115]

Secondly, the compensation awarded to the claimant in *Desert Line* was not only aimed at reparation for 'loss of reputation' of the claimant, a corporation, but also as compensation for moral damages caused to the claimant's executives. The jurisdiction of tribunals in investment treaty arbitration, however, is strictly limited *ratione personae* to investors, as defined both by the applicable international investment treaty and, if applicable, the ICSID Convention. Clearly, the claimant's executives are not 'investors' under these definitions, and they do not, therefore, have standing before the tribunal. Awarding compensation for moral damages caused to individuals who are not *ratione personae* within the jurisdiction of the tribunal is therefore mistaken. It would be a completely different situation if the claimant-corporation had *itself* made pecuniary compensation for moral damages to its executives, and was seeking to be financially compensated for such disbursements. In that case, compensation is not, strictly speaking, for moral damages, but the jurisdictional issues are no longer problematic. This, however, was clearly not the case in *Desert Line*. Although described as 'sensible' by some,[116] the Tribunal's approach on that particular point seems to run counter to the very jurisdictional foundations of investment treaty arbitration, because the claimant's executives were not investors under the applicable BIT and the ICSID Convention, and cannot therefore benefit from the protection of the treaty or have access to the arbitral tribunal.[117]

Thirdly, the jurisdiction *ratione materiae* of investment tribunals may not always allow for the award of compensation for moral damages. It is important to note that the ICJ in the *Diallo* case considered that the award of compensation for moral damages was justified because of Mr Diallo's unlawful detention and expulsion, which

[114] Commentary to Article 2, ILC Articles on the Responsibility of States, UN Doc. A/56/10, paras 3 and 10. See also Daniel Bodansky and John R. Crook, 'Symposium: The ILC's State Responsibility Articles: Introduction and Overview', *American Journal of International Law*, 96(4) (2002): 773, 781. For a criticism of the *Desert Line* decision in this respect, see also Conway Blake, 'Moral Damages in Investment Arbitration: A Role for Human Rights?', *Journal of International Dispute Settlement*, 3(2) (2012): 371, 398 ff.

[115] Dumberry, 'Compensation for Moral Damages in Investor–State Arbitration Disputes', p. 271.

[116] *Ibid.*, p. 267.

[117] See also Schwenzer and Hachem, 'Moral Damages in International Investment Arbitration', p. 422.

constituted breaches of the International Covenant on Civil and Political Rights,[118] but not of an investment treaty. One should keep in mind that investment tribunals, in assessing claims for compensation of moral damages, need to ensure that the link between that claim and the investment and investor protected under the relevant investment treaty is sufficiently established. I recall here the decision of the Tribunal in *Biloune* v. *Ghana*.[119] In that case, which concerned the arrest and detention for thirteen days of a foreign investor, the Tribunal argued that its jurisdiction under the agreement between the investor and the host state was limited to disputes relating to an investment and it was, therefore, only competent to deal with such human rights violations to the extent that it affected the investment and had thus become an investment dispute.[120] In *Generation Ukraine* v. *Ukraine*,[121] the Tribunal similarly dismissed a claim in compensation for moral damages based on the Constitution of Ukraine, considering that its jurisdiction was limited to disputes arising out of an 'alleged breach of any right conferred or created by [the] Treaty'.[122] In the same vein, one could argue that the award of compensation for moral damages to executives of an investor, as was the case in *Desert Line*, is not the consequence of a right conferred or created by an investment agreement.

Fourthly, the amount awarded by the Tribunal in *Desert Line*, although only a fraction of the claimed compensation, by far exceeds the level of compensation usually awarded by international courts and tribunals for moral damages caused to individuals.[123] In *Al-Kharafi*, the compensation was awarded to a corporation, but the amount also far exceeds monetary compensation for moral damages given by courts and tribunals. In this respect, one should also keep in mind, first, that the moral damage suffered by the investors will often already be (partly) remedied through

118 See ICJ, *Diallo*, Compensation owed by the DRC to the Republic of Guinea, Judgment, 19 June 2012, para. 21, referring back to the findings of the court in its judgment on the merits, which explicitly analyses the wrongful acts in relation to the International Covenant on Civil and Political Rights.

119 *Biloune* v. *Ghana*, UNCITRAL, Award on Jurisdiction and Liability.

120 *Ibid.*, paras 188–203.

121 *Generation Ukraine, Inc.* v. *Ukraine*, ICSID Case No. ARB/00/9, Award, 16 September 2003.

122 *Ibid.*, para. 17.6.

123 Cf., for instance, the decision of the International Court of Justice in *Diallo*, Compensation owed by the DRC to the Republic of Guinea, Judgment, 19 June 2012, and the case law of human rights courts (see the case law cited and discussed in Blake, 'Moral Damages in Investment Arbitration').

the award of pecuniary compensation for economic losses, which several tribunals have posited, as mentioned above. This is even more the case when compensation is given for lost profits, as was the case in *Al-Kharafi*. Secondly, it is doubtful that the award of a pecuniary compensation has the effect of 'wip[ing] out all the consequences of the illegal act and reestablish[ing] the situation which would, in all probability, have existed if that act had not been committed', to use the terminology of the PCIJ in the *Chorzów Factory* case. A symbolic amount for moral damage may achieve similar results, but is, however, to be considered more as a form of pecuniary satisfaction than compensation.[124] This criticism was also partially shared by the Tribunal in *Rompetrol* v. *Romania*.[125] The Tribunal not only refused to award compensation for material losses despite having found a limited breach of the FET clause, but also refused to award compensation for moral damages. The Tribunal considered that moral damages should not be awarded as a substitute for the claimant's inability to prove actual economic loss as part of the compensation for material injury caused. Reputational damage, according to the Tribunal, is a subcategory of economic loss that needs to be proven by the claimant, which the claimant had failed to do in this case. More generally, the Tribunal argued that arbitral tribunals should adopt 'a considerable degree of caution' in awarding moral damages.[126]

Fifthly, the principles established in *Desert Line* and *Lemire* are not based on a full and complete analysis of international judgments and awards, with the exception of the need for 'exceptional' circumstances. In the recent *Franck Charles Arif* v. *Moldova* case, the Tribunal refused to award moral damages to the claimant, and confirmed this criticism.[127] While accepting the possibility of awarding compensation for moral damages as a matter of principle and confirming the requirement of 'exceptional circumstances', as embodied in the *Lusitania* case and other investment tribunal decisions, the Tribunal rightly departed from the other conditions set forth in the *Lemire* case. The Tribunal noted that 'the formulation of the principles of the award of moral damages in *Lemire* was based on a limited discussion of three cases, with no broader consideration of underlying principles or policies'.[128] Applied to the facts of the case, the Tribunal refused to award compensation for

[124] Dumberry, 'Satisfaction as a Form of Reparation for Moral Damages', pp. 214–15.
[125] *Rompetrol Group NV* v. *Romania*, ICSID Case No. ARB/06/3, Award, 6 May 2013.
[126] *Ibid.*, paras 289–293.
[127] *Franck Charles Arif* v. *Moldova*, ICSID Case No. ARB/11/23, paras 584 ff.
[128] *Ibid.*, para. 590.

moral damages in the absence of any exceptional circumstances. Interestingly, the Tribunal considered the need to take into consideration the fact that investments take place in states 'where the rule of law and protection against administrative discretion are low and any business is exposed to this risk, irrespective of its conduct'.[129] Finally, it should be added that since the claimant was a physical person, the possibility of awarding compensation for moral damages would not have been as problematic as it has been in *Desert Line* where compensation was awarded to individuals who were not, in and of themselves, investors.

Finally, the above-mentioned cases raise the question of whether, in accordance with the well-established practice in public international law in respect of moral damages to states reflected in the mentioned ILC Articles on the Responsibility of States, moral damages to a corporation, in particular reputational damage, cannot, in certain cases, more adequately be remedied through non-pecuniary reparation, such as satisfaction. This can be achieved, for example, through a statement to this effect in the award of the tribunal.[130] This was posited by the Tribunal in *Pey Casado* v. *Chile* in an *obiter dictum*. Although in that case the Tribunal refused to award compensation based on the lack of evidence of moral damages, it nevertheless noted that 'le prononcé de la présente sentence, notamment par sa reconnaissance des droits des demanderesses et du déni de justice dont elles furent victimes, constitue en soi une satisfaction morale substantielle et suffisante'.[131] This statement cannot be considered a clear affirmation of the fact that satisfaction is the most appropriate remedy for moral damages, since the Tribunal decided that there was insufficient evidence for such damage. It is, nevertheless, indicative in that it considered generally that a declaration of violation may constitute appropriate satisfaction for certain damages, and should be welcomed for this reason.

That satisfaction may be an adequate form of reparation for reputational damages has been confirmed in several cases in which the respondent state had requested reparation for moral damages. In *Europe Cement* v.

[129] *Ibid.*, para. 606.

[130] Wälde and Sabahi, 'Compensation, Damages and Valuation in International Investment Law', pp. 1112–14. See, however, Dumberry, 'Satisfaction as a Form of Reparation for Moral Damages', p. 227, claiming that pecuniary compensation 'should be the only appropriate remedy for moral damages affecting an individual or a corporation'.

[131] *Pey Casado* v. *Chile*, ICSID Case No. ARB/98/2, para. 689.

*Turkey*,[132] for instance, in which Turkey had requested compensation for moral damages because it had suffered reputational damage through a manifestly unfounded claim, the Tribunal considered that, because there were no exceptional circumstances such as physical duress:

> any potential reputational damage suffered by the Respondent will be remedied by the reasoning and conclusions set out in this Award, including an award of costs, which as set out below is significant. This provides a form of 'satisfaction' for the Respondent. In the circumstances, therefore, the Tribunal decides not to make a monetary award of compensation to the Respondent.[133]

In the parallel proceedings in *Cementownia* v. *Turkey*,[134] which involved the same individual, the Tribunal likewise refused to award monetary compensation for moral damages to Turkey, which it had claimed because of the reputational damage suffered by the abusive claims of the claimant. The Tribunal considered that:

> a symbolic compensation for moral damages may indeed aim at indicating a condemnation for abuse of process. However, in the case at hand, the Arbitral Tribunal deems it more appropriate to sanction the Claimant with respect to the allocation of costs. In any case, since the Arbitral Tribunal has already accepted the Respondent's request with respect to the fraudulent claim declaration, the Respondent's objective is already achieved.[135]

Satisfaction, moreover, avoids the overall problem of the quantification of the 'moral damage' of corporations, which is, in any event, difficult to prove financially, in particular, in cases of alleged reputational damage.[136]

[132] *Europe Cement Investment & Trade SA* v. *Republic of Turkey*, ICSID Case No. ARB(AF)/07/2, Award, 13 August 2009.
[133] *Ibid.*, para. 181.
[134] *Cementownia 'Nowa Huta' SA* v. *Republic of Turkey*, ICSID Case No. ARB(AF)/06/2, Award, 17 September 2009.
[135] *Ibid.*, para. 171 (internal references omitted).
[136] Cf. the statement of the Umpire in the *Lusitania* case, that these damages are 'difficult to measure or estimate by monetary standards' (*Lusitania* case, UNRIAA, vol. VII, p. 40). This statement was, moreover, quoted by the Tribunal in *Desert Line* v. *Yemen*, ICSID Case No. ARB/05/17, para. 289.

# Conclusion

This book has argued that investment arbitration is essentially a public international law dispute settlement mechanism. The characterization of investment treaty arbitration as having a 'hybrid' foundation, coupled with the claim that neither international commercial arbitration or private law, nor public international law are adequate legal paradigms to apply in these situations, tends to overlook the effective characterization of the underlying legal relations between foreign investors and host states when claims are brought against the latter for violations of an applicable investment agreement. I have argued that it is both useful and legally necessary to recognize the public international law foundation of investment treaty arbitration. Contemporary investment disputes are primarily concerned with the international responsibility of states for alleged violations of international legal obligations contained in an international legal instrument. Although investment law is characterized by the co-existence of two layers of obligations, which may explain the classification of such relations as dualistic, assessing the responsibility of a state for alleged violations of its international investment obligations is an exercise in applying public international law rules and principles. Such an inquiry, of course, does not imply that private law relations between foreign investors and host states are absent.

Based on this premise, and dissimilar to contemporary theories embracing the hybridity or the public law character of investment treaty arbitration, I have argued that the public international law characteristics of dispute and of investment treaty arbitration generally are visible from the arbitral proceedings, and at the same time have important implications for that procedure. This is so because the acts of the host state, and the public international law dispute settlement mechanism established to judge and evaluate the exercise of this power by the state, are of interest for a broader range of entities and individuals than the mere investor. At the same time, I have made clear that the very concept of international arbitration and the rules inherent to that dispute settlement method should remain intact. In other words, the underlying premise of this book has been to show that investment treaty arbitration is, as such, a viable and functioning dispute settlement system, provided that the necessary implications of the public international law character of the dispute on the rules and principles borrowed from international commercial arbitration are taken into consideration.

This book's main aim has been to provide an analysis and systemic perspective of the various procedural ways in which the public international law character is revealed or has influenced the arbitral proceedings. In doing so, I have balanced these effects with the need to maintain the fundamental foundations of arbitral proceedings. Importantly, this book has shown that the flexibility offered by the use of arbitration as a dispute settlement method is particularly suitable for adaptations that take into account the public international law foundation of investment treaty arbitration.

In certain procedural areas, the public international law dimension of investment treaty arbitration has already been fully recognized and adopted. Such areas include, *inter alia*, the rules relating to transparency and public access to the proceedings. Without doubt, the opening of the proceedings to non-disputing party submissions is a positive development from the perspective of the legitimacy and transparency of the process, in particular, in those cases that are of high public interest, provided that such submissions remain within the boundary set by the very reasons for their admissibility. Similarly, in respect of the legal reasoning and the principles of party autonomy, contemporary practice in investment treaty arbitration has taken into consideration the public international law dimension of the system. Such taking into consideration is visible in certain decisions of arbitral tribunals, and thus reveals again the prevalence of public international law principles in investment treaty arbitration.

In the other areas discussed, however, investment treaty arbitration is still very much subject to tensions between the public international law character of investment treaty arbitration and the rules and principles of international commercial arbitration. In relation to the independence and impartiality of arbitrators, for instance, insufficient account is currently given to the implications of the public availability of awards on questions such as 'issue/role conflicts'. At the same time, and this clearly shows the inherent tensions in the system, arbitration is based on the idea that parties choose the arbitrators that are to decide the dispute. An overly broad regulation of the qualifications of arbitrators may thus be contrary to the flexibility offered by arbitration.

As far as the applicable law is concerned, however, investment tribunals are still reluctant to engage in consideration of issues that are not part of the narrow relation between host states and foreign investors. This is particularly visible in respect of the reluctance of tribunals generally to assess the human rights obligations of host states, often invoked by the latter to 'justify' departures from their obligations under investment protection treaties. There is, however, as was explained, no principled prohibition to this effect. The same is true in respect of remedies. Tribunals have a tendency to favour the award of relatively important amounts of pecuniary compensation, making the system attractive to foreign investors. There is, however, no reason why, as a matter of principle, other forms of reparation should not, under certain circumstances, and in certain situations, accord the same remedy to investors. This would, moreover, be in accordance with well-accepted principles of international law.

This book has confirmed the importance and efficacy of investment treaty arbitration as a method of settling disputes between foreign investors and host states. There is, indeed, no principled reason to dismiss this system because the very reasons behind its creation are judicious and still valid today. This, however, does not imply that its public international law dimension should be disregarded. On the contrary, recognizing the latter may, ironically, ensure the viability of the system for the future.

# Bibliography

ARTICLES

Appleton, Arthur E., '*Amicus Curiae* Submissions in the Carbon Steel Case: Another Rabbit from the Appellate Body's Hat?', *Journal of International Economic Law*, 3(4) (2000): 691.

Baldwin, Edward, Mark Kantor and Michael Nolan, 'Limits to Enforcement of ICSID Awards', *Journal of International Arbitration*, 23(1) (2006): 1.

Bevilacqua, Thomas, 'Voluntary Intervention and Other Participation of Third Parties in Ongoing International Arbitrations: A Survey of the Current State of Play', *World Arbitration & Mediation Review*, 1(4) (2007): 507.

Bingham, Thomas, 'Reasons and Reasons and Reasons: Differences Between a Court Judgment and an Arbitral Award', *Arbitration International*, 4(2) (1988): 141.

Blackaby, Nigel, 'Public Interest and Investment Treaty Arbitration', *Transnational Dispute Management*, 1 (2004): 1.

Blake, Conway, 'Moral Damages in Investment Arbitration: A Role for Human Rights?', *Journal of International Dispute Settlement*, 3(2) (2012): 371.

Bodansky, Daniel and John R. Crook, 'Symposium: The ILC's State Responsibility Articles: Introduction and Overview', *American Journal of International Law*, 96(4) (2002): 773.

Boisson de Chazournes, Laurence, 'Transparency and *Amicus Curiae* Briefs', *Journal of World Investment and Trade*, 5(2) (2004): 333.

Bottini, Gabriel, 'Should Arbitrators Live on Mars? Challenge of Arbitrators in Investment Arbitration', *Suffolk Transnational Law Review*, 32(2) (2009): 341.

Broches, Aron, 'The Convention on the Settlement of Investment Disputes Between States and Nationals of Other States', *Recueil des Cours*, 136 (1972): 329.

Brower II, Charles H., 'Structure, Legitimacy, and NAFTA's Investment Chapter', *Vanderbilt Journal of Transnational Law*, 36(1) (2003): 37.

'The Function and Limits of Arbitration and Judicial Settlement under Private and Public International Law', *Duke Journal of Comparative and International Law*, 18(2) (2007/8): 259.

Brower, Charles N. and Michael N. Ottolenghi, 'Damages in Investor–State Arbitration', *Transnational Dispute Management*, 4 (2007): 6.

Brown, Chester, 'The Inherent Powers of International Courts and Tribunals', *British Yearbook of International Law*, 76 (2005): 195.

Buergenthal, Thomas, 'The Proliferation of Disputes, Dispute Settlement Procedures and Respect for the Rule of Law', *Arbitration International*, 22(4) (2006): 495.

Caron, David, 'The Nature of the Iran–United States Claims Tribunal and the Evolving Structure of International Dispute Resolution', *American Journal of International Law*, 84(1) (1990): 104.

'The ILC Articles on State Responsibility: The Paradoxical Relationship between Form and Authority', *American Journal of International Law*, 96(4) (2002): 857.

Carver, Jeremy, 'The Strengths and Weaknesses of International Arbitration Involving a State as a Party: Practical Implications', *Arbitration International*, 1(2) (1985): 179.

Cheng, Tai-Heng and Robert Trisotto, 'Reasons and Reasoning in Investment Treaty Arbitration', *Suffolk Transnational Law Review*, 32(2) (2009): 409.

Coe, Jack J., 'Transparency in the Resolution of Investor–State Disputes: Adoption, Adaptation and NAFTA Leadership', *University of Kansas Law Review*, 54(4) (2005/6): 1339.

Crawford, James, 'Treaty and Contract in Investment Arbitration', *Arbitration International*, 24(3) (2008): 351.

d'Argent, Pierre, 'Le droit de la responsabilité internationale complété? Examen des Principes fondamentaux et directives concernant le droit à un recours et à réparation des victimes de violations flagrantes du droit international des droits de l'homme et de violations graves du droit international humanitaire', *Annuaire français de droit international*, 51 (2005): 27.

Davis, Megan, 'New Developments in International Advocacy: *Amicus Curiae* and the World Trade Organization', *Indigenous Law Bulletin*, 5 (2003), available at: www.austlii.edu.au/au/journals/ILB/2003/28.html.

De Brabandere, Eric, 'NGOs and the "Public Interest": The Legality and Rationale of *Amicus Curiae* Interventions in International Economic and Investment Disputes', *Chicago Journal of International Law*, 12(1) (2011): 85.

'Individuals in Advisory Proceedings before the International Court of Justice: Equality of the Parties and the Court's Discretionary Authority', *Law and Practice of International Courts and Tribunals*, 11(2) (2012): 253.

Desierto, Diane A., 'Conflict of Treaties, Interpretation, and Decision-making on Human Rights and Investment During Economic Crises', *Transnational Dispute Management*, 10 (2013): 1.

Douglas, Zachary, 'The Hybrid Foundations of Investment Treaty Arbitration', *British Yearbook of International Law*, 74 (2004): 151.

Dumberry, Patrick, 'The Admissibility of *Amicus Curiae* Briefs by NGOs in Investor–States Arbitration: The Precedent Set by the Methanex Case in the

Context of NAFTA Chapter 11 Proceedings', *Non-State Actors and International Law*, 1(3) (2001): 201.
'Compensation for Moral Damages in Investor–State Arbitration Disputes', *Journal of International Arbitration*, 27(3) (2010): 247.
'Satisfaction as a Form of Reparation for Moral Damages Suffered by Investors and Respondent States in Investor–State Arbitration Disputes', *Journal of International Dispute Settlement*, 3(1) (2012): 205.
Fon, Vincy and Francesco Parisi, 'Judicial Precedents in Civil Law Systems: A Dynamic Analysis', *International Review of Law and Economics*, 26(4) (2006): 519.
Fox, Hazel, 'States and the Undertaking to Arbitrate', *International and Comparative Law Quarterly*, 37(1) (1988): 1.
Francioni, Francesco, 'Access to Justice, Denial of Justice and International Investment Law', *European Journal of International Law*, 20(3) (2009): 729.
Galgano, Francesco, 'The New *Lex Mercatoria*', *Annual Survey of International & Comparative Law*, 2 (1995): 99.
García-Bolívar, Omar E., 'Comparing Arbitrator Standards of Conduct in International Commercial, Trade and Investment Disputes', *Dispute Resolution Journal*, 60(4) (2005): 76.
Gerbay, Rémy, 'Confidentiality vs Transparency in International Arbitration: The English Perspective', *Transnational Dispute Management*, 9 (2012): 3.
Giovannini, Teresa, 'International Arbitration and *Jura Novit Curia*: Towards Harmonization', *Transnational Dispute Management*, 9 (2012): 3.
Guillaume, Gilbert, 'The Use of Precedent by International Judges and Arbitrators', *Journal of International Dispute Settlement*, 2(1) (2011): 5.
Hacking, David, 'Ethics, Elitism, Eligibility: A Response – What Happens if the Icelandic Arbitrator Falls Through the Ice?' *Journal of International Arbitration*, 15(4) (1998): 73.
Hardenberg, L., 'The Awards of the Iran–United States Claims Tribunal Seen in Connection with the Law of the Netherlands', *International Business Lawyer*, 12 (1984): 337.
Henry, Robert L., '*Jurisprudence Constante* and *Stare Decisis* Contrasted', *American Bar Association Journal*, 15(1) (1929): 11.
Kaufmann-Kohler, Gabrielle, 'Globalization of Arbitral Procedure', *Vanderbilt Journal of Transnational Law*, 36(4) (2003): 1313.
'Arbitral Precedent: Dream, Necessity or Excuse?', *Arbitration International*, 23(3) (2007): 357.
Kessedjian, Catherine, 'Principe de la contradiction et arbitrage', *Revue de l'arbitrage*, 3 (1995): 381.
Knahr, Christina and August Reinisch, 'Transparency versus Confidentiality in International Investment Arbitration: The Biwater Gauff Compromise', *Law and Practice of International Courts and Tribunals*, 6(1) (2007): 97.
Kriebaum, Ursula, 'Foreign Investments and Human Rights: The Actors and Their Different Roles', *Transnational Dispute Management*, 10 (2013): 1.

Kuo, Houchi, 'The Issue of Repeat Arbitrators: Is it a Problem and How Should the Arbitration Institutions Respond?', *Contemporary Asia Arbitration Journal*, 4(2) (2011): 247.

Laird, Ian and Rebecca Askew, 'Finality versus Consistency: Does Investor–State Arbitration Need an Appellate System', *Journal of Appellate Practice and Process*, 7(2) (2005): 285.

Lake, William and Jane Tucker Dana, 'Judicial Review of Awards of the Iran–United States Claims Tribunal: Are the Tribunal's Awards Dutch?', *Law & Policy in International Business*, 16 (1984): 755.

Lalive, Pierre, 'On the Reasoning of International Arbitral Awards', *Journal of International Dispute Settlement*, 1(1) (2010): 55.

Lee, Ilhyung, 'Practice and Predicament: The Nationality of the International Arbitrator (with Survey Results)', *Fordham International Law Journal*, 31(3) (2007): 603.

Levine, Judith, 'Dealing with Arbitrator "Issue Conflicts" in International Arbitration', *Dispute Resolution Journal*, 61(1) (2006): 60.

Mann, Francis A., 'The Theoretical Approach Towards the Law Governing Contracts Between States and Private Persons', *Revue Belge de Droit International*, 11(2) (1975): 563.

Muchlinski, Peter, 'Human Rights, Social Responsibility and the Regulation of International Business: The Development of International Standards by Intergovernmental Organisations', *Non-State Actors and International Law*, 3(1) (2003): 123.

Mus, Jan B., 'Conflicts between Treaties in International Law', *Netherlands International Law Review*, 45(3) (1998): 208.

Nelson, Timothy G., 'Human Rights and BIT Protection: Areas of Convergence, *Journal of World Investment & Trade*, 11(1) (2011): 27.

Nollkaemper, André, 'The Role of Domestic Courts in the Case Law of the International Court of Justice', *Chinese Journal of International Law*, 5(2) (2006): 301.

Ortino, Federico, 'Legal Reasoning of International Investment Tribunals: A Typology of Egregious Failures', *Journal of International Dispute Settlement*, 3(1) (2012): 31.

Parish, Matthew T., Annalise K. Newlson and Charles B. Rosenberg, 'Awarding Moral Damages to Respondent States in Investment Arbitration', *Berkeley Journal of International Law*, 29(1) (2011): 225.

Paulsson, Jan, 'Arbitration without Privity', *ICSID Review – Foreign Investment Law Journal*, 10(2) (1995): 232.

'Ethics, Elitism, Eligibility', *Journal of International Arbitration*, 14(4) (1997): 13.

'International Arbitration and the Generation of Legal Norms: Treaty Arbitration and International Law', *Transnational Dispute Management*, 3 (2006): 5.

Pauwelyn, Joost, 'Bridging Fragmentation and Unity: International Law as a Universe of Inter-Connected Islands', *Michigan Journal of International Law*, 25(4) (2003/4): 903.

Radi, Yannick, 'The Application of the Most-Favoured-Nation Clause to the Dispute Settlement Provisions of Bilateral Investment Treaties: Domesticating the Trojan Horse', *European Journal of International Law*, 18(4) (2007): 757.

'The "Human Nature" of International Investment Law', *Transnational Dispute Management*, 10 (2013): 1.

Rau, Alan Scott, 'On Integrity in Private Judging', *Arbitration International*, 14(2) (1998): 115.

Roberts, Anthea, 'Clash of Paradigms: Actors and Analogies Shaping the Investment Treaty System', *American Journal of International Law*, 107(1) (2013): 45.

Rodgers, Marie-Louise M., 'Bilateral Investment Treaties and Arbitration: An Argument and a Proposal for the ICSID's Implementation of a System of Binding Precedent', *Transnational Dispute Management*, 5 (2008): 3.

Schachter, Oscar, 'Editorial Comment. Compensation for Expropriation', *American Journal of International Law*, 78(1) (1984): 121.

Schill, Stephan W., 'Enabling Private Ordering: Function, Scope and Effect of Umbrella Clauses in International Investment Treaties', *Minnesota Journal of International Law*, 18(1) (2009): 1.

'Crafting the International Economic Order: The Public Function of Investment Treaty Arbitration and its Significance for the Role of the Arbitrator', *Leiden Journal of International Law*, 23(2) (2010): 401.

Schreuer, Christoph, 'Non-pecuniary Remedies in ICSID', *Arbitration International*, 20(4) (2004): 325.

Shany, Yuval, 'Notes and Comments. Contract Claims v. Treaty Claims: Mapping Conflicts Between ICSID Decisions on Multi-Sourced Investment Claims', *American Journal of International Law*, 99(4) (2005): 835.

Simma, Bruno, 'Foreign Investment Arbitration: A Place for Human Rights?', *International and Comparative Law Quarterly*, 60(3) (2011): 573.

Simmons, Joshua B., 'Valuation in Investor–State Arbitration: Toward a More Exact Science', *Berkeley Journal of International Law*, 30(1) (2012): 196.

Spiermann, Ole, 'Individual Rights, State Interests and the Power to Waive ICSID Jurisdiction under Bilateral Investment Treaties', *Arbitration International*, 20(2) (2004): 179.

Spoorenberg, Frank and Jorge E. Viñuales, 'Conflicting Decisions in International Arbitration', *Law and Practice of International Courts and Tribunals*, 8(1) (2009): 91.

Tate Jr., Albert, 'Techniques of Judicial Interpretation in Louisiana', *Louisiana Law Review*, 22(4) (1962): 727.

Teitelbaum, Ruth, 'A Look at the Public Interest in Investment Arbitration: Is it Unique? What Should We do About It?', *Berkeley Journal of International Law Publicist*, 5 (2010): 54.

Tienhaara, Kyla, 'Third Party Participation in Investment–Environment Disputes: Recent Developments', *Review of European Community & International Environmental Law*, 16(2) (2007): 230.

van den Berg, Albert-Jan, 'Proposed Dutch Law on the Iran–United States Claims Settlement Declaration, A Reaction to Mr. Hardenberg's Article', *International Business Lawyer*, 12 (1984): 341.

Van Harten, Gus and Martin Loughlin, 'Investment Treaty Arbitration as a Species of Global Administrative Law', *European Journal of International Law*, 17(1) (2006): 121.

von Wobeser, Claus, 'The Arbitral Tribunal-Appointed Expert', *Transnational Dispute Management*, 4 (2007): 3.

Wälde, Thomas W., 'The "Umbrella Clause" in Investment Arbitration: A Comment on Original Intentions and Recent Cases', *Journal of World Investment & Trade*, 6(2) (2005): 183.

'Procedural Challenges in Investment Arbitration Under the Shadow of the Dual Role of the State: Asymmetries and Tribunal's Duty to Ensure, Pro-actively, the Equality of Arms', *Arbitration International*, 26(1) (2010): 3.

Williams, Sarah J. and Hannah Woolaver, 'The Role of the *Amicus Curiae* before International Criminal Tribunals', *International Criminal Law Review*, 6(2) (2006): 151.

Wythes, Annika, 'Investor–State Arbitrations: Can the "Fair and Equitable Treatment" Clause Consider International Human Rights Obligations?', *Leiden Journal of International Law*, 23(1) (2010): 241.

## BOOK CHAPTERS

Aguilar Alvarez, Guillermo and W. Michael Reisman, 'How Well are Investment Awards Reasoned?', in Guillermo Aguilar Alvarez and W. Michael Reisman (eds.), *The Reasons Requirement in International Investment Arbitration: Critical Case Studies*. Leiden: Martinus Nijhoff, 2008, pp. 1–33.

Asteriti, Alessandra and Christian Tams, 'Transparency and Representation of the Public Interest in Investment Treaty Arbitration', in Schill (ed.), *International Investment Law and Comparative Public Law*, pp. 787–816.

Audit, Bernard, 'L'arbitrage international et les contrats d'État: bilan et perspectives', in Centre d'étude et de recherche de droit international et de relations internationales, *L'arbitrage transnational et les contrats d'État*. Dordrecht: Martinus Nijhoff, 1987.

Azzali, Stefano, 'Introduction: Balancing Confidentiality and Transparency', in Malatesta and Sali (eds.), *The Rise of Transparency in International Arbitration*, pp. xix–xxxii.

Banifatemi, Yas, 'The Law Applicable in Investment Treaty Arbitration', in Katia Yannaca-Small (ed.), *Arbitration under International Investment Agreements. A Guide to the Key Issues*. Oxford University Press, 2010, pp. 191–210.

Bjorklund, Andrea K., 'Investment Treaty Arbitral Decisions as *Jurisprudence Constante*', in Colin B. Picker, Isabella D. Bunn and Douglas W. Arner (eds.), *International Economic Law: The State and Future of the Discipline*. Oxford: Hart, 2008, pp. 265–80.

'The Participation of Sub-national Government Units as *Amici Curiae* in International Investment Disputes', in Brown and Miles (eds.), *Evolution in Investment Treaty Law and Arbitration*, pp. 298–316.

Böckstiegel, Karl-Heinz, 'The Role of the Arbitrators in Investment Treaty Arbitration', in Albert Jan van den Berg (ed.), *International Commercial Arbitration. Important Contemporary Questions, ICCA Congress Series, 2002, London*, vol. 11. The Hague: Kluwer Law International, 2003, pp. 1–50.

Coe, Jack J., 'The Tribunal's Transparency Features: Some Observations', in Christopher R. Drahozal and Christopher S. Gibson (eds.), *The Iran–U.S. Claims Tribunal at 25: The Cases Everyone Needs to Know for Investor–State and International Arbitration*. Oxford University Press, 2007, pp. 119–64.

Comoglio, Paolo and Chiara Roncarolo, 'Presenting the Guidelines for the Publication of Arbitral Awards: Aiming to the Circulation of a Solid Arbitral Case Law', in Malatesta and Sali (eds.), *The Rise of Transparency in International Arbitration*, pp. 1–37.

Cordero-Moss, Giuditta, 'Tribunal's Powers versus Party Autonomy', in Muchlinski, Ortino and Schreuer (eds.), *The Oxford Handbook of International Investment Law*, pp. 1207–44.

Crawford, James, 'State Responsibility', in Wolfrüm (ed.), *Max Planck Encyclopedia of Public International Law*, vol. IX, pp. 517–32.

d'Aspremont, Jean, 'Customary International Investment Law: Story of a Paradox', in Gazzini and Brabandere (eds.), *International Investment Law*, pp. 5–47.

'Articulating International Human Rights and International Humanitarian Law: Conciliatory Interpretation under the Guise of Conflict of Norms-Resolution', in Fitzmaurice and Merkouris (eds.), *The Interpretation and Application of the European Convention of Human Rights*, pp. 3–32.

De Brabandere, Eric, 'Pragmatism in International Law: Non-State Actor Participation in International Dispute Settlement', in d'Aspremont (ed.), *Participants in the International Legal System*, pp. 342–59.

'Non-State Actors and the Proliferation and Individualization of International Dispute Settlement', in Bob Reinalda (ed.), *The Ashgate Research Companion to Non-State Actors*. Farnham: Ashgate, 2011, pp. 347–59.

'Arbitral Decisions as a Source of International Investment Law', in Gazzini and De Brabandere (eds.), *International Investment Law*, pp. 245–88.

'Human Rights Considerations in International Investment Arbitration', in Fitzmaurice and Merkouris (eds.), *The Interpretation and Application of the European Convention of Human Rights*, pp. 183–215.

'Co-existence and Conflict: Interaction between Preferential Trade and Investment Agreements and the BIT World', in Rainer Hofmann, Christian Tams and Stephan Schill (eds.), *Preferential Trade and Investment Agreements. A New Ordering Paradigm for International Investment Relations?* Baden-Baden: Nomos Publishers, 2013, pp. 37–69.

Douglas, Zachary, 'Other Specific Regimes of Responsibility: Investment Treaty Arbitration and ICSID', in James Crawford, Alain Pellet and Simon Olleson (eds.), *The Law of International Responsibility*. Oxford University Press, 2010, pp. 815–42.

Dumberry, Patrick, 'International Investment Contracts', in Gazzini and De Brabandere (eds.), *International Investment Law*, pp. 215–44.

Dumberry, Patrick and Erik Labelle-Eastaugh, 'Non-state Actors in International Investment Law: The Legal Personality of Corporations and NGOs in the Context of Investor–State Arbitration', in d'Aspremont (ed.), *Participants in the International Legal System*, pp. 360–71.

Dupuy, Pierre-Marie, 'Unification Rather than Fragmentation of International Law? The Case of International Investment Law and Human Rights Law', in Dupuy, Francioni and Petersmann (eds.), *Human Rights in International Investment Law and Arbitration*, pp. 45–62.

Francioni, Francesco, 'Access to Justice, Denial of Justice, and International Investment Law', in Dupuy, Francioni and Petersmann (eds.), *Human Rights in International Investment Law and Arbitration*, pp. 63–81.

Gaillard, Emmanuel, 'Investment Treaty Arbitration and Jurisdiction over Contract Claims: The SGS Cases Considered', in Weiler (ed.), *International Investment Law and Arbitration*, pp. 338–45.

García-Bolívar, Omar E., 'Comparing Arbitrator Standards of Conduct in International Commercial, Trade and Investment Disputes', in American Arbitration Association (ed.), *Handbook on International Arbitration Practice*, Huntington, NY: Juris, 2010, pp. 251–68.

Hirsch, Moshe, 'Investment Tribunals and Human Rights: Divergent Paths', in Dupuy, Francioni and Petersmann (eds.), *Human Rights in International Investment Law and Arbitration*, pp. 97–114.

Kalderminis, Daniel, 'Investment Treaty Arbitration as Global Administrative Law: What this Might Mean in Practice', in Brown and Miles (eds.), *Evolution in Investment Treaty Law and Arbitration*, pp. 145–59.

Kaufmann-Kohler, Gabrielle, 'Iura novit arbiter: Est-ce bien raisonnable?' in Anne Héritier and Laurent Hirsch (eds.), *De Lege Ferenda. Réflexions sur le droit désirable en l'honneur du Professeur Alain Hirsch*. Geneva: Editions Slatkine, 2004, pp. 71–8.

'The Governing Law: Fact or Law? A Transnational Rule on Establishing its Content', in Markus Wirth (ed.), *Best Practices in International Arbitration*, ASA Swiss Arbitration Association Conference of January 27, 2006, Zurich, ASA Special Series No. 26. Basel: Association Suisse de l'Arbitrage, 2006, pp. 79–85.

Kessedjian, Catherine, 'To Give or Not to Give Precedential Value to Investment Arbitration Awards', in Catherine A. Rogers and Roger P. Alford (eds.), *The Future of Investment Arbitration*. Oxford University Press, 2009, pp. 43–68.

Kinnear, Meg, Eloïse Obadia and Michael Gagain, 'The ICSID Approach to Publication of Information in Investor–State Arbitration', in Malatesta and Sali (eds.), *The Rise of Transparency in International Arbitration*, pp. 107–22.

Knoll-Tudor, Ioanna, 'The Fair and Equitable Treatment Standard and Human Rights Norms', in Dupuy, Francioni and Petersmann (eds.), *Human Rights in International Investment Law and Arbitration*, pp. 310–42.

Landau, Toby, 'Reasons for Reasons: The Tribunal's Duty in Investor–State Arbitration', in A. J. van den Berg (ed.), *ICCA Congress Series No. 8 14 Dublin Conference, 2008*. The Hague: Kluwer Law International, 2009, pp. 187–205.

Lutrell, Sam, 'Bias Challenges in Investor–State Arbitration: Lessons from International Commercial Arbitration', in Brown and Miles (eds.), *Evolution in Investment Treaty Law and Arbitration*, pp. 445–82.

McCaffrey, Stephen C., 'The Human Right to Water', in Edith Brown Weiss, Laurence Boisson de Chazournes and Nathalie Bernasconi-Osterwalder (eds.), *Fresh Water and International Economic Law*. Oxford University Press, 2005, pp. 93–115.

Merrills, John, 'The Means of Dispute Settlement', in Malcolm N. Evans (ed.), *International Law*. Oxford University Press, 2011, pp. 313–39.

Paparinskis, Martins, 'Inherent Powers of ICSID Tribunals: Broad and Rightly So', in Todd Weiler and Ian Laird (eds.), *Investment Treaty Arbitration and International Law*. Huntington, NY: JurisNet, 2012, pp. 11–76.

Parra, Antonio, 'Applicable Law in Investor–State Arbitration', in Arthur Rovine (ed.), *Contemporary Issues in International Arbitration and Mediation*. Leiden: Martinus Nijhoff, 2008, pp. 3–12.

Petersmann, Ernst-Ulrich, 'Human Rights and International Trade Law: Defining and Connecting the Two Fields', in Thomas Cottier, Joost Pauwelyn and Elisabeth Bürgi (eds.), *Human Rights and International Trade*. Oxford University Press, 2005, pp. 29–94.

Rigo Sureda, Andrés, 'Precedent in Investment Treaty Arbitration', in Christina Binder, Ursula Kriebaum, August Reinisch and Stephan Wittich (eds.), *International Investment Law for the 21st Century. Essays in Honour of Christoph Schreuer*. Oxford University Press, 2009, pp. 830–42.

Rubins, Noah and Bernhard Lauterburg, 'Independence, Impartiality and Duty of Disclosure in Investment Arbitration', in Christina Knahr, Christian Koller, Walter Rechberger and August Reinisch (eds.), *Investment and Commercial Arbitration. Similarities and Divergences*. Utrecht: Eleven International, 2010, pp. 153–80.

Sands, Philippe, 'Conflict and Conflicts in Investment Treaty Arbitration: Ethical Standards for Counsel', in Brown and Miles (eds.), *Evolution in Investment Treaty Law and Arbitration*, pp. 19–41.

Sands, Philippe and Ruth Mackenzie, 'International Courts and Tribunals, *Amicus Curiae*', in Wolfrüm (ed.), *Max Planck Encyclopedia of Public International Law*, vol. II, pp. 519–26.

Schreuer, Christoph, 'Three Generations of ICSID Annulment Proceedings', in Emmanuel Gaillard and Yas Banifatemi (eds.), *Annulment of ICSID Awards*. Huntington, NY: Juris, 2004, pp. 17–42.

'Investment Treaty Arbitration and Jurisdiction over Contract Claims: The *Vivendi I* Case', in Weiler (ed.), *International Investment Law and Arbitration*, pp. 281–323.

Schreuer, Christoph and Matthew Weiniger, 'A Doctrine of Precedent?', in Muchlinski, Ortino and Schreuer (eds.), *The Oxford Handbook of International Investment Law*, pp. 1188–206.

Schwenzer, Ingeborg and Pascal Hachem, 'Moral Damages in International Investment Arbitration', in Stefan Kröll, Loukas Mistelis, Pilar Perales Viscasillas and Vikki Rogers (eds.), *International Arbitration and International Commercial Law: Synergy, Convergence and Evolution, Liber Amicorum Eric Bergsten*. Alphen aan den Rijn: Kluwer Law International, 2011, pp. 411–30.

Thielbörger, Pierre, 'The Human Right to Water versus Investor Rights: Double-Dilemma or Pseudo-Conflict?', in Dupuy, Francioni and Petersmann (eds.), *Human Rights in International Investment Law and Arbitration*, pp. 487–510.

van Aaken, Anne, 'Primary and Secondary Remedies in International Investment Law and National State Liability: A Functional and Comparative View', in Schill (ed.), *International Investment Law and Comparative Public Law*, pp. 721–54.

van Haersholte-van Hof, Jacomijn J. and Anne K. Hoffmann, 'The Relationship between International Tribunals and Domestic Courts', in Muchlinski, Ortino and Schreuer (eds.), *The Oxford Handbook of International Investment Law*, pp. 962–1007.

Wälde, Thomas W. and Borzu Sabahi, 'Compensation, Damages and Valuation in International Investment Law', in Muchlinski, Ortino and Schreuer (eds.), *The Oxford Handbook of International Investment Law*, pp. 1049–124.

Weil, Prosper, 'Droit international et contrat d'Etat', in *Mélanges offerts à Paul Reuter. Le droit international: unité et diversité*. Paris: Pedone, 1981.

Wittich, Stephan, 'The Limits of Party Autonomy in Investment Arbitration', in Christina Knahr, Christian Koller, Walter Rechberger and August Reinisch (eds.), *Investment and Commercial Arbitration. Similarities and Divergences*, Utrecht: Eleven International Publishing, 2010, pp. 47–71.

## BOOKS

Blackaby, Nigel, Constantine Partasides, Alan Redfern and Martin Hunter, *Redfern & Hunter on International Arbitration*, 5th edn. Oxford University Press, 2009.

Boisson de Chazournes, Laurence, *Fresh Water in International Law*. Oxford University Press, 2013.

Brower, Charles N. and Jason D. Brueschke, *The Iran–United States Claims Tribunal*. The Hague: Martinus Nijhoff, 1998.

Brown, Chester, *A Common Law of International Adjudication*. Oxford University Press, 2007.

Brown, Chester and Kate Miles (eds.), *Evolution in Investment Treaty Law and Arbitration*. Cambridge University Press, 2011.

Caron, David, Matti Pellonpää and Lee M. Caplan, *The UNCITRAL Arbitration Rules. A Commentary*. Oxford University Press, 2006.

Collier, John and Vaughan Lowe, *The Settlement of Disputes in International Law. Institutions and Procedures*. Oxford University Press, 1999.

d'Aspremont, Jean (ed.), *Participants in the International Legal System. Theoretical Perspectives*. London: Routledge, 2010.
Derains, Yves and Laurent Levy (eds.), *Is Arbitration Only as Good as the Arbitrator? Status, Powers and Role of the Arbitrator*. Paris: ICC Institute of World Business Law, 2012.
Derains, Yves and Eric A. Schwartz, *A Guide to the ICC Rules of Arbitration*. The Hague: Kluwer Law International, 2005.
Dolzer, Rudolf and Christoph Schreuer, *Principles of International Investment Law*. Oxford University Press, 2008.
Douglas, Zachary, *The International Law of Investment Treaty Claims*. Cambridge University Press, 2009.
Dupuy, Pierre-Marie, Francesco Francioni and Ernst-Ulrich Petersmann (eds.), *Human Rights in International Investment Law and Arbitration*. Oxford University Press, 2009.
Fitzmaurice, Malgosia and Olufemi Elias, *Contemporary Issues in the Law of Treaties*. Utrecht: Eleven, 2005.
Fitzmaurice, Malgosia and Panos Merkouris (eds.), *The Interpretation and Application of the European Convention of Human Rights: Legal and Practical Implications*. Leiden: Martinus Nijhoff, 2012.
Gazzini, Tarcisio and Eric De Brabandere (eds.), *International Investment Law: The Sources of Rights and Obligations*. Leiden: Martinus Nijhoff, 2012.
Holtzmann, Howard M. and Edda Kristjánsdóttir (eds.), *International Mass Claims Processes. Legal and Practical Perspectives*. Oxford University Press, 2007.
Jennings, Robert and Arthur Watts, *Oppenheim's International Law*, 9th edn. Oxford University Press, 1992.
Klabbers, Jan, *Treaty Conflict and the European Union*. Cambridge University Press 2009.
Kulick, Andreas, *Global Public Interest in International Investment Law*. Cambridge University Press, 2012.
Malatesta, Alberto, and Rinaldo Sali (eds.), *The Rise of Transparency in International Arbitration*. Huntington, NY: Juris, 2013.
McLachlan, Campbell, Laurence Shore and Matthew Weiniger, *International Investment Arbitration. Substantive Principles*. Oxford University Press, 2008.
Mistelis, Loukas, Pilar Perales Viscasillas and Vikki Rogers (eds.), *International Arbitration and International Commercial Law. Synergy, Convergence and Evolution, Liber Amicorum Eric Bergsten*. Alphen aan den Rijn: Kluwer Law International, 2011.
Montt, Santiago, *State Liability in Investment Treaty Arbitration: Global Constitutional and Administrative Law in the BIT Generation*. Oxford: Hart, 2009.
Moses, Margaret L., *The Principles and Practice of International Commercial Arbitration*. Cambridge University Press, 2008.
Muchlinski, Peter, Federico Ortino and Christoph Schreuer (eds.), *The Oxford Handbook of International Investment Law*. Oxford University Press, 2009.
Newcombe, Andrew and Lluis Paradell, *Law and Practice of Investment Treaties: Standards of Treatment*. Alphen aan den Rijn: Kluwer Law International, 2009.

Orrego Vicuña, Francisco, *International Dispute Settlement in an Evolving Global Society. Constitutionalization, Accessibility, Privatization.* Cambridge University Press, 2004.

Parra, Antonio R., *The History of the ICSID.* Oxford University Press, 2012.

Pasqualucci, Jo M., *The Practice and Procedure of the Inter-American Court of Human Rights.* Cambridge University Press, 2003.

Petrochilos, Georgios, *Procedural Law in International Arbitration.* Oxford University Press, 2004.

Ripinksy, Sergey and Kevin Williams, *Damages in International Investment Law.* London: British Institute of International and Comparative Law, 2008.

Rosenne, Shabtai, *Interpretation, Revision and Other Recourse from International Judgments and Awards.* Leiden: Martinus Nijhoff, 2007.

Salacuse, Jeswald W., *The Law of Investment Treaties.* Oxford University Press, 2009.

Schill, Stephan W. (ed.), *International Investment Law and Comparative Public Law.* Oxford University Press, 2010.

Schill, Stephan W., *The Multilateralization of International Investment Law.* Cambridge University Press, 2010.

Schreuer, Christoph, Loretta Malintoppi, August Reinisch and Anthony Sinclair, *The ICSID Convention. A Commentary.* Cambridge University Press, 2009.

Shahabuddeen, Mohamed, *Precedent in the World Court.* Cambridge University Press, 1996.

Van Harten, Gus, *Investment Treaty Arbitration and Public Law*, Oxford University Press, 2007.

Weiler, Todd (ed.), *International Investment Law and Arbitration. Leading Cases from the ICSID, NAFTA, Bilateral Treaties and Customary International Law.* London: Cameron May, 2005.

Wolfrüm, Rüdiger (ed.), *Max Planck Encyclopedia of Public International Law.* Oxford University Press, 2012.

## INTERNATIONAL CONVENTIONS

African Charter on Human and Peoples' Rights, 27 June 1981, 1520 UNTS 217.

American Convention on Human Rights, 21 November 1969, 1144 UNTS 143.

Convention for the Protection of Human Rights and Fundamental Freedoms, 4 November 1950, 213 UNTS 222.

Convention on the Recognition and Enforcement of Foreign Arbitral Awards, 10 June 1958, 330 UNTS 38 (1959).

Convention on the Settlement of Investment Disputes between States and Nationals of Other States, 18 March 1965, 575 UNTS 159.

United Nations Convention on the Law of the Sea, 10 December 1982, 1833 UNTS 3.

Vienna Convention on Consular Relations, 24 April 1963, 596 UNTS 261.

Vienna Convention on the Law of Treaties, 23 May 1969, 1155 UNTS 331.

## OFFICIAL DOCUMENTS


Declaration of the Democratic and Popular Republic of Algeria Concerning the Settlement of Claims by the Government of the United States of America and the Government of the Islamic Republic of Iran, *International Legal Materials*, 20 (1981): 223.

International Bar Association, IBA Guidelines on Conflicts of Interest in International Arbitration, approved on 22 May 2004 by the Council of the International Bar Association, available at: www.ibanet.org/Publications/publications_IBA_guides_and_free_materials.aspx#conflictsofinterest.

'IBA Rules on the Taking of Evidence in International Arbitration', Adopted by a resolution of the IBA Council 29 May 2010, available at: www.ibanet.org/Publications/publications_IBA_guides_and_free_materials.aspx.

*ICSID Caseload – Statistics*, Issue 2013-1, available at: https://icsid.worldbank.org/ICSID/FrontServlet?requestType=ICSIDDocRH&actionVal=CaseLoadStatistics.

ICSID News Release, *United Parcel Service of America, Inc.* v. *Government of Canada*, NAFTA/UNCITRAL Arbitration Rules Proceeding, 28 May 2001, available at: https://icsid.worldbank.org/ICSID/FrontServlet?requestType=CasesRH&actionVal=OpenPage&PageType=AnnouncementsFrame&FromPage=NewsReleases&pageName=Archive_%20Announcement6.

*United Parcel Service of America, Inc.* v. *Government of Canada*, NAFTA/UNCITRAL Arbitration Rules Proceeding, 7 December 2005, available at: https://icsid.worldbank.org/ICSID/FrontServlet?requestType=CasesRH&actionVal=OpenPage&PageType=AnnouncementsFrame&FromPage=NewsReleases&pageName=Archive_%.

ICSID Secretariat, 'Suggested Changes to the ICSID Rules and Regulations', Working Paper of the ICSID Secretariat, 12 May 2005, available at: http://icsid.worldbank.org/ICSID/FrontServlet?requestType=ICSIDPublicationsRH&actionVal=ViewAnnouncePDF&AnnouncementType=archive&AnnounceNo=14_1.pdf.

International Law Association, Committee on International Commercial Arbitration, Final Report: 'Ascertaining the Contents of the Applicable Law in International Commercial Arbitration', Rio de Janeiro Conference, 2008, available at: www.ila-hq.org/en/committees/index.cfm/cid/19.

International Law Commission, 'Articles on the Responsibility of States for Internationally Wrongful Acts', Report of the International Law Commission on the Work of its 53rd Session, Official Records of the General Assembly, 56th Session, Supplement No. 10, UN Doc. A/56/10, November 2001.

Draft Articles on Diplomatic Protection, International Law Commission, Report on the Work of its 58th Session, 1 May–9 June and 3 July–11 August 2006, General Assembly Official Records, 61st Session, Supplement No. 10, UN Doc. A/61/10, 1006, p. 26.

Final Report of the ILC Study Group on the issue of Fragmentation of International Law, UN Doc. A/CN.4/L.682, 13 April 2006.

Iran–United States Claims Tribunal, Tribunal Rules of Procedure, Notes to Article 15, para. 5, 3 May 1983, available at: www.iusct.org/tribunal-rules.pdf.

NAFTA Free Trade Commission, Notes of Interpretation of Certain Chapter 11 Provisions, 31 July 2001, available at: www.international.gc.ca/trade-agreements-accords-commerciaux/disp-diff/NAFTA-Interpr.aspx?lang=en&view=d.

Statement of the Free Trade Commission on Non-Disputing Party Participation, available at: www.international.gc.ca/trade-agreements-accords-commerciaux/assets/pdfs/Nondisputing-en.pdf, accessed 7 April 2010.

Permanent Court of Arbitration, 111th Annual Report, 2011, available at: www.pca-cpa.org/showpage.asp?pag_id=1069.

112th Annual Report, 2012, available at: www.wx4all.net/pca/PCA-annualreport_2012.pdf

United Nations General Assembly, United Nations Commission on International Trade Law, Settlement of Commercial Disputes: Preparation of a Legal Standard on Transparency in Treaty-based Investor–State Arbitration, Note by the Secretariat, UN Doc. A/CN.9/WG.II/WP.176, 30 November 2012.

Report of Working Group II (Arbitration and Conciliation) on the Work of its 58th Session, New York, 4–8 February 2013, UN Doc. A/CN.9/765, 13 February 2013.

## OTHER

Crawford, James, 'The Permanent Court of Arbitration and Mixed Arbitration, Remarks on the Occasion of a Celebration of the Centenary of the PCA', 18 October 2007, available at: www.pca-cpa.org/upload/files/Crawford%20EN.pdf.

Jacob, Marc, 'International Investment Agreements and Human Rights', INEF Research Paper Series on Human Rights, Corporate Responsibility and Sustainable Development 03/2010. Duisburg: Institute for Development and Peace, University of Duisburg-Essen, 2010, available at: www.humanrights-business.org/files/international_investment_agreements_and_human_rights.pdf.

Kingsbury, Benedict and Stephan Schill, 'Investor–State Arbitration as Governance: Fair and Equitable Treatment, Proportionality and the Emerging Global Administrative Law', IILJ Working Paper 2009/6, Global Administrative Law Series, available at: http://lsr.nellco.org/nyu_plltwp/146.

# Index

CAMBRIDGE STUDIES IN INTERNATIONAL AND COMPARATIVE LAW

*Books in the series*

*Investment Treaty Arbitration as Public International Law: Procedural Aspects and Implications*
Eric De Brabandere

*The New Entrants Problem in International Fisheries Law*
Andrew Serdy

*Substantive Protection under Investment Treaties: A Legal and Economic Analysis*
Jonathan Bonnitcha

*Popular Governance of Post-Conflict Reconstruction: The Role of International Law*
Matthew Saul

*Evolution of International Environmental Regimes: The Case of Climate Change*
Simone Schiele

*Judges, Law and War: The Judicial Development of International Humanitarian Law*
Shane Darcy

*Religious Offence and Human Rights: The Implications of Defamation of Religions*
Lorenz Langer

*Forum Shopping in International Adjudication: The Role of Preliminary Objections*
Luiz Eduardo Ribeiro Salles

*International Law and the Arctic*
Michael Byers

*Cooperation in the Law of Transboundary Water Resources*
Christina Leb

*Underwater Cultural Heritage and International Law*
Sarah Dromgoole

*State Responsibility: The General Part*
James Crawford

*The Origins of International Investment Law*
Kate Miles

*The Crime of Aggression under the Rome Statute of the International Criminal Court*
Carrie McDougall

*Crimes against Peace and International Law*
Kirsten Sellars

*The Non-Legal in International Law*
Fleur Johns

*Armed Conflict and Displacement: The Protection of Refugees and Displaced Persons under International Humanitarian Law*
Mélanie Jacques

*Foreign Investment and the Environment in International Law*
Jorge Viñuales

*The Human Rights Treaty Obligations of Peacekeepers*
Kjetil Larsen

*Cyberwarfare and the Laws of War*
Heather Harrison Dinniss

*The Right to Reparation in International Law for Victims of Armed Conflict*
Christine Evans

*Global Public Interest in International Investment Law*
Andreas Kulick

*State Immunity in International Law*
Xiaodong Yang

*Reparations and Victim Support in the International Criminal Court*
Conor McCarthy

*Reducing Genocide to Law: Definition, Meaning, and the Ultimate Crime*
Payam Akhavan

*Decolonizing International Law: Development, Economic Growth and the Politics of Universality*
Sundhya Pahuja

*Complicity and the Law of State Responsibility*
Helmut Philipp Aust

*State Control over Private Military and Security Companies in Armed Conflict*
Hannah Tonkin

*'Fair and Equitable Treatment' in International Investment Law*
Roland Kläger

*The UN and Human Rights: Who Guards the Guardians?*
Guglielmo Verdirame

*Sovereign Defaults before International Courts and Tribunals*
Michael Waibel

*Making the Law of the Sea: A Study in the Development of International Law*
James Harrison

*Science and the Precautionary Principle in International Courts and Tribunals: Expert Evidence, Burden of Proof and Finality*
Caroline E. Foster

*Transition from Illegal Regimes in International Law*
Yaël Ronen

*Access to Asylum: International Refugee Law and the Globalisation of Migration Control*
Thomas Gammeltoft-Hansen

*Trading Fish, Saving Fish: The Interaction between Regimes in International Law*
Margaret Young

*The Individual in the International Legal System: Continuity and Change in International Law*
Kate Parlett

*The Participation of States in International Organisations: The Role of Human Rights and Democracy*
Alison Duxbury

*'Armed Attack' and Article 51 of the UN Charter: Evolutions in Customary Law and Practice*
Tom Ruys

*Science and Risk Regulation in International Law*
Jacqueline Peel

*Theatre of the Rule of Law: Transnational Legal Intervention in Theory and Practice*
Stephen Humphreys

*The Public International Law Theory of Hans Kelsen: Believing in Universal Law*
Jochen von Bernstorff

*Vicarious Liability in Tort: A Comparative Perspective*
Paula Giliker

*Legal Personality in International Law*
Roland Portmann

*Legitimacy and Legality in International Law: An Interactional Account*
Jutta Brunnée and Stephen J. Toope

*The Concept of Non-International Armed Conflict in International Humanitarian Law*
Anthony Cullen

*The Challenge of Child Labour in International Law*
Franziska Humbert

*Shipping Interdiction and the Law of the Sea*
Douglas Guilfoyle

*International Courts and Environmental Protection*
Tim Stephens

*Legal Principles in WTO Disputes*
Andrew D. Mitchell

*War Crimes in Internal Armed Conflicts*
Eve La Haye

*Humanitarian Occupation*
Gregory H. Fox

*The International Law of Environmental Impact Assessment: Process, Substance and Integration*
Neil Craik

*The Law and Practice of International Territorial Administration: Versailles to Iraq and Beyond*
Carsten Stahn

*Cultural Products and the World Trade Organization*
Tania Voon

*United Nations Sanctions and the Rule of Law*
Jeremy Farrall

*National Law in WTO Law: Effectiveness and Good Governance in the World Trading System*
Sharif Bhuiyan

*The Threat of Force in International Law*
Nikolas Stürchler

*Indigenous Rights and United Nations Standards*
Alexandra Xanthaki

*International Refugee Law and Socio-Economic Rights*
Michelle Foster

*The Protection of Cultural Property in Armed Conflict*
Roger O'Keefe

*Interpretation and Revision of International Boundary Decisions*
Kaiyan Homi Kaikobad

*Multinationals and Corporate Social Responsibility: Limitations and Opportunities in International Law*
Jennifer A. Zerk

*Judiciaries within Europe: A Comparative Review*
John Bell

*Law in Times of Crisis: Emergency Powers in Theory and Practice*
Oren Gross and Fionnuala Ní Aoláin

*Vessel-Source Marine Pollution: The Law and Politics of International Regulation*
Alan Tan

*Enforcing Obligations* Erga Omnes *in International Law*
Christian J. Tams

*Non-Governmental Organisations in International Law*
Anna-Karin Lindblom

*Democracy, Minorities and International Law*
Steven Wheatley

*Prosecuting International Crimes: Selectivity and the International Law Regime*
Robert Cryer

*Compensation for Personal Injury in English, German and Italian Law: A Comparative Outline*
Basil Markesinis, Michael Coester, Guido Alpa and Augustus Ullstein

*Dispute Settlement in the UN Convention on the Law of the Sea*
Natalie Klein

*The International Protection of Internally Displaced Persons*
Catherine Phuong

*Remedies against International Organisations*
Karel Wellens

*Diversity and Self-Determination in International Law*
Karen Knop

*The Law of Internal Armed Conflict*
Lindsay Moir

*International Commercial Arbitration and African States: Practice, Participation and Institutional Development*
Amazu A. Asouzu

*The Enforceability of Promises in European Contract Law*
James Gordley

*International Law in Antiquity*
David J. Bederman

*Money Laundering: A New International Law Enforcement Model*
Guy Stessens

*Good Faith in European Contract Law*
Reinhard Zimmermann and Simon Whittaker

*On Civil Procedure*
J. A. Jolowicz

*Trusts: A Comparative Study*
Maurizio Lupoi

*The Right to Property in Commonwealth Constitutions*
Tom Allen

*International Organizations Before National Courts*
August Reinisch

*The Changing International Law of High Seas Fisheries*
Francisco Orrego Vicuña

*Trade and the Environment: A Comparative Study of EC and US Law*
Damien Geradin

*Unjust Enrichment: A Study of Private Law and Public Values*
Hanoch Dagan

*Religious Liberty and International Law in Europe*
Malcolm D. Evans

*Ethics and Authority in International Law*
Alfred P. Rubin

*Sovereignty Over Natural Resources: Balancing Rights and Duties*
Nico Schrijver

*The Polar Regions and the Development of International Law*
Donald R. Rothwell

*Fragmentation and the International Relations of Micro-States: Self-determination and Statehood*
Jorri Duursma

*Principles of the Institutional Law of International Organizations*
C. F. Amerasinghe